Identifying and Managing Project Risk

Identifying and Managing Project Risk

Essential Tools for Failure-Proofing Your Project

Tom Kendrick

AMACOM

American Management Association

New York • Atlanta • Brussels • Buenos Aires • Chicago • London • Mexico City
San Francisco • Shanghai • Tokyo • Toronto • Washington, D.C.

Special discounts on bulk quantities of AMACOM books are available to corporations, professional associations, and other organizations. For details, contact Special Sales Department, AMACOM, a division of American Management Association, 1601 Broadway, New York, NY 10019.
Tel.: 212-903-8316. Fax: 212-903-8083.
Web Site: www.amacombooks.org

This publication is designed to provide accurate and authoritative information in regard to the subject matter covered. It is sold with the understanding that the publisher is not engaged in rendering legal, accounting, or other professional service. If legal advice or other expert assistance is required, the services of a competent professional person should be sought.

"PMI" and the PMI logo are service and trademarks registered in the United States and other nations; "PMP" and the PMP logo are certification marks registered in the United States and other nations; "PMBOK", "PM Network", and "PMI Today" are trademarks registered in the United States and other nations; and "Project Management Journal" and "Building professionalism in project management" are trademarks of the Project Management Institute, Inc.

Library of Congress Cataloging-in-Publication Data

Kendrick, Tom.
     Identifying and managing project risk: essential tools for failure-proofing your project / Tom Kendrick.
          p. cm.
     Includes bibliographical references and index.
     ISBN 0-8144-0761-7
     1. Risk management. 2. Project management. I. Title.

HD61 .K46 2003
658. 4'04—dc21   *2002152001*

Printing number

10 9 8 7 6 5 4 3 2 1

CONTENTS

ACKNOWLEDGMENTS

This book is the result of decades of project work and thousands of hours of discussion about project management and project risk (including more than a little good-humored disagreement). It is also the consequence of hundreds of workshops on project risk management. Project work described in this book includes both projects I have led within Hewlett-Packard, DuPont, and other places where I have worked and other projects done by colleagues, friends, and workshop participants from an enormous diversity of project environments. The large number of project situations that serve as the foundation of this book ensures that it is aligned with the real world and that it contains ideas that are practical and effective—not just based on interesting theories.

It is not possible to specifically acknowledge all of the people who have contributed useful content about projects and risk that are found in this book, but there are a few names that I need to single out. The members of the Hewlett-Packard Project Management Initiative team that I worked with for a dozen years served as a boundless source of wisdom and good examples, and they were always quick to point out anything that I said that was nonsense. Although all of us have now moved on, that group largely remains close as friends, as critics, and as associates. From this group, I am particularly indebted to Richard Simonds, who diligently read and reread several early drafts of the book and pointed out where I was incoherent, incomplete, or less than grammatical. Richard Bauhaus, who for several years served as my manager and remains a mentor, also read early drafts and provided valuable feedback. Many of the main points of the book are the result of long and fruitful debates with Charlie Elman, who has forgotten more about process measurement than most people would guess there is to know. Others from that group that I am indebted to are Patrick Neal, John Lamy, Jo Killen, Kathy Meikle, and Randy Englund. Several others from Hewlett-Packard participated frequently and productively in our efforts, although they were never formally part of the HP Project Management Initiative team. Denis Lambert was particularly helpful, as he never agreed with anything until all of it was demonstrably useful. Ron Benton, similarly, worked tirelessly to keep us all honest. Many colleagues from Europe and Asia also provided invaluable assistance, particularly Patrick Schmid in Germany and Ashok Waran in India. Consultants from outside also offered frequent and useful feedback, including Charlie Hoerner, Cathy Tonne, and Janet Ellison.

I also need to acknowledge others who diligently read through the early versions of this book, particularly John Kennedy, who ensured that anything I said about statistics was within defendable confidence limits, and Dennis Hong, who provided valuable feedback and suggestions related to emerging information technology trends.

Finally, my largest debt of gratitude in this endeavor goes to my wife, Barbara, who encouraged this project, supported it, and repeatedly read all the versions of the manuscript (even the boring parts). She provided the book with most of its clarity and a good deal of its logical structure. If the book proves useful to you, it is largely due to her efforts.

While others have contributed mightily to the content of this book, any errors, omissions, or other problems are strictly my own. Should you run into any, let me know.

Tom Kendrick, San Carlos, CA
kendrict@alumni.princeton.edu

INTRODUCTION

"Your mission, Jim, should you decide to accept it. . . ."

So began each episode of the TV series *Mission: Impossible*, and what followed chronicled the execution of that week's impossible mission. The missions were seldom literally impossible, though; careful planning, staffing, and use of the (seemingly unlimited) budget resulted in a satisfactory conclusion just before the deadline—the final commercial.

High-technology projects today should also probably arrive on a tape that "will self-destruct in five seconds." Compared with project work done in the past, all high-tech projects are more time-constrained, pose greater technical challenges, and rarely seem to have enough resources. All of this leads to increased project risk—culminating too often in a doomed project.

As a leader of high-tech projects, you need to know that techniques do exist to better deal with risk in projects like yours. When used, they will help you recognize and manage potential problems. Often, they can make the difference between a project that is possible and one that is impossible. This is what *Identifying and Managing Project Risk* is about. Throughout this book, examples from technical projects show how the ideas presented may be applied to meet challenges you may face. This is not a book of theories; it is based on data collected from hundreds of technical projects worldwide over the past ten years. A database filled with this information, the Project Experience Risk Information Library (PERIL), forms much of the foundation for this book. These examples are used to examine sources of risk, and they demonstrate practical responses that do not always resort to brute force.

The structure of the book also reflects the changes adopted in the 2000 edition of the *Guide to the Project Management Body of Knowledge (PMBOK® Guide)* from the Project Management Institute (PMI®, the professional society for project managers). The Risk section of the *PMBOK® Guide* is one of the key areas tested on the

Project Management Professional (PMP®) certification examination administered by PMI. This section was extensively revised for the 2000 edition, and the material here is consistent with those changes.

The first half of the book addresses risk identification, which relies heavily on thorough project definition and planning. The initial six chapters show the value of these activities in uncovering sources of risk. The remainder of the book covers assessment and management of risk, both at the detail (activity) and at the project levels. These chapters cover methods for assessing each identified risk, establishing the overall risk profile for the project, making project adjustments, ongoing risk tracking, and project closure.

It is especially easy on high-tech projects to convince yourself that there is little to be learned from the past and that established ideas and techniques "don't really apply to *my* project." Tempting though it is to wear these "hindsight blinders," wise project managers realize that their chances of success are always improved when they take full advantage of what has gone before. Neither project management in general nor risk management in particular is all that new. Broad principles and techniques for both have been successfully used for more than a century. While there are many lessons to be learned from current projects (as the PERIL database illustrates), there is also much to be absorbed from earlier work.

As a graphic reminder of this connection, each chapter in this book concludes with a short description of how some of the principles discussed relate to a very large historical project: the construction of the Panama Canal. Taking a moment every so often to consider this remarkable project reinforces the importance of good project management practices—and may provide some tropical relief from what can be occasionally dry subject matter.

The construction of the Panama Canal nearly one hundred years ago was the risky, high-tech project of its day. There were no earlier similar projects to learn from, and much of the engineering was necessarily innovative. It was, for its time, breathtakingly expensive. The Panama Canal represents the single largest project investment prior to the late twentieth century. The construction effort stretched over several decades, required a series of project leaders, and provides a wealth of project management examples, both positive and disastrous. The examples cited here are drawn from a number of sources, but the best one by far is *The Path Between the Seas: The Creation of the Panama Canal, 1870–1914*, by David McCullough (Touchstone Books, 1977).

The story of the Panama Canal is especially instructive because it is actually the story of two projects. The first failed for many reasons, but lack of good project and risk management played a large part. The second succeeded largely because of the rigorous and disciplined application of good project practices. The Panama Canal projects illustrate many of the points made in this book, and they demonstrate important concepts applicable to current projects.

First, as stated before, successful project management practices are not new. They are well established and have worked effectively for more than a century. Modern project management was developed in the late 1800s to deal with the increasingly enormous civil engineering projects of that era all over the world—the bridges, the transcontinental railroads, the dams, and other massive projects made possible by Machine Age technology. *Many basic lessons learned on earlier projects can be usefully applied to your high-tech projects today.*

Second, tools for managing projects have evolved significantly, but the fundamental principles have changed little. Henry Gantt, the gentleman who developed the chart that bears his name, contributed to the planning of many projects. He did all of this with a ruler and a straight edge. Never in his whole life did he fire up Microsoft Project, not even once. *Having the very newest tool may or may not help your project, but understanding why management tools are important and how best to use them will always serve you well.*

Finally, systematic application of good methods leads to successful outcomes in projects of all types. All projects are fundamentally dependent on people, and human beings are not very different today than we were hundreds, or even thousands, of years ago. *To motivate people and enhance performance on your project team, you can look to what has worked before—because, by and large, it still does.*

Risk in projects comes from many sources, including two that are generally left out of even the better books on the subject—inadequate application (or even discouragement) of project management practices and the all-too-common situation of wildly aggressive project objectives that are established without the backing of any realistic plan. These risks are related, because only through adequate understanding of the work can you detect whether objectives are impossible and only by using the information you develop can you hope to do anything about it.

Identifying and Managing Project Risk is intended to help leaders of technical projects (and their managers) successfully deliver on their commitments. Whether you develop technical products, provide services, create information technology solutions, or apply technology in other types of projects, you will find easy-to-follow, practical guidance to improve your management of project risk as well as effective practices for aligning your projects with reality. You will learn how to failure-proof difficult projects by reducing your risks, with minimal incremental effort.

CHAPTER 1

WHY PROJECT RISK MANAGEMENT?

"Those who cannot remember the past are condemned to repeat it."
                                                    —GEORGE SANTAYANA

Far too many technical projects retrace the shortcomings and errors of earlier work. Projects that successfully avoid such pitfalls are often viewed as "lucky," but there is usually more to it than that.

The Doomed Project

Every project has risk. There is always at least some level of uncertainty in a project's outcome, no matter what the Microsoft Project Gantt chart on the wall seems to imply. High-tech projects are particularly risky, for a number of reasons. First, technical projects have high variation. While there are invariably aspects of a project that resemble earlier work, every project has unique aspects and has objectives that differ from previous work in some material way. Because the environment of technical projects evolves very quickly, there can be much larger differences from one project to the next than may be found in other types of projects. In addition, technical projects are frequently staffed "lean" and may also do their work with inadequate funding and equipment. To make matters worse, there is a pervasive expectation that, however fast the most recent project may have been, the next one should be even quicker. Technical projects chronically accept aggressive challenges to execute ever more rapidly. Risks on technical projects are significant, and their number and severity continue

1

to grow. To successfully lead such projects, you must consistently use the best practices available.

Good practices come from experience. Experience, unfortunately, generally comes from unsuccessful practices and mistakes. People learn what *not* to do, all too often, by doing it and then suffering the consequences. Experience can be an invaluable resource, even when it is not your own. The foundation of this book is the experiences of others—a large collection of mostly plausible ideas that did not work out as hoped.

Projects that succeed generally do so because their leaders do two things well. One is to recognize that, among the unique aspects of a new project, some parts of the work ahead have been done before and that the notes, records, and lessons learned on earlier projects can be a road map for identifying, and in many cases avoiding, the problems of earlier projects. The second thing that these leaders do well is to plan the work thoroughly, including the portions that require innovation, in order to understand the challenges ahead and to anticipate at least some of the potential problems. Using this plan, they guide and monitor the work.

Effective project risk management relies on both of these ideas. By looking backward, managers may avoid repeating past failures, and by looking forward through project planning, they can eliminate or minimize many future potential problems.

The principal ideas addressed in this chapter are:

❒ A definition of risk

❒ Macro-risk management

❒ Micro-risk management

❒ Benefits of risk management

❒ The overall risk management process

Risk

In projects, a risk can be almost any undesirable event associated with the work. There are many ways to characterize these risks. One of the simplest, from the insurance industry, is:

"Loss" multiplied by "Likelihood"

Risk is the product of these two factors: the expected *consequences* of the event and the *probability* that the event might occur. All risks have these two related, but distinctly different, components. Employing this concept, risk may be characterized in the aggregate for a large population of events ("macro-risk"), or it may be considered on an event-by-event basis ("micro-risk").

Both characterizations are useful for risk management, but which of these is most applicable depends on the situation. In most fields, risk is managed primarily in the aggregate, in the "macro" sense. As examples, insurance companies sell a large number of policies, commercial banks make many loans, gambling casinos and lotteries attract crowds of players, and managers of mutual funds hold large portfolios of investments. The literature of risk management for these fields (which is extensive) tends to focus on large-scale risk management, with secondary treatment for managing single-event risks.

To take a very simple example, consider throwing two fair, six-sided dice. In advance, the outcome of the event is unknown, but, through analysis, experimenting, or guessing, you can develop some expectations. The only possible outcomes for the sum of the faces of the two dice are the integers between two and twelve. One way to establish expectations is to figure out the number of possible ways there are to reach each of these totals. (For example, the total 4 can occur three ways from two dice: $1 + 3$, $2 + 2$, and $3 + 1$.) Arranging this analysis in a histogram results in Figure 1-1. Since each of the thirty-six possible combinations is equally likely, this histogram can be used to predict the relative probability for each possible total.

If you throw many dice, the empirical data collected (which is another method for establishing the probabilities) will generally resemble the theoretical histogram, but since the events are random it is extraordinarily unlikely that your experiments rolling dice

Figure 1-1. Histogram of sums from two dice.

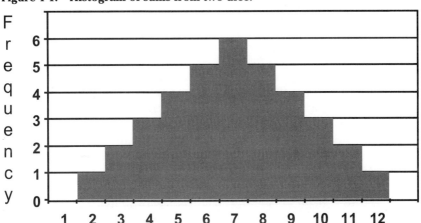

will ever precisely match the theory. What will emerge, though, is that the *average* sum generated in large populations (one hundred or more throws) will be close to the calculated mean, and the *shape* of the histogram will also resemble the predicted theoretical distribution. Risk analysis in the macro sense takes notice of the mean, seven (which for this case is also the most likely outcome, due to symmetry), and casino games of chance played with dice are designed to make money using this fact. On the other hand, risk in the micro sense, noting the range of possible outcomes, dominates the analysis for the casino visitors, who may play such games only once; the risk associated with a single event—their next throw of the dice—is what matters.

For projects, risk management in the large sense is useful, but, from the perspective of the leader of a single project, there is no population; there is only one project. Risk management for projects reverses the emphasis of the other fields, focusing primarily on management of risk in the small sense. Both types of risk management are discussed in this book, but risk management for single events dominates.

MACRO-RISK MANAGEMENT

In the literature of the insurance and finance industries, risk is described and managed using statistical tools: data collection, sampling, and data analysis. In these fields, analysts collect and aggregate a large population of individual examples and then calculate statistics for the "loss and likelihood." Even though the individual cases in the population may vary widely, the average "loss times likelihood" tends to be fairly predictable and stable over time. When a large number of cases in the population representing various levels of loss have been collected, the population can be characterized using distributions and histograms, similar to the plot in Figure 1-2. In this case, each "loss" result that falls into a defined range is counted, and the number of observations in each range is plotted against the ranges to show the overall results.

Various statistics and methods are used to study such populations, but the mean is the main one used for managing risk in such a population. The mean represents the *typical* loss—the total of all the losses divided by the number of data points. The uncertainty, or the amount of spread for the data on each side of the mean, also matters, but the mean sufficiently characterizes the population for most decisions.

In fields such as these, risk is managed mostly in the macro sense, using a large population to forecast the mean. This information may be used to set interest rates for loans, premiums for insur-

Figure 1-2. Histogram of population data.

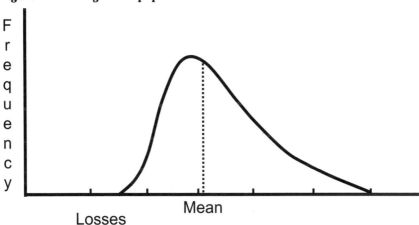

ance policies, and expectations for stock portfolios. Because there are many loans, investments, and insurance policies, the overall expectations depend much more on the typical result. It does not matter so much how large or small the extremes are; as long as the average results remain consistent with the business objectives, risk is managed by allowing the high and low values to balance each other, providing a stable and predictable overall result.

Some project risk management in this macro sense is common at the level of an overall business. If all the projects undertaken are considered together, performance of the portfolio will depend primarily on the results of the "average" project. Some projects will fail and others may achieve spectacular results, but the aggregate performance is what impacts the business bottom line. Business performance will be judged successful as long as most projects achieve results close to expectations.

MICRO-RISK MANAGEMENT

Passive measurement, even in the fields that manage risk using large populations, is never the whole job. Studying averages is necessary, but it is never sufficient. Managing risk also involves taking action to modify the outcomes.

In the world of gambling, which is filled with students of risk on both sides of the table, knowing the odds in each game is a good starting point. Both parties also know that if they can shift the odds, they will be more successful. Casinos shift the game in roulette by adding zeros to the wheel but not including them in the calculation of the payoffs. In many casino games that use cards, such as blackjack, casino owners employ the dealers, knowing that the dealer has a statistical advantage. In blackjack the players may also shift the odds by paying attention and counting the cards, but establishments minimize this advantage through frequent shuffling of the decks and by barring known card counters from play. There are even more effective methods for shifting the odds in games of chance, but most are not legal; tactics like stacking decks of cards and loading dice are frowned upon. Fortunately, in project risk management, shifting the odds is not only completely fair; it is an excellent idea.

Managing risk in this *small* sense considers each case separately—every investment in a portfolio, each individual bank loan, each insurance policy, and, in the case of projects, every exposure faced by the current project. In all of these cases, standards and criteria are used to minimize the possibility of large individual variances above the mean, and actions are taken to move the expected result. Screening criteria are applied at the bank to avoid making loans to borrowers who appear to be poor credit risks. Insurers either raise the price of coverage or refuse to sell insurance to people who seem statistically more likely to generate claims. Insurance companies also use tactics, such as auto safety campaigns, aimed at reducing the frequency or severity of events that result in claims. Managers of mutual funds work to influence the boards of directors of companies whose stocks are held by the fund. All these tactics work to shift the odds—actively managing risk in the small sense.

For projects, risk management is almost entirely similar to these examples, considering each project individually. Thorough screening of projects at the overall business level attempts to select only the best opportunities. It would be excellent risk management to pick out and abort (or avoid altogether) the projects that will ultimately fail—if only it were that easy. As David Packard noted, "Half the projects at Hewlett-Packard are a waste of time. If I knew which half, I would cancel them." Risk management at the portfolio level for projects is covered in the next chapter, but the majority of this book focuses on project risk management for the single project—risk management in the small sense.

As said before, for the leader of a project, there is no population. There is only the single project, and there will be only one outcome. In most other fields, risk management is concerned primarily with the mean values of large numbers of independent events, but for project risk management, what generally matters most is predictability—managing the variation expected in the result.

For a given project, you can never know the precise outcome in advance, but, through review of data from earlier work and project planning, you can predict the range and frequency of potential outcomes that may be expected. Through analysis and planning, you can better understand the odds and take action to improve them. The goals of risk management for a single project are to establish a credible plan consistent with business objectives and then to minimize the range of possible outcomes.

One type of "loss" for a project may be measured in time. The distributions in Figure 1-3 compare timing expectations graphically for two similar projects. These plots are very different from what was shown in Figure 1-2. In that case, the plot was based on empirical measurements of a large number of actual, historical cases. The plots in Figure 1-3 are *projections* of what might happen for the two projects, based on assumptions and data for each. These histograms are speculative and require you to pretend that you will execute the project many times, with varying results. Developing this sort of risk characterization for projects is explored in Chapter 9, where quantifying and analyzing project risk are discussed. For the present, assume that the two projects have expectations as displayed in the two distributions.

For these two projects, the mean (or expected) duration is the same, but the range of expected durations for Project A is much larger. Project B has a much narrower spread (the *statistical variance*, or *standard deviation*), and so it will be more likely to com-

Figure 1-3. Possible outcomes for two projects.

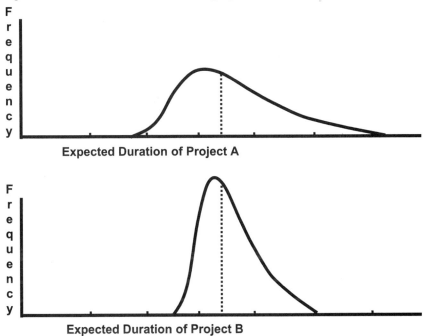

Expected Duration of Project A

Expected Duration of Project B

plete close to the expected duration. The larger range of possible durations for Project A represents higher risk, even though it also includes a small possibility of an outcome even shorter than expected for Project B. Project risk increases with the level of uncertainty.

Managing project risk requires the project team to understand the sources of variation in projects and then to minimize them wherever it is feasible. Since no project is likely to be repeated enough times to develop distributions like those in Figure 1-3 using measured, empirical data, project risk analyses depend on projections and range estimates.

Benefits and Uses of Risk Data

Developing a project plan with thorough risk analysis can involve significant effort, which may not seem necessary to many project stakeholders and even to some project leaders. In fact, the benefits and uses of appropriate project risk analysis more than justify this effort. Some of the reasons for risk management follow, and each of these is amplified in detail later in this book.

PROJECT JUSTIFICATION

Project risk management is undertaken primarily to improve the chances that a project will achieve its objectives. While there are never any guarantees, broader awareness of common failure modes and ideas that make projects more robust can significantly improve the odds of success. The primary goal of project risk management is either to develop a credible foundation for each project, showing that it is possible, or to demonstrate that the project is not feasible so that it can be avoided, aborted, or transformed.

LOWER COSTS AND LESS CHAOS

Adequate risk analysis reduces both the overall cost and the frustration caused by avoidable problems. The amount of rework and of unforeseen late project effort is minimized. Knowledge of the root causes of the potentially severe project problems enables project leaders and teams to work in ways that avoid these problems. Dealing with the causes of risk also minimizes "fire-fighting" and chaos during projects, much of which is focused short-term and deals primarily with symptoms rather than the intrinsic sources of the problems.

PROJECT PRIORITY AND MANAGEMENT SUPPORT

Support from managers and other project stakeholders and commitment from the project team are more easily won when projects are based on thorough, understandable information. High-risk projects may begin with lower priority, but a thorough risk plan, displaying competence and good preparation for possible problems, can improve the project priority. Whenever you are successful in raising the priority of your project, you significantly reduce project risk—by opening doors, reducing obstacles, making resources available, and shortening queues for services.

PROJECT PORTFOLIO MANAGEMENT

Achieving and maintaining an appropriate mix of ongoing projects for an organization uses risk data as a key factor. The ideal project portfolio includes both lower- and higher-risk projects in proportions that are consistent with the business objectives. The process of project portfolio management and its relationship to project risk is covered in Chapter 2.

FINE-TUNING PLANS TO REDUCE RISK

Risk analysis uncovers weaknesses in a project plan and triggers changes, new activities, and resource shifts that improve the project. Risk analysis at the project level may also reveal needed shifts in overall project structure or basic assumptions.

ESTABLISHING MANAGEMENT RESERVE

Risk analysis demonstrates the uncertainty of project outcomes and is useful in setting reserves for schedule and/or resources. Risky projects really require a window of time (or budget), instead of a single-point objective. While the project targets can be based on expectations (the "most likely" versions of the analysis), project commitments should be established with less aggressive goals, reflecting overall project risk. The target and committed objectives set a range for acceptable project results and provide visible recognition of project risk. For example, the target schedule for a risky project might be twelve months, but the committed schedule, reflecting the uncertainty, may be set at fourteen months. Completion within (or before) this range defines a successful project; only if the project takes more than fourteen months will it be considered a failure. Project risk assessment data provides both the rationale and the magnitude for the required reserve. More detail on this is found in Chapter 10.

PROJECT COMMUNICATION AND CONTROL

Project communication is more effective when there is a solid, credible plan. Risk assessments also build awareness of project exposures for the project team, showing how painful the problems might be and when and where they might occur. This causes people to work in ways that avoid project difficulties. Risk data can also be very useful in negotiations with project sponsors. Using information about the likelihood and consequences of potential problems gives project teams more influence in defining objectives, determining budgets, obtaining staff, setting deadlines, and negotiating project changes.

The Risk Management Process

The overall structure of this book mirrors the information in the *Guide to the Project Management Body of Knowledge*, 2000 edition (or *PMBOK®* Guide). This guide from the Project Management Institute (PMI) is widely used as a comprehensive summary of project management processes and principles, and it is the foundation for PMI certification. The *PMBOK®* Guide has nine Project Management Knowledge Areas:

☐ *Project Risk Management* outlines processes for identifying, analyzing, and responding to project risk.

☐ *Project Integration Management* describes processes for overall project coordination.

☐ *Project Scope Management* covers project processes that ensure that the project defines the deliverable(s) and that it includes all the work required, and only the work required, for successful project completion.

☐ *Project Time Management* describes the processes for scheduling and timely project completion.

☐ *Project Cost Management* details the processes for budgeting and project completion within the approved budget.

☐ *Project Quality Management* discusses the processes for ensuring that the project will satisfy the need(s) for which it was undertaken.

☐ *Project Human Resource Management* outlines processes for staffing and working with the people involved with the project.

❏ *Project Communications Management* covers project information management processes.

❏ *Project Procurement Management* describes the processes required to acquire outside goods and services.

Of these areas, Project Risk Management is the most central to this book, but the other eight topics are strongly related.

The *PMBOK®* Guide is also built around five Process Groups: Initiating, Planning, Executing, Controlling, and Closing. In the *PMBOK®* Guide, the processes are related as shown in Figure 1-4. Project Risk Management is included in two of these groups, Planning Processes and Controlling Processes.

In this book, Risk Management Planning is discussed in Chapter 2. Risk Identification is covered in Chapters 3 through 6, on scope risk, schedule risk, resource risk, and management of project constraints. The analysis and management of project risk is covered first at a detail level and then for projects as a whole. (This is a distinction not explicit in the *PMBOK®* Guide, which addresses project-level risk only superficially.) Both Quantitative and Qualitative Risk Analysis are covered on two levels, for activity risks in Chapter 7 and for project risk in Chapter 9. Risk Response Planning is also discussed twice, in Chapter 8 for activities and in Chapter 10 for the project as a whole. The final *PMBOK®* Guide process, Risk Monitoring and Control, is the topic of Chapter 11, and Project Closure is covered in Chapter 12.

As in the *PMBOK®* Guide, the majority of the book aligns with project planning, but the material here goes beyond the coverage in the *PMBOK®* Guide to focus on the "how to" of effective risk

Figure 1-4. PMBOK links among process groups.

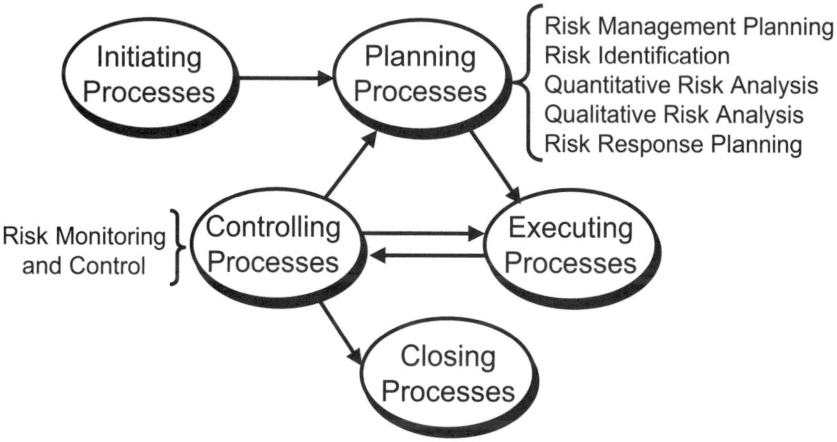

management, from the practitioner's standpoint. There is particular emphasis on ideas and tools that work well and can be easily adopted in technical projects. This book also goes significantly beyond the *PMBOK®* Guide in many areas to include risk topics not included there. All risk management topics in the *PMBOK®* Guide are included here, for people who may be using this book to prepare for the PMP® Certification test, but not every topic will get equal coverage.

Anatomy of a Failed Project: The First Panama Canal Project

Risk management is never just about looking forward. Heeding the lessons learned on projects of all types—even some very distant examples—can help you avoid problems on new projects. One such example, illustrating that people have been making similar mistakes for a long, long time, is the initial effort by the French to construct a canal across Panama.

For obvious reasons, the building of the Panama Canal was not, strictly speaking, impossible. However, the initial undertaking was certainly premature; the first canal project, begun in the late 1800s, was a massive challenge for the technology of the day. That said, lack of project management contributed significantly to the decision to go forward in the first place, the many project problems, and the ultimate failure.

Precise definition for the project was unclear, even years after it began. Planning was never thorough, and changes in the work were frequent and managed informally. Reporting on the project was sporadic and generally inaccurate (or even dishonest). Risks were not identified effectively or were ignored, and the primary risk management strategy seems to have been "hoping for the best."

Although people speculated about a canal in Central America years before actual construction began, the first serious investigation of the possibility of such a project was undertaken in the mid-1800s. Estimates were that such a canal would provide $48 million a year in shipping savings and that it might be built for less than $100 million. Further study on-site was less optimistic, but in 1850 construction of a railroad across the Isthmus of Panama started. The railroad was ultimately completed, but the $1.5 million, two-year project swelled to $8 million before it was finished, three years late, in 1855. After a slow start, the railroad did prove a financial success, but its construction problems foreshadowed the canal efforts to come.

A few years later, on the other side of the world, the Suez Canal was completed and opened in 1869. This project was sponsored and led successfully from Paris by Ferdinand de Lesseps. This triumph earned him the nickname "The Great Engineer," although he was actually a diplomat by training, not an engineer at all. He had no technical background and only modest skills as an administrator. However, he had completed a project many thought to be impossible and was now world-famous. The Suez project was a huge financial success, and de Lesseps and his backers were eager to take on new challenges.

Examining the world map, de Lesseps decided that a canal at Panama would be his next triumph, so, in the late 1870s, a French syndicate negotiated the necessary agreements in Bogota, Colombia, as Panama was then the northernmost part of Colombia. They were granted rights to build and operate a canal in exchange for a small percentage of the revenue to be generated over ninety-nine years.

While it might seem curious today that these projects so far from France originated there, in the late 1800s Paris was the center of the engineering universe. The best schools in the world were there, and many engineering giants of the day lived in Paris, including Gustave Eiffel (then planning his tower). These canal projects could hardly have arisen anywhere else.

The process of defining the Panama project started promisingly enough. In 1879, Ferdinand de Lesseps sponsored an "International Congress" to study the feasibility of a canal connecting the Atlantic and Pacific oceans through Central America. More than a hundred delegates from a large number of nations (although most of the delegates were French) gathered in Paris. A number of routes were considered, and canals through Nicaragua and Panama both were recommended as possibilities. Construction ideas, including a very realistic "lock-and-dam" concept (somewhat similar to the canal in service today), were also proposed. In the end, though, the Congress voted to support a sea-level canal project at Panama, even though nearly all the engineers present thought the idea infeasible and voted against it. Not listening to technical people is a perilous way to start a project. The Panama Canal was neither the first nor the last project to create its own problems through insufficient technical input.

Planning for the project was also a low priority. De Lesseps paid little attention to technical problems. He believed that need would result in innovation, as it had at Suez, and that the future would take care of itself. He valued his own opinions and ignored the views of those who disagreed with him, even when they were recognized authorities. An inveterate optimist, he was convinced, on the basis only of self-confidence, that he could not fail. These attitudes are not conducive to good risk management; there are few things more dangerous to a project than an overly optimistic project leader.

The broad objective de Lesseps set for his Compagnie Universelle du Canal Interoceanique was to build a sea-level canal in twelve years, to open in 1892. He raised $60 million from investors through public offerings—a lot of money, but still less than one-third of the initial engineering cost estimate of more than $200 million. In addition to this financial shortfall, the project was dogged by the fact that very little detailed planning was done before work actually commenced, and most of that occurred at the 1879 meeting in Paris. Even on the visits that de Lesseps made to Panama and New York to build support for the project, he failed to involve his technical people.

Eventually the engineers did travel to Panama, and digging started in 1882. Quickly, estimates of the volume of excavation required started to rise, to 120 million cubic meters—almost triple the estimates used in 1879. As the magnitude of the effort rose, de Lesseps made no public changes to his cost estimates or to the completion date.

Management of risks on the project, inadequate at the start, improved little in the early stages of execution. There were many problems. Panama is in the tropics, and torrential rains for much of the year created floods that impeded the digging and made the work very dangerous. The frequent rains turned Panama's clay into a flowing, sticky sludge that bogged down work, and the moist, tropical salt air combined with the viscous mud to destroy the machinery. There was also the issue of elevation. The continental divide in Panama is not too high by North or South American standards, but it does rise to more than 130 meters. For a canal to cross the central portion of Panama, it would be necessary to dig a trench more than fifteen kilometers long to this depth, an unprecedented amount of excavation. Digging the remainder of the eighty-kilometer transit across the isthmus was nearly as daunting. Adequate funding for the work was also a problem, as only a portion of the money that was raised was allocated to construction (most of the money went for publicity, including a very impressive periodic *Canal Bulletin*, used to build interest and support). Worst of all, diseases, especially malaria and yellow fever, were lethal to many workers not native to the tropics, and they died by the hundreds. As work progressed, the engineers, already dubious, increasingly believed the plan to dig a sea-level canal doomed.

Intense interest in the project and a steady stream of new workers kept work going, and the *Canal Bulletin* reported good progress (regardless of what was actually happening). As the project progressed, there were changes. Several years into the project, in 1885, the cost estimates were finally raised, and investors provided new funds that quadrupled the project budget to $240 million. The expected opening of the canal was delayed "somewhat," but no specific date was offered. Claims were made at this time that the canal was half dug, but the truth was probably less than 15 percent. Information on the project was far from trustworthy.

In 1887, costs were again revised upward, exceeding $330 million. The additional money was borrowed, as de Lesseps could find no new investors. Following years of struggle and frustration, the engineers finally won the debate over construction of a canal at sea level. Plans were shifted to construct dams on the rivers near each coast to create large lakes that would serve as much of the transit. Sets of locks would be needed to bring ships up to, and down from, these manmade lakes. While this would slow the transit of ships somewhat, it significantly reduced the necessary excavation.

Even with these changes, problems continued to mount, and, by 1889, more revisions and even more money were needed. After repeated failures to raise funding, de Lesseps liquidated the Compagnie Universelle du Canal Interoceanique, and the project ended. This collapse caused complete financial losses for all the investors. By 1892, scandals were rampant, and the bad press and blame spread far and wide. Soon the lawyers and courts of France were very busy dealing with the project's aftermath.

The French do not seem to have done a formal postproject analysis, but a look at the project in retrospect reveals more than a decade of work, in excess of $300 million spent, lots of digging, and no canal. In the wake of the years of effort, the site was ugly and an ecological mess. The cost of this project also included at least 20,000 lives lost (many workers who came to Panama died so soon after their arrival that their deaths were never recorded; some estimates of the death toll run as high as 25,000). Directly as a result of this project failure, the French government fell in 1892, ending one of the messiest and most costly project failures in history.

The leader of this project did not fare well in the wake of this disaster. Ferdinand de Lesseps was not technical, and he was misguided in his beliefs that equipment and medicines would appear when needed. He also chronically reported more progress than was real (through either poor analysis or deception; the records are not clear enough to tell). He died a broken man, in poverty. Had he never undertaken the project at Panama, he would have been remembered as the heroic builder of the Suez Canal. Instead, his name is also linked forever to the failure at Panama.

Perhaps the one positive outcome from all this was clear evidence that building a sea-level canal at Panama was all but impossible because of the rains, flooding, geology, and other challenges. These are problems that probably could not be surmounted even with current technology.

While it is not possible ever to know whether a canal at Panama could have been constructed in the 1880s, better project and risk management practices, widely available at the time, would have helped substantially. Setting a more appropriate initial objective, or at least modifying it sooner, would have improved the likelihood of success. Honest, more frequent communication—the foundation of well-run projects—would almost certainly have either forced these changes or led to earlier abandonment of the work, saving thousands of lives and a great deal of money.

CHAPTER 2

PLANNING FOR RISK MANAGEMENT

"You can observe a lot just by watching." —YOGI BERRA

Planning for risk involves paying attention. The practices that worked before are the foundation of future work, and the problems of the past trigger necessary changes.

Projects fail for one of three reasons. First, some projects fail because they actually *are* impossible; the objective lies outside the technical capabilities available, at least currently. "Design an antigravity device" is such a project. A second failure mode occurs when the project has a perfectly possible deliverable, but the rest of the objective is unrealistic. "Rewrite all the corporate accounting software so that it can use a different database package in two weeks using two part-time university students" is an example. The third reason projects fail is avoidable but all too common. Here, the deliverable is feasible, and the rest of the objective is also plausible. These projects fail simply because too little thought is put into the work, and no useful results emerge.

Risk and project planning enable you to distinguish among and to deal with all three of these situations. For projects that are demonstrably beyond the state of the art, planning and other data generally provide sufficient information to terminate consideration of the project or at least to redirect the objective ("buy a helicopter," for example, instead of developing antigravity). Chapter 3, on project scope risk identification, discusses these projects. For projects with unrealistic timing, resource, or other constraints, risk and planning data provide you with a compelling basis for project negotiation, resulting in a more plausible objective (or, in some cases, the conclusion that the project should not be undertaken because its cost would exceed its value or it would take too long). Chapters 4, 5, and 6, on schedule, resource, and other risk identification, discuss issues common for these failure-prone projects.

The third situation, a credible project that fails due to faulty execution, is definitely avoidable. Through adequate attention to project and risk planning, these projects can succeed. Well-planned projects begin quickly, limiting unproductive chaos. Rework and defects are minimized, and people remain busy performing activities that efficiently move the project forward. A solid foundation of project analysis also reveals problems that might lead to failure and prepares the project team for their prompt resolution. In addition to making project execution more efficient, risk planning also provides insight for faster, better project decisions. While changes are required to succeed with the first two types of doomed projects, this third type depends only on you, your project team, and application of the concepts in this book. The last half of this book, Chapters 7 through 13, specifically addresses these projects.

Most of the content of this chapter falls into the "Risk Management Planning" portion of the Planning Processes in the *PMBOK®* Guide, but it also draws from Project Integration Management and from other Planning Processes. The principal ideas in this chapter include:

- ❐ Project selection
- ❐ Overall project planning processes
- ❐ Risk management planning
- ❐ The Project Experience Risk Information Library (PERIL) database

Project Selection

Project risk is a significant factor even before there is a project. Projects begin as a result of an organization's business decision to create something new or to change something old. Projects are a large portion of the overall work done in organizations, and there are nearly always many more attractive project ideas than can be undertaken at any given time. The process for choosing projects both creates project risk and relies on project risk analysis, so the processes for project selection and project risk management are tightly linked.

Project selection affects project risk in a number of ways. Appropriate project selection can minimize several problems: too many projects; project priorities misaligned with business and technical strategies; and overestimated resources and resource capabilities. Inadequate analysis during project selection creates these risks.

Project risk management data are also a critical input to the project selection process. Decisions about which projects to initiate (and continue) should reflect the overall risk tolerances of the organization. Companies just starting up normally have a high tolerance for risky projects, and their project mix contains mainly projects with considerable uncertainty. Organizations that provide custom solutions for fixed fees typically avoid risky projects to protect their reputation and to avoid financial penalties. Risk data are necessary to make appropriate selection decisions. Since these decisions are generally made before there is much detailed planning, the project risk information available is often not very precise. Revisiting the decisions on a regular basis is crucial for both managing overall risk and keeping the project portfolio balanced.

An effective project selection process has only three possible outcomes for a new or continuing project. The first possibility is that the project is authorized and it becomes or remains an active project. The second option is that the project may require changes (to scope, schedule, or resources) before it becomes or continues to be an active part of the portfolio. The third option is rejection; some (perhaps most) project ideas are turned down or postponed for later reconsideration.

Decisions about which projects to select, change, or reject are generally based on the relative costs and benefits of each option. Expected project benefits and returns are estimated in a number of ways for these portfolio decisions, including predictions of financial metrics for return on investment (ROI metrics are covered in Chapter 9). Risk management information is critical to the portfolio decisions. It allows you to assess the credibility of the estimates for overall return, and it is often the primary factor that triggers changes in the project objectives. Best-in-class companies reject questionable projects early, before too much investment is made. Best-in-class high-technology companies spend less than 5 percent of their research and development budget on failed projects. In the typical high-tech company, the figure is far higher.

The most effective project selection processes include frequent reviews, at least once per quarter, to update project information, revisit the assumptions, and rebalance the project load. This ensures that inappropriate projects are weeded out early and the mix of ongoing projects contains the best available opportunities.

Project selection decisions also directly impact the risk of the selected projects. If choices are made on the basis of unrealistic assumptions about resource requirements, too many projects will be started. It is not uncommon for the project load in high-tech organizations to have resource requirements that are double, or even triple, what is actually available, due to chronic underestimation of the actual resources required. If projects expected to complete are delayed, or hiring new staff takes longer than expected, there may also be insufficient resources for the approved projects. Inadequate staffing on projects creates increased risk for all the projects in the portfolio. Project risk and resource information can minimize the "too many projects" problem.

Project risk also arises from the type of projects selected. The mix of projects by type—such as new research and development, next generation, evolutionary, partner or joint venture, maintenance, support, and infrastructure—also needs to be kept in balance. The proportions will vary over time and from organization to organization, but the target mix should consistently reflect strategic planning decisions and staffing constraints. It requires ongoing discipline to ensure that the project load does not become overloaded with too many projects of a given type—for example, too many maintenance projects or too many projects that depend on speculative technology. When the project load deviates from the overall business objectives, it increases business risk for the organization as a whole. Project selection should result in an appropriate mix of projects with risk and benefit profiles consistent with business objectives and adequate staffing for a focused portfolio of good projects.

Overall Project Planning Processes

The project selection process is one source of project risk for all projects, but another factor, the overall approach used for project management, is even more influential. When projects are undertaken in organizations that lack adequate project management processes, risks will be unknown, and probably unacceptably high. Without adequate analysis of projects, no one has much idea of what "going right" looks like, so it is not possible to identify and manage the risks—the things that may go wrong. The project management processes provide the magnifying glass you need to inspect your project to discover its possible failure modes.

Regular review of the overall methods and processes used to manage projects is an essential foundation for good risk management. If project information and control is sufficient across the organization and most of the projects undertaken are successful, then your processes are working well. For many high-tech projects, though, this is not the case. The methods used for managing project work are too informal, and they lack adequate structure. Exactly what process you choose matters less than that you are using one. If elaborate, formal, PMBOK®–inspired heavyweight project management works for you, great. If agile, lightweight, adaptive methodologies provide what you need, that's fine, too. The important requirement for risk management is that you adopt and *use* a project management process.

Too many technical projects are undertaken with indifference or even hostility to planning. This occurs for a number of reasons, and it originates in organizations at several levels. At the project level, other work may carry higher priority, or planning may be viewed as a waste of time. Above the project level, project management processes may appear to be unnecessary overhead, or they may be discouraged to deprive project teams of data that could be used to win arguments with their managers. Whatever the rationalizations used, there can be little risk management without planning. Until you have a basic plan, most of the potential problems and failure modes for your project will remain undetected.

The next several pages provide support for the investment in project processes. If you or your management need convincing that project management is worthwhile, read on. If project planning and related management processes are adequate in your organization, skip ahead.

AT THE PROJECT LEVEL

Project leaders frequently cite a number of reasons for avoiding project planning. Some projects are not thoroughly planned because changes to them are so frequent that planning seems futile. Quite a few leaders know that project management methodology is beneficial, but with their limited time they feel they must do only "real work." An increasingly common reason offered is the belief that in "Internet time," thinking and planning are no longer affordable luxuries. There is a response for each of these assertions.

Inevitable project change is a poor reason not to plan. In fact, frequent change is one of the most damaging risk factors, and managing this risk requires good project information. Project teams that have solid planning data are better able to resist inappropriate change, rejecting or deferring proposed changes on the basis of the consequences demonstrated by the project plan. When changes are necessary, it is easier to continue the work by modifying an existing plan than by starting over in a vacuum. In addition, many high-tech project changes directly result from faulty project assumptions that persist because of inadequate planning information. Better understanding leads to clearer definition of project deliverables and fewer reasons for change.

The time required to plan is also not a very good reason to avoid project management processes. While it is universally true that no project has enough time, the belief that there is no time to plan is difficult to understand. All the work in any project must always be planned. There is a choice as to whether planning will be done primarily in a focused, early-project exercise or by identifying the work one activity at a time, day by day, all through the project. All necessary analysis must be done by someone, eventually. The incremental approach requires comparable, if not more, overall effort, and it carries a number of disadvantages. First, project tracking is not very useful, as progress measurement is at best a guess. Second, most project risks, even the easily identifiable ones, come as unexpected surprises when they occur. Early, more thorough planning provides other advantages, and it is always preferable to have project information sooner than later. Why not invest in planning when the benefits are greatest?

Assertions about "Internet time" are also difficult to accept. Projects that must execute as quickly as possible need more, not less, project planning. Delivering a result with value requires sequencing the work for efficiency and ensuring that the activities undertaken are truly necessary and of high priority. There is no time for rework, excessive defect correction, or unnecessary activity on fast-track projects. Project planning, particularly on time-constrained projects, *is* real work.

Above the Project Level

Projects are undertaken on the basis of the assumption that whatever the project produces will have value, but there is often little consideration of the type and amount of *process* that projects need. In many high-tech environments, little to no formal project management is mandated, and often it is even discouraged.

Whenever the current standards and project management practices are inadequate in an organization, strive to improve them. There are two possible ways to do this. Your best option is to convince the managers and other stakeholders that more formal project definition, planning, and tracking will deliver an overall benefit for the business. When this is successful, all projects benefit. For situations where this is unsuccessful, a second option is to adopt greater formalism just for your current project. It may even be necessary to do this in secret, to avoid criticism and comments like "Why are you wasting time with all that planning stuff? Why aren't you working?"

In organizations where expenses and overhead are tightly controlled, it can be difficult to convince managers to adopt greater project formalism. Building a case for this takes time and requires metrics and examples, and you may find that some upper-level managers are highly resistant even to credible data. The benefits are substantial, though, so it is well worth trying; anything you can do to build support for project processes over time will help.

If you have credible, local data that demonstrate the value of project management or the costs associated with inadequate process, assemble them. Most organizations that have such data also have good processes. If you have a problem that is related to inadequate project management, it is likely that you will also not have a great deal of information to draw from. For projects lacking a structured methodology, few metrics are established for the work, so mounting a compelling case for project management processes using your own data may be difficult.

Typical metrics that may be useful in supporting your case relate to achieving specifications, managing budgets, meeting schedules, and delivering business value. Project processes directly impact the first three but only indirectly influence the last one. The ultimate value of a project deliverable is determined by a large number of factors in addition to the project management approach, many of which are totally out of the control of the project team. Business value data may be the best information you have available, though, so make effective use of what you can find.

Even if you can find or create only modest evidence that better project management processes will be beneficial, it is not hopeless. There are other approaches that may suffice, using anecdotal information, models, and case studies.

Determining which approaches to use depends on your situation. There is a wide continuum of beliefs about project management among upper-level managers. Some managers favor project management naturally. These folks require little or no convincing, and any approach you use is likely to succeed. Other managers are highly skeptical about project management and focus heavily on the visible costs (which are unquestionably real), while doubting the benefits. The best approach in this case is to gather local information, lots of it, that shows as clearly as possible the high costs of *not* using better processes. Trying to convince an extreme skeptic that project management is necessary may even be a waste of time for both of you. Good risk management in such a skeptical environment is up to you and is probably best done "below the radar."

Fortunately, most managers are somewhere in the middle, neither "true believers" in project management nor chronic process adversaries. The greatest potential for process improvement is with this ambivalent group, and the following approaches can be very effective.

Anecdotal Information

Building a case for more project process with stories depends on outlining the benefits and costs, and showing there is a net benefit. Project management lore is filled with stated benefits, among them:

❏ Better communication

❏ Less rework

❏ Lowered costs, reduced time

❏ Earlier identification of gaps and inadequate specifications

❏ Fewer surprises

❏ Less chaos and fire-fighting

Finding situations that show either where project management delivered on these or where lack of process created a related problem should not be hard.

Project management does have costs, some direct and some more subtle, and you need to address these. One obvious cost is the "overhead" it represents: meetings, paperwork, time invested in project management activities. Another is the initial (and ongoing) cost of establishing good practices in an organization, such as training, job aids, and new process documentation. Do some assessment of the investment required, and summarize the results.

There is a more subtle cost to managers in organizations that set high project management standards: the shift that occurs in the balance of power in an organization. Without project management processes, all the power in an organization is in the hands of management; all negotiations tend to be resolved using political and emotional tactics. Having little or no data, project teams are fairly easily backed into whatever corners their management chooses. With data, the discussion shifts and negotiations are based more on reality. Even if you choose not to directly address this "cost," be aware of it in your discussions.

Your decision to answer the question "Is project management worth it?" with anecdotal information depends on whether you can credibly show the benefits to outweigh the costs. Your case will be most effective if you find the best examples you can, using projects from environments as similar to yours as possible.

Models: Estimating Project Management Costs

Another possible approach for establishing the value of process relies on logical models. The need for process increases with scale and complexity, and managing projects is no exception to this. Scaling projects may be done in a variety of ways, but one common technique segregates them into three categories: small, medium, and large.

Small projects are universal; everyone does them. There is usually no particular process or formality applied, and more often than not these simple projects are successful. Nike-style ("Just Do It") project management is good enough, and, although there may well be any number of slightly better ways to approach the work (very apparent in hindsight, more often than not), the penalties associated with simply diving into the work are modest enough that it doesn't matter much. Project management processes are rarely applied with any rigor, even by project management zealots, as the overhead involved may double the work required for the project.

Medium-size projects last longer and are more complex. The benefits of thinking about the work, at least a little, are obvious to most people. At a minimum, there is a "to do" list. Rolling up your sleeves and beginning work with no advance thought often costs significant additional time and money. As the "to do" list spills over a single page, project management processes start to look useful. At what exact level of complexity this occurs has a lot to do with experience, background, and individual disposition. Many midsize projects succeed, but the possibility of falling short of some key goal (or complete project failure) is increasing.

For large projects, the case for project management should never really be in doubt. Beyond a certain scale, all projects with no process for managing the work will fail to meet at least some part of the stated objective. For the largest of projects, success rates are low even *with* program management and systems engineering processes in addition to thorough project management practices.

For projects of different sizes, costs of execution with and without good project management will vary. Figure 2-1 shows the cost of a "best effort," or brute force, approach to a project contrasted with a project management approach. The assumption for this graph is that costs will vary linearly with project scale if project management is applied and geometrically with scale if it is not.

Figure 2-1. Cost benefit of project management.

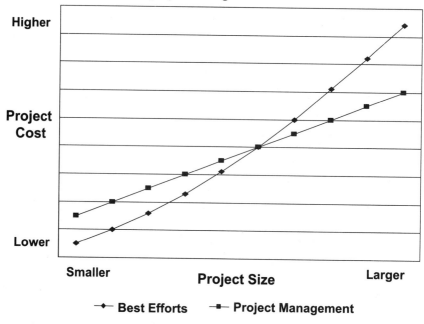

This figure, though not based on empirical data, is solidly rooted in a large amount of anecdotal information.

The figure has no units, because the point at which the crossover occurs (in total project size and cost) is highly situational. If project size is measured in effort-months, a common metric, a typical crossover might be between one and four total effort-months.

Wherever the crossover point is, the cost benefit is very minor near this point and negative below it. For these smaller projects, project management is a net cost or of very small financial benefit. (Cost may not be the only, or even the most important, consideration, though. Project management methodologies may also be employed for other reasons, such as to meet legal requirements, to manage risk better, or to improve coordination between independent projects.)

A model similar to this, especially if it is accompanied by project success and failure data, can be a compelling argument for adopting better project management practices.

Case Studies

To offset the costs of project management, you need to establish measurable (or at least plausible) benefits. Many studies and cases have been developed over the years to assess this, including the one summarized in Figure 2-2. The data in this particular study were collected over a three-year period in the early 1990s from more than 200 projects at Hewlett-Packard. For every project included, all schedule changes were noted and characterized. All changes attributed to the same root cause were aggregated, and the summations were sorted for the Pareto diagram in the figure, displaying the magnitude of the change on the vertical axis and the root causes along the horizontal axis.

Figure 2-2. Schedule change Pareto diagram.

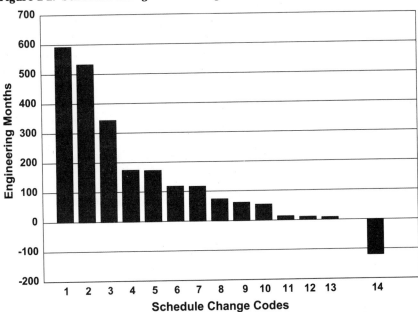

Additional project effort—hundreds of engineer months—was associated with the most common root causes. The codes for the root causes, sorted by severity, were:

1. Unforeseen technical problems
2. Poor estimation of effort/top-down schedules
3. Poor product/system design or integration problems
4. Changing product definition
5. Other
6. Unforeseen activities/too many unrelated activities
7. Understaffed, or resources not on time

8. Software development system/process problems

9. Related project slip (also internal vendor slip)

10. Insufficient support from service areas

11. Hardware development system/process problems

12. Financial constraints (tooling, capital, prototypes)

13. Project placed on hold

14. Acceleration

Not every one of these root causes directly correlates with project management principles, but most of them clearly do. The largest one is unforeseen technical problems, many of which were probably caused by insufficient planning. The second, faulty estimation is also a project management factor. While better project management would not have eliminated all these slippages, it surely would have reduced them. The top two reasons in the study by themselves represent an average of roughly five unanticipated engineer-months per project; reducing this by half would save thousands of dollars per project.

Case study data such as these, particularly if they directly relate to the sort of project work you do, can be very convincing. You very likely have access to data similar to these, or could estimate it, for rework, fire-fighting, crisis management, missing work, and the cost of defects on recent projects.

Other Reasons for Project Management

One of the principal motivators in organizations that adopt project principles is reduction of uncertainty. Most technical people hate risk and will go to great lengths to avoid it. One manager who strongly supports project management practices uses the metaphor of going down the rapids of a white-water river. Without project management, you are down in the water—you have no visibility, it is cold, it is hard to breathe, and your head is hitting lots of rocks. With project management, you are up on a raft. It is still a wild ride, but you can see a few dozen feet ahead and steer around the worst obstacles. You can breathe more easily, you are not freezing and are less wet, and you have some confidence that you will survive the trip. In this manager's group, minimizing uncertainty is important, and planning is never optional.

Another motivator is a desire (or requirement) to become more process-oriented. Some industries have adopted ISO standards so widely that individual companies have no choice but to comply. In companies that provide solutions to customers, use of a defined methodology is a competitive advantage that can help win business. In some organizations, evidence of process maturity is deemed important, and standards set by organizations such as the Software Engineering Institute for higher maturity are pursued. In other instances, specific process requirements are tied to the work, as with many government contracts. In all of these cases, project management is used, at least to some extent, whether or not the individuals and managers involved think it is a good idea.

THE PROJECT MANAGEMENT METHODOLOGY

Project risk management depends on thorough, sustained application of effective project management principles. The precise nature of the project management methodology can vary widely, but management of risk is most successful when consistent processes are adopted by the organization as a whole, because there is more information to work with and more durable support for the ongoing effort required. If you need to manage risk better on your project and it proves impossible to gain support for more effective project management principles broadly, resolve to apply them, project by project, with sufficient rigor to develop the information you need to manage risk.

Defining Risk Management for the Project

Beyond basic project planning, risk management also involves specific planning for risk. Risk planning begins by reviewing the initial project assumptions. Project charters, datasheets, or other documents used to initiate a project often include information concerning risk, as well as goals, staffing assumptions, and other information. Any risk information included in these early project descriptions is worth noting; sometimes projects believed to be risky are described as such, or there may be other evidence of project risk. Projects that are thought to be low-risk may use assumptions that lead to unrealistically low staffing and funding. Take note of any differences in *your* perception of project risk and the stated (or implied) risks perceived by the project sponsors. Risk planning builds on a foundation that is consistent with the overall assumptions and project objectives. In particular, work to understand the expectations of the project stakeholders, and adopt an approach to risk management that reflects your environment.

STAKEHOLDER RISK TOLERANCE

Organizations in different businesses deal with risk in their own ways. Start-ups and speculative endeavors such as oil exploration generally have a high tolerance for risk; many projects undertaken are expected to fail, but these are compensated for by a small number that are extremely successful. More conservative enterprises and organizations that provide solutions to customers for a fee generally are very risk-averse, expecting consistent success but more modest returns on each project. Organizational risk tolerance is reflected in the organizational policies, such as preestablished prohibitions on pursuing fixed-price contract projects.

In addition, the stakeholders of the project may have strong individual opinions on project risk. While some stakeholders may be risk-tolerant, others may wish to staff and structure the work to minimize extreme outcomes. Technical contributors tend to prefer low risk. One often repeated example of stakeholder risk preference is attributed to the NASA astronauts, who observed that they were sitting on the launch pad atop hundreds of systems, each constructed by the lowest bidder. Risk tolerance frequently depends on your perspective.

PLANNING DATA

Project planning information supports risk planning. As you define the project scope and create planning documents such as the project work breakdown structure, you will uncover potential project risks. The planning processes also support your efforts in managing risk. The linkages between project planning and risk identification are explored in Chapters 3 through 6.

TEMPLATES AND METRICS

Risk management is easier and more thorough when you have access to predefined templates for planning, project information gathering, and risk assessment. Templates that are preloaded with information common to most projects make planning faster and decrease the likelihood that necessary work will be overlooked. Consistent templates created for use with project scheduling applications organizationwide make sharing information easier and improve communication. If such templates exist, use them. If there are none, create and share proposed versions of common documents with others who do similar project work, and begin to establish standards.

Risk planning also relies on a solid base of historical data.

Archived project data support project estimating, quantitative project risk analysis, and project tracking and control. Examples of metrics useful for risk management are covered in Chapter 9.

RISK MANAGEMENT PLAN

For small projects, risk planning may be informal, but for large, complex projects, you should develop and publish a written risk management plan. A risk management plan includes information on stakeholders, planning processes, project tools, and metrics, and it states the standards and objectives for risk management on your project. While much of the information in a risk plan can be developed generally for all projects in an organization, each specific project has at least some unique risk elements.

A risk plan usually starts by summarizing your risk management approach, listing the methodologies and processes that you will use, and defining the roles of the people involved. It may also include information such as definitions and standards for use with risk management tools; the frequency and agenda for periodic risk reviews; any formats to be used for required inputs and for risk management reports; and requirements for status collection and other tracking. In addition, each project may determine specific trigger events and thresholds for metrics associated with project risks and the budgets for risk analysis, contingency planning, and risk monitoring.

The PERIL Database

Over the past ten years, in the context of a series of workshops on risk management, I have asked hundreds of project leaders to describe typical past project problems, defining both what went wrong and the impact it had on their projects. These data are collected in the Project Experience Risk Information Library (PERIL) database and serve as the basis for the following analysis of high-tech project risk.

One useful dichotomy in risk management is between the "known" risks, the risks that occur frequently enough to be analyzed in advance, and the "unknown" risks, those that result from the uniqueness of the work and are difficult or impossible to anticipate. While the PERIL database contains a few unusual situations that are unlikely to recur, nearly all of the data represent situations that are typical of technical projects, so PERIL also provides a template for identifying risk situations that might otherwise fall into the "unknown" category.

THE DATA

First, what the information in PERIL is not. It is not comprehensive. It represents a small fraction of the tens of thousands of projects undertaken during this time by the project managers from whom it was collected, and it does not represent *all* the problems encountered even for the projects that are included. It is not unbiased. Several sources of potential bias are obvious: the data were not collected randomly, they are self-reported, and the information comes from a constituency at least interested enough in project and risk management to invest time attending the workshop. Another bias is toward more significant risks; few minor risks are reported here, as the point of the exercise was to collect data on major problems. Having said all this, the risk information collected represents a wide range of risks typical of current projects, and, even with its flaws, a number of patterns emerge. Some of the bias may even make the data more useful, as a focus on more significant problems is consistent with accepted strategies for risk management. However, in extending this analysis to other situations, be aware that "your mileage may vary."

Now, what the PERIL database is. The information collected covers a wide range of projects. Slightly more than half are product development projects, and the rest are information technology, customer solution, or process improvement projects. The projects are worldwide, with a majority from the Americas (primarily United States, Canada, and Mexico). The rest of the cases are from Asia (Singapore and India) and from Europe and the Middle East (from a number of nations, but mainly Germany and the United Kingdom). Whatever the type or location, most of these projects share a strong dependence on new or relatively new technology and significant investment in software development. Both longer and shorter projects are represented, but most had durations between six months and one year. While there are some very large programs in PERIL, typical staffing on these projects was between ten and twenty-five people.

The raw project numbers in the PERIL database are:

	AMERICAS	ASIA	EUROPE/ MIDDLE EAST	Total
IT/Solution	67	25	13	105
Product Development	56	45	16	117
Total	**123**	**70**	**29**	**222**

In order to normalize the data for analysis and comparison purposes, a consistent measure for "impact" is used. The most typical serious impact reported was deadline slip (in weeks), so I estimated a slippage equivalent to this whenever the impact was primarily unplanned overtime, scope reduction, or some other project change. In cases where the deadline was mandatory, the data reported are the equivalent duration that would have been required if the overtime had been worked on a standard schedule or the duration that would have been required to restore any deletions from the project scope. When this was necessary, very conservative estimates were used in making these transformations. The average impact for all records was slightly over five weeks, representing about a 20 percent slip for a typical nine-month project. The averages by project type and by region were consistently very close to the average for all of the data, ranging from about four and a half weeks up to six and a half weeks.

Risk Types

Categorizing risks is a useful way to identify specific problems. Categories suggested by the project triple constraint—scope, schedule, and resources—are used to organize the PERIL database. The relative occurrence and impact of risks of various types provide the basis for improved risk discovery and for more selective and cost-effective risk management. The resource, schedule, and scope risks in PERIL are further subdivided into categories and subcategories on the basis of the sources of the risks.

For most of the risks, the categorization was fairly obvious. For others, the risk spanned a number of factors, and the categorization was a judgment call. In each case, however, the risk was grouped under the project parameter where it had the largest effect, and then by its primary perceived root cause. While schedule risks are most numerous, they seem slightly less damaging, on average, than the other risks (but they still typically caused nearly a month of project slip). Scope risks represent the most impact on project delivery, followed by resource risks. The data are shown here:

	COUNT	CUMULATIVE IMPACT (WEEKS)	AVERAGE IMPACT (WEEKS)
Scope	76	478	6.3
Schedule	82	306	3.7
Resource	64	361	5.6
Total	**222**	**1145**	**5.2**

Scope risks dominate the data, but all categories are significant. A Pareto chart summarizing this total impact by category is in Figure 2-3.

Figure 2-3. Risks in the PERIL database.

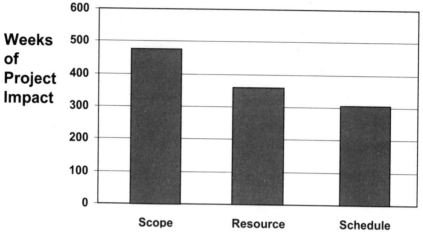

Each of these three categories is further characterized by root cause, and a summary of this data appears in Figure 2-4. The PERIL database offers insight into the sources and magnitudes of technical project risk, and detailed descriptions of the analysis for each category are spread through the next three chapters, with scope risks discussed in Chapter 3, schedule risks in Chapter 4, and resource risks in Chapter 5.

Figure 2-4. Subcategory risks in the PERIL database.

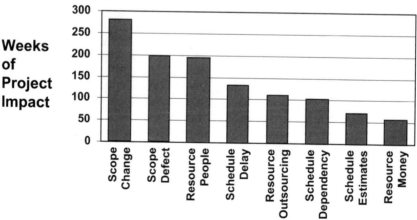

A Second Panama Canal Project: Sponsorship and Initiation (1902–1904)

"A man, a plan, a canal. Panama."

Successful projects are often not the first attempt to do something. Often, there is a recognized opportunity that triggers a project. If the first attempted project fails, it discourages people for a time. Soon, however, if the opportunity remains attractive, another project will begin, building on the work and the experiences of the first project. A canal at Panama remained such an attractive opportunity. When Theodore Roosevelt became president in 1901, he decided to make successful completion of a Central American canal part of his presidential legacy. (And so it is. He is the "man" in the famous palindrome.)

As much as the earlier French project failed due to lapses in project management, the U.S. project ultimately succeeded as a direct result of the application of good project principles. The results of better project and risk management on this second project unfold throughout the remainder of this book.

Unlike the initial attempt to build a canal, the U.S. effort was not a commercial venture. Maintaining separate U.S. navies on the east and west coasts had become increasingly costly. Consolidation into a single larger navy required easy transit between the Atlantic and Pacific, so Theodore Roosevelt saw the Panama Canal as a strategic military project, not a commercial one.

The U.S. venture started with the Battle of the Routes—Nicaragua versus Panama—and, on the basis of technical analysis, they selected Panama. Unlike Ferdinand de Lesseps, Theodore Roosevelt was a more typical project sponsor. He delegated the management of the project to others. His greatest direct contribution to the project was in "engineering" the independence of Panama from Colombia. (This "revolution" was accomplished by a pair of gunboats, one at Colon, on the Gulf of Mexico side of Panama, and another at Panama City, on the Pacific. Without the firing of a single shot, the independent nation of Panama was created in 1902. Repercussions from this U.S. foreign policy decision persist a century later.) To get the project started quickly, Roosevelt also moved to acquire the assets of the Nouvelle Compagnie (which returned some relief to shareholders of the original company, but not much).

"I took the isthmus!" Roosevelt said. He then went to the U.S. Congress to get approval to go forward with the building of the canal. Following all this activity and the public support it generated, Congress had little choice but to support the project. While the specifics for the project were still vague, the intention of the United States was clear: to build a canal at Panama capable of transporting even the largest U.S. warships and to build it as quickly as was practical.

Insight into Roosevelt's thinking concerning the project is found in this quotation from 1899, two years before his presidency:

> Far better it is to dare mighty things, to win glorious triumphs, even though checkered by failure, than to take rank with those poor spirits who neither enjoy much nor suffer much, because they live in the gray twilight that knows not victory nor defeat.

Project sponsors often aspire to "dare mighty things." They are much more risk-tolerant than most project leaders and teams. Good risk management planning serves to balance the process of setting project objectives so that we undertake projects that are not only worthwhile and challenging but also *possible*.

CHAPTER 3

IDENTIFYING PROJECT SCOPE RISK

"Well begun is half done."

—ARISTOTLE

While beginning well never actually completes half of a project, beginning poorly leads to disappointment, rework, stress, and potential failure. A great deal of project risk can be discovered at the earliest stages of project work, when project leaders are defining the scope of the project.

For risks associated with the elements of the project management triple constraint (scope, schedule, and resources), scope risk generally is considered first. Of the three types of doomed projects—those that are beyond your capabilities, those that are over-constrained, and those that are ineffectively executed—the first type is the most significant, because this type of project is *literally* impossible. Identification of scope risks reveals either that your project is probably feasible or that it lies beyond the state of your art. Early decisions to shift the scope or abandon the project are essential on projects with significant scope risks.

There is little consensus in project management circles on a precise definition of "scope." Very broad definitions use scope to refer to everything in the project, and very narrow definitions limit project scope to include only project deliverables. For the purposes of this chapter, project scope is defined to be consistent with the *Guide to the Project Management Body of Knowledge*, 2000 edition *(PMBOK® Guide)*. The type of scope risk considered here relates primarily to the project deliverable(s). Other types of project risk are covered in later chapters.

The principal risk ideas covered in this chapter are:

❐   Sources of scope risk

❐   Deliverable definition

❐   High-level risk assessment

❐   Setting limits

❐   Work breakdown structure

❐   Market and confidentiality risk

Sources of Scope Risk

While scope risks represent roughly one-third of the data in the Project Experience Risk Information Library (PERIL) database, they account for close to half of the total impact. The two broad categories of scope risk in PERIL relate to *changes* and to *defects*. By far the most damage was due to poorly managed change, but all scope risks represent significant exposure in typical high-tech projects. While some of the risk situations, particularly in the category of defects, were legitimately "unknown" risks, quite a few common problems could have been identified in advance through better definition of deliverables and a more thorough work breakdown structure. The summary:

SCOPE RISKS	COUNT	CUMULATIVE IMPACT (WEEKS)	AVERAGE IMPACT (WEEKS)
Changes	46	280	6.1
Defect	30	198	6.6

These root causes were further characterized by type, and a Pareto chart of overall impact by type of risk is summarized in Figure 3-1.

Change Risks

Change risk represents well over half the scope risks reported in the PERIL database. There are three categories of scope change risks:

❐   *Scope creep*: requirements that evolve and mutate as a project runs

❐   *Gaps*: specifications or activities added to the project late

❐   *Scope dependencies*: inputs or other needs of the project not anticipated at the start of a project

Figure 3-1. Scope risks in the PERIL database.

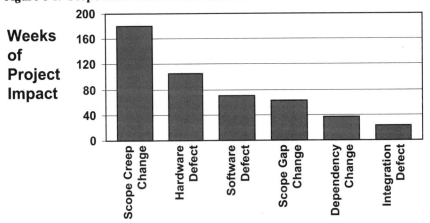

Scope creep is the most serious category and the one in which the majority of the change risks in PERIL fall. Nearly all of these incidents represented unanticipated additional investment of time and money that could have been predicted with clearer scope definition. The average impact on projects that reported scope creep was more than two months of slip. Some of the changes were a result of a shift in the specifications. Others were specifications above and beyond the stated project objective that were added as the project ran. While in some, perhaps even most, of these cases, the changes represented good business decisions, there is no question that the projects would have been shorter, less expensive, and easier to run if the definitions ultimately used had been determined earlier. In some particularly severe cases, the changes in scope delayed the project so much that the product had little or no value. The need was no longer pressing, or it had been met by some other means. The tool that uncovers these problems most effectively is early establishment of a better, clearer, more thorough definition.

Scope creep also comes from within, generally from well-intentioned attempts by some part of the project team to "improve" the deliverable. While internally generated changes may have value, often they do not have enough to warrant the project impact they cause. Whatever the source, meandering definition of scope creates a great deal of scope risk. Scope creep is a universal and pervasive issue for technical projects.

Other project changes in the PERIL database resulted from gaps in the project scope that were discovered late in the project. Most of these risks were due to overlooked requirements—work required for the project objective that went unrecognized until late in the project. In a small number of cases, the project objective was so unlike earlier work that the gaps were probably unavoidable. The additional insights provided in midproject by customers, managers, team members, or other project stakeholders were not available at the start of the project, so the work required was not visible. In most of the cases, however, the gaps came from incomplete analysis and could have been avoided. More thorough scope definition and project work breakdown would have clearly shown the missing and incomplete portions of the project plan.

A third category of change relates to unexpected scope dependencies. (Dependency risks that primarily affect the project timeline, rather than the scope, are included with schedule risks in the database.) Again, there were some changes that no amount of realistic analysis would have uncovered. While the legal requirements and other factors external to the project are generally stable, they may occasionally shift quickly and without warning. In the risk database, however, most of the situations were due to factors that should not have come as complete surprises. Some were due to changes in the infrastructure the project was depending upon, such as a new version of system or application software or hardware upgrades. Some projects in the database were hurt by unplanned delays in access to new software versions or product releases. Investigation and more thorough analysis of the systems, software, and the infrastructure your project requires can uncover many dependency risks.

DEFECT RISKS

Technical projects rely on many complicated things to work as expected. Unfortunately, new things do not always operate as promised or as required. Even normally reliable things may break down or fail to perform as desired in a novel application. Hardware failure was the most common defect risk of this sort in the PERIL database, followed by software problems. In several cases, the root cause was new, untried technology that the project was unable to use for the project because it lacked functionality or reliability. In other cases, a component created by the project (such as a custom integrated circuit, a board, or a software module) did not work initially and had to be redone. In still other cases, critical purchased components delivered to the project failed to work and required replacement. Nearly all of these risks are visible, at least as possibilities, through adequate analysis and planning.

Some hardware and software functional failures related to quality. In many projects, some components may work but fail to meet a stated standard of performance. Hardware may fail to meet a throughput standard or require too much power or emit excessive electromagnetic interference. Software may not be easy enough to operate or may not work in unusual circumstances. As with other defects, the definition, planning, and analysis of project work helps in anticipating many of these potential quality risks.

The third type of defect risk, after hardware and software problems, occurs above the component level. In many large technical programs, the work is decomposed into smaller, related subprojects that execute in parallel. Successful integration of the outputs of each of the subprojects into a single system deliverable requires not only that each of the components delivered operate as specified but also that the combination of all these parts also work as a functioning system. As computer users, we are more familiar with this exposure than we would care to be. When the various software programs we use fail to play nicely together, we see a characteristic "blue screen of death" or the crash of a system or application with notification of some sort of "illegal operation." Integration risk is particularly problematic in projects, as it generally occurs very near the deadline and is rarely simple to diagnose and correct. Again, thorough analysis using disciplines such as software architecture and systems engineering can reveal much of this sort of risk early.

A more complete listing of the scope risks in the PERIL database is included in the Appendix. While uncovering scope risks begins with a review of past problems such as these, each new project you take on will also pose unique scope risks that can be uncovered only as you define deliverables and develop the project work breakdown structure.

Defining Deliverables

Defining deliverables thoroughly is a powerful tool for uncovering potential change-oriented scope risks.

The process for specifying deliverables for a project varies greatly depending on the type and the scale of the project. For small projects, informal methods can work well, but for most projects, adopting a more rigorous approach is where good risk management begins. Defining the deliverables for a project gives the project leader and the team their first indication of the risks in the proposed project. Whatever the process, the goal is to develop specific, written requirements that are clear, unambiguous, and agreed to by all project stakeholders and project contributors.

A good, thorough process for defining project deliverables

begins with identifying the people who should participate, including all who must agree with the definition. Much project scope risk arises because key project contributors are not involved with the project early, when initial definition work is done. Some scope problems become visible only late in the project, when these staff members finally join the project team. Whenever it is not possible to work with the specific people who will later be part of the project team, locate and work with people who *are* available and who can represent each needed perspective and functional area. In establishing this team, strive to include all functions that are essential to the project: call in favors, beg, plead, or do whatever you need to do to get qualified people involved. The definition effort includes all of the core project team, but it rarely ends there. You nearly always need to include others from outside your project who may not be directly involved with the work, from functions such as marketing, sales, and support. Outside your organization, you probably also need input from customers, users, other related project teams, and potential subcontractors. Consider the project over its entire development life cycle. Think about who will be involved with all stages of design, development, manufacturing or assembly, testing, documentation, selling, installation, distribution, support, and other aspects of the work.

Even when the right people are available and involved early in the early project definition activities, it is difficult to be thorough. The answers for many questions may not yet be available, and much of your data may be ranges or even guesses. Specifics concerning new methods and technologies add more uncertainty. Three useful techniques for managing scope risk are:

❐ Using a documented definition process

❐ Developing a straw-man definition document

❐ Adopting a rigorous evolutionary methodology

DELIVERABLE DEFINITION PROCESS

Processes for defining deliverables vary depending on the nature of the project. For product development projects, a list of guidelines similar to the one that follows is a typical starting point. By reviewing such a list and documenting both what is known and what is still needed, you build a firm foundation for defining project scope and also begin to capture activities that need to be integrated into the project plan.

Topics for a typical deliverable definition process are:

1. Alignment with business strategy (How does this project contribute to stated high-level business objectives?)

2. User and customer needs (Has the project team captured the ultimate end user requirements that must be met by the deliverable?)

3. Compliance (Has the team identified all relevant regulatory, environmental, and manufacturing requirements, as well as any relevant industry standards?)

4. Competition (Has the team identified both current and projected alternatives to the proposed deliverable, including *not* undertaking the project?)

5. Positioning (Is there a clear and compelling benefit-oriented project objective that supports the business case for the project?)

6. Decision criteria (Does this project team have an agreed-upon hierarchy of measurable priorities for cost, time, and scope?)

7. Delivery (Are logistical requirements understood and manageable? These include, but are not limited to, sales, distribution, installation, sign-off, and support.)

8. Sponsorship (Does the management hierarchy collectively support the project, and will it provide timely decisions and ongoing resources?)

9. Resources (Does the project have, and will it continue to have, the staffing and funding needed to meet the project goals within the allotted time?)

10. Technical risk (Has the team assessed the overall level of risk it is taking? Are technical and other exposures well documented?)

(This list is based on the 1972 SAPPHO Project at the University of Sussex, England.)

While this list is not exhaustive, a thorough examination of each criterion and written documentation of available information provides a firm foundation for defining specific requirements. Assessment of the *degree* to which each element of the list is adequately understood (on a scale ranging from "Clueless" on one extreme to "Omniscient" on the other) also begins to identify what is missing. The gaps identified in the process may be used to define tasks and activities that will be added to the project plan. While some level of uncertainty will always remain, this sort of analysis makes it clear where the biggest exposures are. It also allows the project team and sponsor to make intelligent choices and decide whether the level of risk is inappropriately high. The last point on this list, technical risk, is most central to the subject at hand. High-level project risk assessment is discussed in some detail later in this chapter.

STRAW-MAN DEFINITION DOCUMENT

Most books on project management prattle on about identifying and documenting all the known project requirements. This is much easier said than done for projects in the real world; it is very hard to get users and stakeholders of technical projects to cooperate with this strategy. When too little about a project is clear, many people see only two options: accept the risks associated with incomplete definition, or abandon the project. Between these, however, lies a third option. By constructing a straw-man definition, instead of simply accepting the lack of data, the *project team* defines the specific requirements. These requirements may be based on earlier projects, assumptions, guesses, or the team's best understanding of the problem that the project deliverable is supposed to solve. Any definition constructed this way is certain to be inaccurate and incomplete, but formalizing requirements leads to one of two very beneficial results.

The first possibility is that the invented requirements will be accepted and approved, giving the project team a solid basis for planning. Once sign-off has occurred, anything that is not quite right or deemed incomplete can be changed only through a formal project change management process. (Some contracting firms use this to get rich. They win business by quoting fixed fees that are below the cost of delivering all the stated requirements, knowing full well that there will be changes. They then make their profits by charging for the inevitable changes that occur, generating large incremental billings for the project.) Even for projects where the sponsors and project team are in the same organization, the sign-off process gives the project team a great deal of leverage when negotiating changes. (This whole process brings to mind the old riddle: "How do you make a statue of an elephant?" Answer: "You get an enormous chunk of marble and chip off anything that does not look like an elephant.")

The second possible outcome is a flood of criticism, corrections, edits, and "improvements." While most people are intimidated by a blank piece of paper or an open-ended question, *everyone* seems to enjoy being a critic. Once a straw-man requirements document is created, the project leader can circulate it far and wide as "pretty close, but everything is not exactly right yet." Using such a document to gather comments (and providing big, red pens to get things rolling) is very effective for the project, even if it is humbling to the original authors. In any case, it is better to identify these issues early than to find out what you missed during acceptance testing.

EVOLUTIONARY METHODOLOGIES

A third approach to scope definition used for software development relies on firm definitions for project scope, but only for the short-term future. Evolutionary (or cyclic) methodologies used for this have enjoyed some popularity since the 1980s and are still widely discussed and applied to development of software applications by small project teams that have ready access to their end users. Rather than defining a system as a whole, these methodologies set out a more general objective and then describe incremental stages, each producing a functional deliverable. The system built at the end of each cycle adds more functionality, and each release brings the project closer to its destination. As the work continues, very specific scope is defined for the next several cycles (each varying from about two to six weeks, depending on the specific methodology), but the deliverables for later cycles are defined only in more general terms. These will be revised and specified later, on the basis of evaluations by users during preceding development cycles and other data collected along the way.

While this can be an effective technique for managing revolutionary projects where fundamental definition is initially not possible, it does carry the risk of institutionalizing scope creep (a significant source of scope risk in the PERIL database) and may even be an invitation to "gold plating." It also starts the project with no certain end or budget, as the number of cycles is indeterminate and, without careful management, can even be perpetual.

Historically, evolutionary methodologies have carried higher costs than other project approaches. Compared with projects that are able to define project deliverables with good precision in the early stages (within the first 10 to 15 percent of the proposed schedule) and then execute using a more traditional "waterfall" life cycle, evolutionary development has been both slower and more expensive. Due to rework and other effort associated with a meandering definition process and the need to deliver to users every cycle and then evaluate their feedback, evolutionary methodologies may triple a project's cost and double its timeline. From a risk standpoint, evolutionary methodologies have a tendency to focus exclusively on scope risk, while accepting potentially unlimited schedule and resource risk. Risk management using an evolutionary approach for technical projects is more incremental, and it requires frequent reevaluation of the current risks, as well as extremely disciplined use of scope change assessment. In managing risk using evolutionary methodologies, it is also prudent to set limits for both time and money, not only for the complete project but also for key checkpoints no more than a few months apart.

Current thinking on evolutionary software development includes a number of methodologies described as agile, adaptive, or lightweight. These methods adopt more robust scope control and incorporate project management practices intended to avoid the "license to hack" nature of earlier evolutionary development models. "Extreme programming" (XP) is a good example of this. XP is intended for use on relatively small software development projects by project teams collocated with their users. It adopts effective project management principles for estimating, scope management, setting acceptance criteria, planning, and project communication. XP puts pressure on the users to determine the overall scope initially, and on this basis the project team determines the effort required for the work. Development cycles of a few weeks are used to implement the scope incrementally, as prioritized by the users, but the quantity of scope (which is carved up into "stories") in each cycle is determined exclusively by the programmers. XP allows revision of scope as the project runs, but only as a zero-sum game—any additions cause something to be bumped out or deferred until later. XP rigorously avoids scope creep in the current cycle.

Even for projects adopting this incremental approach to scope definition, you must outline the overall project objective, as in XP, in order to identify scope risk.

SCOPE DOCUMENTATION

However you go about defining scope, the next step is to write it down. Managing scope risk requires a clear scope statement that defines both what you will deliver and what you will not deliver. Without thorough scope definition, you cannot even understand the scope risks, let alone manage them. One common type of inadequate scope definition lists project requirements as "musts" and "wants." While it may be fine to have some flexibility during the earliest project investigation, the longer final decisions are delayed, the more problematic they become. Dragging a list of desirable, "want to have" features well into the development phase of a project is a major scope risk faced by many high-tech projects. Because project scope is not well-defined, project schedules and resource plans will be unclear, and estimates will be inexact.

From a risk management standpoint, the "is/is not" technique is far superior to "musts and wants." The "is" list is equivalent to the "musts," but the "is not" list serves to limit scope. Determining what *is not* in the project specification is never easy, but if you fail to do it, many of your scope risks will remain hidden behind a moving target. The "is/is not" technique is particularly important for projects that will have a fixed deadline and limited resources in order to establish a constraint for scope that is consistent with the limits on timing and budget. It is nearly always better to define the minimum requirements and deliver them as early as possible than to be aggressive with scope and either deliver late or have to drop promised features late in the project in order to meet the deadline. As you document your project scope, establish boundaries that define what the project *will not* include, to minimize scope creep.

There are dozens of formats for a document that defines scope. In product development, it may be a reference specification or a product data sheet. In a custom solution project (and for many other types of projects), it may be a key portion of the project proposal. For information technology projects, it may be part of the project charter document. In other types of projects, it may be included in a statement of work or a plan of record. For agile software methodologies, it may be a brief summary on a Web page and a collection of index cards tacked to a wall or forms taped to a whiteboard. Whatever it may be called or be a part of, an effective definition for project deliverables must be *in writing*. Specific information typically includes:

- ❐ A description of the project (what are you doing?)
- ❐ Project purpose (why are you doing it?)
- ❐ Completion criteria (project end, acceptance criteria)
- ❐ Planned project start
- ❐ Intended customer(s) and/or users
- ❐ What the project will and will not include ("is/is not")
- ❐ Dependencies (both internal and external)
- ❐ Staffing requirements (in terms of skills and experience)
- ❐ High-level risks
- ❐ Cost (rough order-of-magnitude, at least)
- ❐ Technology required

❏ Hardware, software, and other infrastructure required

❏ Detailed requirements, outlining functionality, usability, reliability, performance, supportability, and any other significant issues

❏ Other data customary and appropriate to your project

High-Level Risk Assessment Tools

Technical project risk assessment is part of the earliest phases of project work. (Item 10 of the deliverable definition process on page 43 states this need.) While there is usually very little concrete information on which to base an early project risk assessment, there are several tools that do provide useful insight into project risk even in the beginning stages. These tools are:

❏ Risk framework

❏ Risk complexity index

❏ Risk assessment grid

The first two are useful in any project that creates a tangible, physical deliverable through technical development processes. The third is appropriate for projects that have less tangible results, such as software modules, new processes, commercial applications, network architectures, or Internet service offerings. These tools all start by asking the same question: "How much experience do you have with the work the project will require?" How the tools use this information differs, and each builds on the assessment of technical risk in different ways. These tools are not mutually exclusive; depending on the type of project, one or more of them may help in assessing risk.

While any of these tools may be used at the start of a project to get an indication of project risk, none of the three is very precise. The purpose of each is to provide information about the *relative* risk of a new project. Each of these three techniques does have the advantage of being quick, and each can provide an assessment of project risk very early in a new project. None of the three is foolproof, but the results provide as good a basis as you are likely to have for deciding whether to go further with investigation and other project work. (You may also use these three tools to reassess project risk later in the project. Chapter 9 discusses reusing these three tools, as well as several additional project risk assessment methods that require planning details, to refine project risk assessment.)

RISK FRAMEWORK

This is the simplest of the three high-level techniques. To assess risk, consider the following three project factors:

☐ Technology (the work)

☐ Marketing (the user)

☐ Manufacturing (the production and delivery)

For each of these factors, assess the amount of change required by the project. For technology, does the project use only well-understood methods and skills, or will new skills be required (or developed)? For marketing, will the deliverable be used by someone (or by a class of users) you know well, or does this project address a need for someone unknown to you? For manufacturing, consider what is required to provide the intended end user with your project deliverable: are there any unresolved or changing manufacturing or delivery channel issues?

For each factor, the assessment is binary: change is either trivial (small) or significant (large). Assess conservatively; if the change required seems somewhere between these choices, treat it as significant.

Nearly all projects will require significant change to at least one of these three factors. Projects representing no (or very little) change may not be worth doing, and they may not even meet the requirement for a project that the effort be unique. Some projects, however, may require large changes in two or even all three factors. For technical projects, changes correlate with risk. The more change inherent in a project, and the more different types of change, the higher the risk.

In general, if your project has significant changes in only one factor, it probably has an acceptable, manageable level of risk. Evolutionary-type projects, where existing products or solutions are upgraded, leveraged, or improved, often fall into this category. If your project changes two factors simultaneously, it has higher relative risk, and the management decision to proceed, even into further investigation and planning, ought to reflect this. Projects that develop new platforms intended as the foundation of future project work frequently depend upon new methods for both technical development and manufacturing. For projects in this category,

the higher risks must be balanced against potential business benefits.

If your project requires large shifts in all three categories,
the risks are greatest of all. Many, if not most, projects in this risk
category are unsuccessful. Projects that represent this much
change are revolutionary and are justified by the very substantial
financial or other benefits that will result from successful completion. Often the risks seem so great—or so unknowable—that a truly
revolutionary project requires the backing of a very high-level
sponsor with a vision.

A commonly heard story around Hewlett-Packard from the
early 1970s involves a proposed project pitched to Bill Hewlett, the
more technical of the two HP founders. The team brought a mock-
up of a handheld device capable of scientific calculations with ten
significant digits of accuracy. The model was made out of wood,
but it had all the buttons labeled and was weighted to feel like the
completed device. Bill Hewlett examined the functions and display,
lifted the device, slipped it in his shirt pocket, and smiled. The HP-
35 calculator represented massive change in all three factors; the
market was unknown, manufacturing for it was unlike anything HP
had done before, and it was even debatable whether the electronics
could be developed on the small number of chips that could fit in
the tiny device. The HP-35 was developed primarily because Bill
Hewlett wanted one. It was also a hugely successful product, selling
more units in a month than had been forecasted for the entire year
and yielding a spectacular profit. The HP-35 also changed the direction of the calculator market completely, and it destroyed the market for mechanical slide rules and gear-driven computing machines
forever.

This story is known because the project was successful.
Similar stories surround many other revolutionary products, like
the Apple Macintosh, the Yahoo search engine, and home video-
cassette recorders. Stories about the risky projects that fail (or fall
far short of their objectives) are harder to uncover; most people
and companies would prefer to forget them. The percentage of revolutionary ideas that crash and burn is usually estimated to be at
least 90 percent. The higher risks of such projects should always
be justified by very substantial benefits and a strong, clear vision.

RISK COMPLEXITY INDEX

A second technique for assessing risk on projects that develop technical products is the risk complexity index. As in the risk
framework tool, technology is the starting point. This tool looks
more deeply at the technology being employed, separating it into

three parts and assigning to each an assessment of difficulty. In addition to the technical complexity, the index also looks at another source of project risk: the complexity arising from larger project teams, or scale. The following formula combines these four factors:

Index = (Technology + Architecture + System) × Scale

For the index, Technology is defined as new, custom development unique to this project. Architecture refers to the high-level functional components and any external interfaces, and System is the internal software and hardware that will be used in the product. Assess each of these three against your experience and capabilities, assigning each a value from 0 to 5:

- 0—Only existing technology required
- 1—Minor extensions to existing technology needed in a few areas
- 2—Significant extensions to existing technology needed in a few areas
- 3—Almost certainly possible, but innovation needed in some areas
- 4—Probably feasible, but innovation required in many areas
- 5—Completely new, technological feasibility in doubt

The three technology factors generally correlate, but some variation is common. Add these three factors, to a sum between 0 and 15.

For Scale, assign a value based on the number of people (including all full-time contributors, both internal and external) expected on the project:

- 0.8— Up to twelve people
- 2.4—thirteen to forty people
- 4.3—forty-one to one hundred people
- 6.6—More than one hundred people

The calculation for the index yields a result between 0 and 99. Projects with an index below 20 are generally low-risk projects with durations of well under a year. Projects assessed between 20 and 40 are medium risk. These projects are more likely to get into trouble and often take a year or longer. Most projects with an index above 40 finish long past their stated deadline, if they complete at all.

RISK ASSESSMENT GRID

The first two high-level risk tools are appropriate for hardware deliverables. Technical projects with intangible deliverables may not easily fit these models, so the risk assessment grid is a better approach to use for early risk assessment on these projects.

This tool examines three project factors, similar to the risk framework technique. Assessment here also provides two choices for each factor, and technology is again the first. The other factors are different, and here the three factors carry different weights. The factors, in order of priority, are:

- ❐ Technology
- ❐ Structure
- ❐ Size

The highest weight factor, Technology, is based on required change, and it is either Low or High, depending on whether the required technology is well known to the project team and whether it is well established for uses similar to the current project.

The second factor, Structure, is also assessed as either Low or High, on the basis of factors such as solid formal specifications, project sponsorship, and organizational practices appropriate to the project. Structure is Low when there are significant unknowns in staffing, responsibilities, infrastructure issues, objectives, or decision processes. Good up-front definition indicates high structure.

The third factor, Size, is similar to the Scale factor in the risk complexity index. A project is either considered Large or Small. For this tool, size is not an absolute assessment. It is measured relative to the size of teams that the project leader has successfully led in the past. Teams that are only 20 percent larger than the size a project leader has successfully led with should be considered Large. Other considerations in assessing size are the expected length of the project, the overall budget for the project, and the number of separate locations where project work will be performed.

After you have assessed each of the three factors, the project will fall into one of the sections of the grid, A through H (see

Figure 3-2). Projects in the right column are most risky; those to the left are more easily managed.

Figure 3-2. Risk assessment grid.

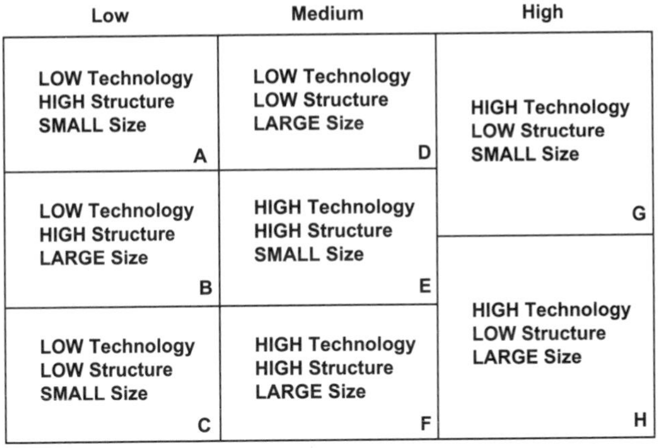

Low	Medium	High
LOW Technology HIGH Structure SMALL Size A	LOW Technology LOW Structure LARGE Size D	HIGH Technology LOW Structure SMALL Size
LOW Technology HIGH Structure LARGE Size B	HIGH Technology HIGH Structure SMALL Size E	G
LOW Technology LOW Structure SMALL Size C	HIGH Technology HIGH Structure LARGE Size F	HIGH Technology LOW Structure LARGE Size H

A = Lowest Risk; H = Highest Risk

This technique has been used to assess risk on a wide variety of project types. A consulting team in England used it very effectively by making it a central part of their decision process when considering whether to respond to a Request for Proposal (RFP). After an initial review of the RFP, they used the risk assessment grid to decide whether to respond, to "No Bid," or to develop and counterpropose a somewhat different solution.

Beyond risk assessment, these tools may also guide early project risk management, indicating ways to lower project risk by using alternative technologies, making changes to reduce staffing, decomposing longer projects into a sequence of shorter projects with less aggressive goals, or improving the proposed structure. Use of these and other tools to manage project risk is the topic of Chapter 10.

Setting Limits

While many scope risks come from specifics of the deliverable and the overall technology, scope risk also arises from failure to establish firm, early limits for the project.

Running workshops on risk management, I demonstrate this aspect of scope risk using an exercise that begins by getting out a single U.S. one-dollar bill. After showing it to the group, two rules are established:

❒ The dollar bill will go to the highest bidder, who will pay the amount bid. All bids must be for a real amount—no fractional cents. The first bid must be at least a penny, and each succeeding bid must be higher than earlier bids. (This is the same as in any auction.)

❒ The second-highest bidder *also* pays the amount he or she bid (the bid just prior to the winning bid) but gets *nothing* in return. (This is unlike a normal auction.)

As the auctioneer, I start by asking whether anyone wants to buy the dollar for one cent. Following the first bid, I solicit a second low bid: "Does anyone think the dollar is worth five cents?" After two low bids are made, the auction is off and running. The bidding is allowed to proceed to (and nearly always past) one dollar, until it ends. If one dollar is bid and things slow down, a reminder to the person who has the next highest bid that he or she will spend almost one dollar to buy *nothing* will usually get things moving again. The bidding ends when no new bids are made. The two final bids nearly always total well over two dollars.

By now everything is quite exciting. Someone has bought a dollar for more than a dollar. A second person has bought nothing but paid nearly as much. To calm things down, I put the dollar away, explain that this is a lesson in risk management (not a robbery), and apologize to people who seem upset.

So, what does the dollar auction have to do with risk management? This game's outcome is very similar to what happens when a project that hits its deadline (or budget) creeps past and just keeps going. "But we are *so* close. It's almost done; we *can't* stop now."

People point out that the dollar auction is not fair and is unrealistic. They are only half right; while it is not fair, it does approximate quite a few common situations in real life. It effectively models any case where people have, or think they have, too much invested in an undertaking to quit. The dollar auction was originally developed in the 1950s as a part of game theory, to study decision making in situations similar to the scenario of the game. In social settings, the inventors of the game found that the sum of the two highest bids in the auction generally rose to between three and five dollars.

Decisions to continue or to quit in situations that involve spending more time, more money, or both are common: Do you hold or hang up in a telephone queue for airlines, catalog merchants, or help desks? Continue to wait for a bus or hail a taxi? Repair an old car or invest in a new one? Continue or quit at a slot machine? Hold or sell a falling stock investment? Even submitting a competitive proposal where only the winner will get any reward is a variant of the dollar auction.

Dollar auction losses can be minimized by anticipating the possibility of an uncompensated investment, setting limits in advance, and then enforcing them. Rationally, the dollar auction has an expected return of half a dollar (the total return, one dollar, spread between the two active participants). If everyone participating adopted this rule, the auctioneer would always lose. For projects, clearly defining limits and then monitoring intermediate results will provide early indication that you may be in trouble. Project metrics, such as earned value (described in Chapter 9), are very useful in detecting project overrun early enough to abort or modify impossible or unjustified projects, minimizing unproductive investments. Defining project scope with sufficient detail and limits is an essential foundation for risk management and project planning.

Work Breakdown Structure (WBS)

While scope definition reveals some risks, scope planning digs deeper into the project and uncovers even more. Product definition documents, scope statements, and other written materials provide the basis for decomposing of project work into increasingly finer detail so that it can be understood, delegated, estimated, and tracked. The process used to do this—to create the project work breakdown structure (WBS)—also identifies potential defect risks.

One common approach to developing a WBS starts at the scope or objective statement and proceeds to carve the project into smaller parts, working "top-down" from the whole project concept. Decomposition of work that is well understood is straightforward and quickly done. Project risk becomes visible whenever it is confusing or difficult to decompose project work into smaller, more manageable pieces. The most common starting point for the process is the project deliverable or deliverables, which is why the WBS process is considered part of scope management in the *PM-BOK®* Guide. Developing a project WBS often begins by breaking the expected project results into components, features, or specifications that represent subsets of major deliverables for the overall project. There are other possible organizing principles for decomposing project work:

❒ By organizational function (marketing, R&D, manufacturing)

❒ By discipline (hardware, software, quality, support)

❒ By skill set (programming, accounting, assembly)

❒ By geography (Stuttgart, Bangalore, Boise, Taipei)

❒ By life-cycle phase (investigation, design, development, test)

If any part of the project resists breakdown using these ideas, that portion of the project is not well understood, and it is inherently risky. As with many aspects of project management, there is significant variation in how the WBS concept is applied. The *PMBOK®* Guide takes a hard line, insisting that a project WBS be deliverable-oriented, and suggests an alphabet soup of acronyms for breakdowns of other types. However, the examples offered in the *PMBOK®* Guide, and eleven more in the *PMI® Practice Standard for Work Breakdown Structures* (2001), are not organized exclusively on the basis of project deliverables. Most are project phase–oriented, or at least partially organized by discipline or skill set. In practice, it is very difficult to include all the project work in a strictly deliverable-oriented WBS.

From a risk management standpoint, any name you choose and any basis for organizing the work that helps you decompose your project thoroughly into more understandable pieces will provide the foundation you need.

WORK PACKAGES

The ultimate goal of the WBS process is to describe the entire project in much smaller pieces, often called work packages. The WBS is typically developed by breaking the overall project deliverable into major subsets of work and then continuing the process of decomposition down through multiple levels into a hierarchy, where each portion of the project is described at the lowest level by work packages of modest size. However your WBS may be organized at higher levels, each lowest-level work package must be deliverable-oriented, having a clearly defined output. General guidelines for the size of the work represented by the work packages at the lowest level of the WBS are usually in terms of duration (between two and twenty workdays) or effort (roughly eighty person-hours or less). While guidelines such as these are common, WBS standards for projects vary widely. These guidelines illustrate the connections among scope, schedule, and resource risk and foreshadow the discussions of estimating in Chapters 4 and 5. Project work broken down to this level of detail gives the project leader and team the information they need to understand, estimate, schedule, and monitor project work. It also provides a powerful tool for identifying the parts of the project most likely to cause trouble.

The terminology used for the work at the lowest level also varies a good deal for projects of various types. It is common practice to refer to the lowest-level work package as an "activity" or "task," but project methodologies adopt many other names. The extreme programming methodology has adopted the term "story" for the work packages that constitute project work in each development cycle. What you call the results of the decomposition process does not matter much (though inconsistency between related projects can increase communication risks); what matters from a risk management standpoint is that the work be defined with sufficient detail that it is clear what you must do to complete it. Any portion of a project that you do not understand well enough to break into small, clearly defined work packages is risky. Whenever a portion of your project resists logical decomposition, resulting in work at the lowest level of the WBS that is likely to last longer than a month or will probably require more than eighty hours of effort, you lack an adequate understanding of that part of the project. Note such work as a project risk.

Bottom-Up

Work breakdown can also be approached from the other direction, "bottom-up." Instead of starting at the top and carving the project into pieces, some teams prefer to brainstorm a list of required activities and organize it into a WBS after the initial list is developed. Risky portions of the project will emerge from this process, also. To develop the WBS, the identified activities that are similar are clustered, using affinity groupings or some other method to aggregate them. The groupings are then organized further, building up a hierarchy similar to that in the top-down method. Examination of the resulting WBS often reveals gaps— parts of the project for which there are no defined activities—and (again) a few relatively large, hard-to-decompose pieces at the lowest level of the WBS. Note any gaps in the WBS that you are unable to fill in and any work you cannot sufficiently decompose as project risks.

Aggregation

The principle of "aggregation" in a WBS provides one method for detecting missing work, as the defined work at each level of the hierarchical decomposition must plausibly include everything needed at the next higher level. If the work you identified in decomposing a higher-level work package does not represent a complete "to do" list for the higher level, your WBS is incomplete. You need to describe the missing work and add it to the WBS. All the work in the WBS that you cannot describe well contributes to your growing accumulation of identified risks.

Your initial WBS will seldom be complete. Another method for identifying missing activities is to take all the activities at the lowest level and reorganize them using a different method at the first level (for example, convert from a life-cycle model to a functional view). The resulting WBS often reveals holes and gaps, identifying additional work and potential scope risks.

If you are asked to dig a hole in the ground, the work is sometimes easy. A typical approach is to remove the soil, a small amount at a time, until you have cleared out the size hole you need. If there is nothing in the volume to be cleared except soft, moist earth, a good shovel and some effort will get the job done quickly. However, anyone who digs holes regularly knows that it is rarely that easy. The place where you want the hole may have roots growing through it, or, even worse, it may be filled with rocks. Small rocks and roots may be not much trouble for a good shovel, but they will slow you down (just as small risks do in projects). Larger tree roots may require additional technology—an ax, or perhaps a saw. Rocks, depending on the size, may require the assistance of others, levers, power excavation equipment, a hammer and chisel, or even explosives. These obstacles that cannot be broken apart with a shovel are problematic, time-consuming, and potentially expensive. In some cases, you may decide to move the location of the hole or give up completely after assessing the situation.

Like the obstacles hidden beneath the ground, parts of a project that resist easy decomposition are not visible until you systematically seek them. The WBS development process provides a tool for separating the parts of the project that you understand well from those that you do not. As with the large, unruly objects in the hole, you may be able to break activities down using new approaches, technologies, or resources. Before proceeding with a project filled with such challenges, you also must determine whether the associated costs and other consequences are justified.

OWNERSHIP

There are many reasons why some project work is difficult to break into smaller parts, but the root cause is often a lack of experience with the work required. While this is a very common sort of risk discovered in developing a WBS, it is not the only one. A key objective in completing the project WBS is the delegation of each lowest-level work package (or whatever you may choose to call it) to someone who will take responsibility for the completion of that part of the project. Delegation and ownership are well established in management theory as motivators, and they also contribute to team development and broader project understanding.

Delegation is most effective when responsibilities are assumed by team members voluntarily. It is fairly common on projects to allow people to assume ownership of project activities in the WBS by signing up for them, at least on the first pass. While there is generally some conflict over activities that more than one person wants, sorting this out by balancing the workload, selecting the more experienced person, or using some other logical decision process is rarely difficult. The risk discovery opportunity here is when the opposite occurs—when *no one* wants to be the owner.

Activities where no one volunteers to be responsible are risky, and you need to probe to find out why. There are a number of common root causes, including the one discussed before: no one understands the work very well. It may be that no one currently on the project has developed key skills that the work requires or that the work is technically so uncertain that no one believes it can be done at all. It could even be the case that the work is feasible but that no one believes that it can be completed in the "roughly two weeks" expected for activities defined at the lowest level of the WBS. In other cases, the description of deliverables may be so fuzzy or unclear that no one wants to be involved.

There are many other possible reasons, and these are also risks. Of these, availability is usually the most common. If everyone on the project is already working beyond full capacity on other work and other projects, no one will volunteer.

Another possible cause might be that the activity requires working with people that no one wants to work with. If the required working relationships are likely to be difficult or unpleasant, no one will volunteer, and successful completion of the work is uncertain. Some activities may depend on outside support or require external inputs that the project team is skeptical about. Few people willingly assume responsibility for work that is likely to fail due to causes beyond their control.

In addition, the work itself might be the problem. Even easy work can be risky, if people see it as thankless or unnecessary. All projects have at least some required work that no one likes to do. It may involve documentation or some other dull, routine part of the work. If it is done successfully, no one notices; this is simply expected. If something goes wrong, though, there is a lot of attention. The activity owner has managed to turn an easy part of the project into a disaster, and he or she will at least get yelled at. Most people avoid these activities.

Another situation is the "unnecessary" activity. Projects are full of these, too, at least from the perspective of the team. Life-cycle, phase gate, and project methodologies place requirements on projects that seem to be (and, in many cases, may actually be) unnecessary overhead. Other project work may be scheduled primarily because it is part of a planning template or because "that's the way we always do it." If the work is actually not needed, good project managers seek to eliminate it.

To the project risk list, add clear descriptions of each risk identified while developing the WBS, including your best understanding of the root cause for each. These risks may emerge from difficulties in developing the WBS to an appropriate level of detail or in finding willing owners for the lowest-level activities. A typical risk listed might be: "The project requires conversion of an existing database from Sybase to Oracle, and no one on the project staff has relevant experience."

WBS SIZE

Project risk correlates with size; when projects get too large, risk becomes overwhelming. Scope risk rises with complexity, and one measure of complexity is the size of the WBS. Once your project work has been decomposed into work packages that are sufficiently detailed (for example, with an average duration of about two weeks), count up the number at the lowest levels. When the number exceeds about 200, project risk rises very rapidly.

The more separate bits of work that a single project leader is responsible for, the more likely it becomes that he or she will miss something crucial to the project. As the volume of work and project complexity expands, the tools and practices of basic project management, as applied by a single project leader, become more and more inadequate.

At high levels of complexity, the overall effort is best managed in one of two ways: as a series of shorter projects in sequence that deliver what is required in stages or as a program made up of a collection of smaller projects. In both cases, the process of decomposing the total project into sequential or parallel parts is done using a decomposition very like a WBS. In the case of sequential execution, the process is essentially similar to the evolutionary methodologies discussed previously in this chapter. For programs, the resulting decomposition creates a number of projects, each of which will be managed by a separate project leader using project management principles, and the overall effort will be the responsibility of a program manager. Project risk is managed by the project leaders, and overall program risk is the responsibility of the program leader.

When excessively lengthy or complex projects are left as the responsibility of a single project leader to plan, manage risk, and execute, the probability of successful completion is low.

Other Risks

Not all scope risks are strictly within the practice of project management. Examples are *market* risk and *confidentiality* risk. These risks are related, and, although they may not show up in all projects, they are often present at least to some degree. Ignoring these risks is inappropriate and dangerous.

A business balance sheet has two sides: assets and liabilities. Project management primarily focuses on "liabilities," the expense and execution side, using measures related to "scope/ schedule/resources." Market and confidentiality risks tend to be on the asset, or *value*, side of the business ledger, where project techniques and teams are involved indirectly, if at all. Project management is primarily about delivering what you have been asked to deliver, and this does not always equate to "success" in the marketplace. While it is obvious that "on time, on budget, within scope" does not necessarily make a project an unqualified success, managing these aspects alone is a big job, and in a perfect world it is really all the project team ought to be held responsible for. The primary owners for market and confidentiality risks may not even be active participants in the project, although trends in many kinds of technical projects are toward assigning projects to cross-functional business teams—making these risks more central to the project. In any case, these risks are real, and they relate to scope. Unless identified and managed, they too can lead to project failure.

MARKET RISK

This first type of risk is mostly about getting something in the definition wrong. Market risk relates to features, to timing, to cost, or to almost any facet of the deliverable. It can happen when long development efforts are initiated, during which time the problem to be solved changes, goes away, or is addressed by an unexpected new technology. It can happen because a satisfactory deliverable is brought to market a week after an essentially identical offering from a competitor. It can even result when a project produces exactly what was requested by a sponsor or economic buyer but that product is rejected by the intended end user. Sometimes the people responsible for promoting and selling a good product do not (or cannot) follow through. Many paths can lead to a result that meets the specifications and is delivered on time and on budget, yet is never deployed or fails to achieve the expectations set at the beginning of the project.

The longer and the more complicated the project is, the greater the market risk tends to be. Project leaders contribute to the management of these risks through active, continuing participation in any market research and customer interaction and by frequently communicating with (ideally, without annoying) all the people surrounding the project who will be involved with deployment of the deliverable.

Some of the techniques already discussed may help manage this. A thorough process for deliverable definition probes for many of the sources of this sort of risk and the high-level risk tools outlined previously also provide opportunities to understand the environment surrounding the project.

In addition, ongoing contact with the intended users, through interviews, surveys, market research, and other techniques, will help to uncover problems and shifts in the assumptions the project is based upon. Agile methodologies employ ongoing user involvement in the definition of short, sequential project cycles, minimizing the "wrong" deliverable risk greatly for small project teams co-located with their users.

If the project is developing a product that will compete with similar offerings from competitors, ongoing competitive analysis to predict what others are planning can be useful (but, of course, competitors will not make this straightforward or easy—confidentiality risks are addressed next). Responsibility for this work may be fully within the project, but if it is not, the project team must still review what is learned and, if necessary, encourage the marketing staff (or other stakeholders) to keep the information up-to-date.

The project team should always probe beyond the specific requirements (the *stated* need) to understand where the specifications come from (the *actual* need). Understanding what is actually needed is generally much more important than simply understanding what was requested. Early use of models, prototypes, mock-ups, and other simulations of the deliverable will help you find out whether the requested specifications are in fact likely to provide what is needed. Short cycles of development with periodic releases of meaningful functionality (and value) throughout the project also minimize this category of risk. Standards, testing requirements, and acceptance criteria need to be established in clear, specific terms and periodically reviewed with those who will certify the deliverable.

CONFIDENTIALITY RISK

The second type of risk that is generally not exclusively in the hands of the project team relates to secrecy. While some projects are done in an open and relatively unconstrained environment, confidentiality is crucial to many high-tech product development projects, particularly long ones. If the information on what is under way is made public, the value of the project might decrease or even disappear. Better-funded competitors with more staff might learn what you are working on and build it first, making your work irrelevant. Of course, managing this risk well potentially *increases* the market risk, as you will be less free to gather information from end users and the market. The use of prototypes, models, mock-ups, or even detailed descriptions might provide data to competitors that you want to keep in the dark. On some technical projects, the need for secrecy may also be a specific contractual obligation, as with government projects. Even if the product is not a secret, you may be using techniques or methodologies that are proprietary competitive advantages, and loss of this sort of intellectual property also represents a confidentiality risk.

Within the project team, several techniques may help. Some projects work on a "need to know" basis and provide to team members only the information required to do their current work. While this usually hurts teamwork and motivation, and may even lead to substandard results (people will optimize only for what they know, not for the overall project), it can effectively protect confidential information.

Emphasizing the importance of confidentiality also helps. Periodically reinforce the need for confidentiality with all team members, and especially with contractors and other outsiders. Be specific on the requirements for confidentiality in contract terms when you bring in outside help, and discuss the requirements with them to ensure that the terms are clearly understood. Any external market research or customer contact also requires effective non-disclosure agreements, again with enough discussion to make the need for secrecy clear.

In addition to all of this, project documents and other communication must be appropriately marked "confidential" (or according to the requirements set by your organization). Restrict distribution of project information, particularly electronic versions, to people who need it and who understand, and agree with, the reasons for secrecy. Protect information stored on computer networks or the Internet with passwords that are changed often enough to limit inappropriate access. Use legal protections such as copyrights and patents as appropriate to establish ownership of intellectual property. (Timing of patents can be tricky. On the one hand, they protect your work. On the other hand, they are public and may reveal to competitors what you are working on.)

While the confidentiality risks are partially the responsibility of the project team, many lapses are well out of their control. Managers, sponsors, marketing staffs, and favorite customers are the sources for many leaks. Project management tools address principally execution of the work, not secrecy. Effective project management relies heavily on good, frequent communication, so projects with heavy confidentiality requirements can be very difficult and inefficient to lead. Managing confidentiality risk requires discipline, frequent reminders of the need for secrecy to all involved (especially those involved indirectly), limits on the number of people involved, and more than a little luck.

Document the Risks

As the requirements, scope definition documents, WBS, and other project data start to take shape, you can begin to develop a list of specific issues, concerns, and risks related to the scope and deliverables of the project. When the definitions are completed, review the risk list, and inspect it for missing or incomplete information. If some portion of the project scope seems likely to change, note this in the list, as well. Typical scope risks involve performance, reliability, untested methods or technology, or combinations of deliverable requirements that are beyond your experience base. Make very clear why each item listed is an exposure for the project; cite any relevant specifications and measures that go beyond those successfully achieved in the past in the risk description, using explicitly quantified criteria. An example might be, "The system delivered must execute at double the fastest speed achieved in the prior generation."

Sources of specific scope risks include:

- ❐ Requirements that seem likely to change
- ❐ Mandatory use of new technology
- ❐ Requirements to invent or discover new capabilities
- ❐ Unfamiliar or untried development tools or methods
- ❐ Extreme reliability or quality requirements

- ❑ External sourcing for a key subcomponent or tool
- ❑ Incomplete or poorly defined acceptance tests or criteria
- ❑ Technical complexity
- ❑ Conflicting or inconsistent specifications
- ❑ Incomplete product definition
- ❑ Very large WBS

Using the processes for scope planning and definition will reveal many specific technical and other potential risks. List these risks for your project, with information about causes and consequences. The list of risks will expand throughout the project planning process and will serve as your foundation for project risk analysis and management.

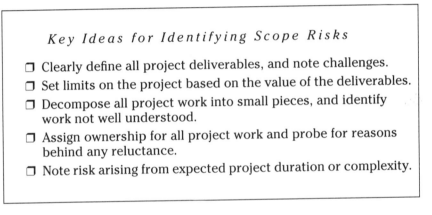

Key Ideas for Identifying Scope Risks

- ❑ Clearly define all project deliverables, and note challenges.
- ❑ Set limits on the project based on the value of the deliverables.
- ❑ Decompose all project work into small pieces, and identify work not well understood.
- ❑ Assign ownership for all project work and probe for reasons behind any reluctance.
- ❑ Note risk arising from expected project duration or complexity.

Panama Canal: Setting the Objective (1905–1906)

One of the principal differences between the earlier unsuccessful attempt to build the Panama Canal and the later project was the application of good project management practices. While this was ultimately true, the new project had a shaky beginning. The scope and objectives of the revived Panama Canal project, conceived as a military project and funded by the U.S. government, should have been very clear, even at the start. They were not.

The initial manager for the project when work commenced in 1904 was John Findlay Wallace, formerly the general manager of the Illinois Central Railroad. Wallace was visionary; he did a lot of investigating and experimenting, but he accomplished very little in

Panama. His background included no similar project experience. In addition to his other difficulties, he could do almost nothing without the consent of a seven-man commission set up back in the United States, a commission that rarely agreed on anything. Also, nearly every decision, regardless of size, required massive amounts of paperwork. A year later, in 1905, $128 million had been spent but still there was no final plan, and most of the workers were still waiting for something to do. The project had in most ways picked up just where the earlier French project had left off, problems and all. Even after a year, it was still not clear whether the canal would be at sea level or constructed with locks and dams. In 1905, mired in red tape, Wallace announced that the canal was a mistake, and he resigned.

John Wallace was promptly replaced by John Stevens. Stevens was also from the railroad business, but his experience was on the building side, not the operating side. He built a reputation as one of the best engineers in the United States by constructing railroads throughout the Pacific frontier. Prior to appointing Stevens, Theodore Roosevelt eliminated the problematic seven-man commission, and he significantly reduced the red tape, complication, and delay. As chief engineer, Stevens, unlike Wallace, effectively had full control of the work. Arriving in Panama, Stevens took stock and immediately stopped all work on the canal, stating, "I was determined to prepare well before construction, regardless of clamor of criticism. I am confident that if this policy is adhered to, the future will show its wisdom." And so it did.

With the arrival of John Stevens, managing project scope became the highest priority. He directed all his initial efforts at preparation for the work. He built dormitories for workers to live in, dining halls to feed them, warehouses for equipment and materials, and other infrastructure for the project. The doctor responsible for the health of the workers on the project, William Crawford Gorgas, had been trying for over a year to gain support from John Wallace for measures needed to deal with the mosquitoes, by then known to spread both yellow fever and malaria. Stevens quickly gave this work his full support, and Dr. Gorgas proceeded to eradicate these diseases. Yellow fever was conquered in Panama just six months after Dr. Gorgas received Stevens's support, and he made good progress combating malaria as well.

Under the guidance of Stevens, all the work was defined and planned employing well-established, modern project management principles. He said, "Intelligent management must be based on exact knowledge of facts. Guesswork will not do." He did not talk much, but he asked lots of questions. People commented, "He turned me inside out and shook out the last drop of information."

His meticulous documentation served as the basis for work throughout the project.

Stevens also determined exactly how the canal should be built, to the smallest detail. The objective for the project was ultimately set in 1907 according to his recommendations: The United States would build an eighty-kilometer (fifty-mile) lock-and-dam canal at Panama connecting the Atlantic and Pacific oceans, with a budget of $375 million, to open in 1915. With the scope defined, the path forward became clear.

CHAPTER 4

IDENTIFYING PROJECT SCHEDULE RISK

"Work expands so as to fill the time available for its completion."
                    —C. NORTHCOTE PARKINSON, *Parkinson's Law*

Although Parkinson's observation was not backed up with any empirical data, the truth of his "law" is rarely questioned. It seems particularly appropriate for technical projects, because, in addition to all the obvious reasons that people have for using up the time available to complete their work, on technical projects there is an additional reason. Most people who are drawn to technical projects are very analytical, and they like to be precise, accurate, and thorough. If there is time available to attempt to make something perfect, most engineers will try.

Projects, however, are rarely about perfection. They are about pragmatism, delivering a result that is "good enough." Practicality is not particularly motivating, and it is rarely much fun, so technical projects often diverge from the direct path and out into the weeds. Thoroughly identifying schedule risks requires awareness of this, and disciplined use of project management planning tools to create appropriate schedules that avoid overengineering.

In the previous chapter, factors that make projects literally impossible were considered. In this chapter, and in Chapter 5, concerning resource risks, the focus is on constraints—factors that transform otherwise reasonable projects into failures. Project processes for scheduling and resource planning provide a fertile source for discovery of project risks that arise from these constraints.

Much of the content of this chapter falls into the "Project Time Management" segment of the *PMBOK®* Guide. In particular, the principal project schedule risk ideas covered in this chapter include:

❐ Sources of schedule risk

❐ Activity definition

❐ Estimating activity duration

❐ Activity sequencing

Sources of Schedule Risk

Schedule risks are the most numerous in the Project Experience Risk Information Library (PERIL) database, representing well over a third of the records. They fall into three categories: *delays*, *dependencies*, and *estimates*. Delays occurred whenever something expected by the project—a part, a decision, a piece of information—was late. Schedule dependency risks relate to unanticipated linkages or missing inputs that affect primarily the project timeline (dependencies that affect primarily the project deliverables or the work are grouped with the risks associated with scope changes). The other category of schedule risk comes from duration estimates that are insufficient for completion of scheduled project activities. The summary:

SCHEDULE RISKS	COUNT	CUMULATIVE IMPACT (WEEKS)	AVERAGE IMPACT (WEEKS)
Delay	46	134	2.9
Dependency	21	102	4.9
Estimates	15	70	4.7

Project problems sorted by subcategories within the three categories are summarized in Figure 4-1. As shown, the largest total impact came from various sources of dependency and delay. Although delay risk caused more problems overall, dependencies on other project work was the dominant subcategory.

DELAY RISKS

Delay risk represents more than half of the schedule risks and nearly a sixth of all the risks in the PERIL database. Impact from delays was lower on average than for other risks, slightly less

Figure 4-1. Schedule risks in the PERIL database.

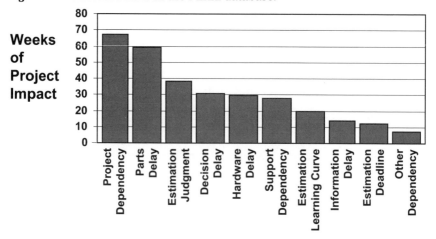

than three weeks. Most of the reported delays related to parts that were required for the project deliverable or hardware that was required to do project work. Delivery and availability problems were a common root cause for the delay, but there were also quite a few issues around international shipping, including customs, paperwork, and other associated concerns. Delays were also a result of parts or other hardware that arrived on time but were found to be defective. Time required to replace or repair things that did not work properly was a significant source of project slip. Delay of parts caused both the largest number of the delay risks and the most severe impact, almost four weeks on average.

Slow decisions caused quite a few project slips. Almost a quarter of the delay examples were due to inaction by managers or other stakeholders who did not act as quickly as necessary to keep the project on schedule. Sometimes the cause was poor access to the decision makers, or their lack of interest in the project. For other projects, delays were the result of extended debates, discussions, or indecision. Projects facing these issues lost nearly three weeks on average waiting for a response to a project request.

Projects also were delayed because they lacked information. Some of the delay was due to time differences separating parts of global project teams. Losing one or more days on a regular basis was common, due to misunderstandings and communication time lags. In other cases, access to information was poor, or delivery of needed reports was interrupted.

Potential delay risks may be difficult to anticipate, and many of them seem to be legitimately "unknown" risks. Thorough analysis of the input requirements at each stage of the project plan, however, will highlight many of them.

DEPENDENCY RISKS

Dependencies are the most severe category of schedule risk in the PERIL database, averaging almost five weeks of impact per incident. There are a number of dependency types, but the most numerous ones in the database are dependencies on other projects and on project support.

Dependency risks from other projects are not only the most numerous of the dependency risks; they also are the most damaging, with an average of more than five weeks. In larger projects (often classified as programs), a number of smaller projects interact and link to one another. In addition to providing one another with information and deliverables that meet well-defined specifications (which is a scope risk exposure), each project within a larger program must also synchronize the timing of schedule dependencies to avoid being slowed down by (or slowing) other projects. Managing all these connections is difficult in complex programs, and the amount of damage increases with time; many of these risks in the PERIL database were noticed only late in the project. Even for the interfaces that were defined in advance, delay was fairly common because of the uncertainty in each project and the likelihood that at least one of the related projects would encounter some sort of difficulty. With so many possible failure modes, it becomes almost certain that something will go wrong. Analysis of the connections and interfaces between projects is a key aspect of program management, and many of the risks faced by the projects become visible through interface management techniques.

Other dependencies that interfere with project schedules in the PERIL database are support problems. These include interruption of hardware services, such as computer systems or networks required by the project, and inadequate access to resources such as help desks, system support, and people who understood older but necessary applications. Several projects were delayed by outages for maintenance that was scheduled in advance but unknown to the project team. One project had severe impact when the legal and paperwork requirements for international shipments changed abruptly. Monitoring the environment of the project and its infrastructure for planned or likely changes can forewarn of many of these potential problems.

ESTIMATING RISKS

Of all the types of schedule risk found in technical projects, estimating seems to be the most visible. People who work on technical projects are usually well aware of how inadequate their estimates are and freely admit it. Despite this, the number of misestimated incidents in the PERIL database is not large, and their impact is about equal to the average for the database as a whole. One source of difficulty with estimating in technical projects is the relatively rapid change in the work, which makes the standard advice offered for improvement less useful. Good estimates, we are told, rely on history. If the environment is in constant flux, history may not seem so useful (more on this later in the chapter).

The most frequent type of estimating problem reported in the PERIL database is related to judgment. For a good number of projects, the issue was estimates that were consistently overoptimistic. Some estimates reported were too short by factors of three and four. Dealing with this source of estimating risk requires thorough planning, with appropriate understanding and decomposition of the work, so that the effort and steps required are known. It also requires good record-keeping. Metrics and project data archives are invaluable in creating future estimates that are more consistent with reality than past estimates have been, even for projects where things change rapidly. Having *some* data always beats having to guess. Another powerful tool in revealing and combating optimistic estimates is worst-case analysis. Not only will the answer to the question "What might go wrong?" reveal something about the likely duration; it will also uncover new potential sources of risk.

A small number of cases of estimating risk involve learning curve issues. The impact of this was well above the average for the database, nearly seven weeks. The quality of the estimates when new technologies or new people (or, even worse, new technologies *and* new people) are involved is not good. The portions of project work that require staff to do things they have never done before are always risky, and thorough analysis of the work can show which parts of the project plan are most exposed. Training plans must be established for the project whenever new skills and capabilities are necessary, and these need to be explicit in the project timeline and budget.

There are also a number of cases in the PERIL database where the estimates used by the project were poor, but the root cause was outside the project. Technical projects frequently have aggressive deadlines determined in advance for them with little or no input from the project team. Even when the project plan shows the deadline to be unrealistic, the objective is retained. These projects are often doomed from the start; they represent a common type of overconstrained project.

Schedule risks are generally uncovered through planning processes. Creating a comprehensive schedule using better processes for estimating, more thorough analysis of linkages and dependencies, and careful worst-case analysis will reveal many of the schedule exposures.

Activity Definition

Building a project schedule starts with defining project work at an appropriate level of decomposition. Both estimating and sequencing of work in a project are most easily and appropriately done using small parts of the project. Where the entire project may be big, complicated, and confusing, the principle of "divide and conquer" allows independent consideration of each little piece and lets the project team bring order out of chaos. The starting point for most schedule development (as well as resource planning) is the project work breakdown structure (WBS). If the work described at the lowest level of your WBS is consistent with the "two to twenty day" guideline, it may be used as it is to create your schedule. If your WBS decomposition is not yet to that level of granularity, you need to do further analysis and decomposition. The ultimate goal of the process, however you approach it, is small, self-contained, deliverable-oriented bits of work that you can estimate, schedule, track, and generally use to manage your project.

Unfortunately, although the processes for developing a project schedule are generally consistent for various types of technical projects, the terminology is not. In project management literature, scheduling tools, and methodologies, many different terms are used to describe small pieces of project work. In "Project Time Management," the *PMBOK*® Guide refers to these pieces of work as *activities*, defined there as "an extension to the WBS." Other common terms for project work at the lowest WBS level are "work packages" and "tasks," and in practice all of this terminology tends to be used interchangeably with "activities," the term used generally throughout the rest of this book. In agile software methodologies such as extreme programming, work decomposed to the level used for scheduling is called a "story."

As noted in Chapter 3, what you name these bits of project work matters little. What matters a great deal for risk management, though, is that you do define them. In most project methodologies, activities (or whatever name you prefer) are defined by the lowest levels of the project WBS. Project activities, once defined, provide the foundation for project planning and risk identification.

Both estimating and sequencing of activities are necessary processes for creating a project schedule. Which of these planning tasks is undertaken first is largely a matter of personal preference. The *PMBOK*® Guide shows these two processes in parallel, which is realistic. Both estimating and sequencing project activities are iterative, and there is a good deal of interaction between these two processes when building a project plan. If starting to sequence project activities prior to estimating them seems more natural to your projects, use the material in this chapter in that order. What is most important is that both processes be conducted thoroughly, as each reveals different schedule risks during project planning.

Estimating Activity Duration

Estimating risk provides a substantial number of the entries in the PERIL database. A good estimating process is a powerful tool for identifying this type of schedule risk. When the estimates that are precise can be separated from those that are uncertain, the risky parts of the project are more visible. When estimates are "top-down," or based on guesses, the exposures in the project plan remain hidden. Quite a few failed projects are the result of inaccurate estimates.

In the dictionary, an estimate is "a rough or approximate calculation." Projects require approximations of both time and cost. The focus of this section is on the risks associated with time estimates. However, project estimates are all related. A number of concepts introduced here are expanded in Chapter 5 and used there to identify resource risks through the process of refining estimates of effort and cost. Estimates of varying accuracy are derived throughout a project, from the "rough-order-of-magnitude" estimates used to initiate projects to fairly precise estimates that are refined as the project runs to control and execute the work in the project plan. Single-point estimates imply accuracy that is rarely justified in technical projects. Estimates that make risk visible are therefore stated as ranges, or include percentages (plus and minus) to indicate the precision, or specify a probability distribution of expected possibilities.

ESTIMATION PITFALLS

As mentioned before, estimating project work is challenging, and most people admit that they do not do it very well. Understanding the factors that make accurate estimating hard to do for technical projects provides insight into sources of project risk, and it may also indicate how to improve future estimates. Four key impediments to estimating well are:

❐ Avoidance

❐ Optimism

❐ Lack of information

❐ Granularity

Probably the most significant problem with estimating is that people who work on technical projects do not like to estimate, and they avoid it. The appeal of technical projects is the work—designing, programming, engineering, building, and other activities that the analytical people on these projects like to do. People avoid estimating (and planning in general) because it is seen as overhead, or boring "administrivia." Estimates are done quickly, and only grudgingly. Most technical people have little estimating experience or training for estimating, so their skill level is low. Few people like doing things that they are not very good at. To make matters worse, since the estimates provided are so often inaccurate, most of the feedback they get is negative. It is human nature to avoid activities that are likely to result in criticism and punishment.

Too much optimism is another enemy of good estimates. In the PERIL database, the most common cause for risk due to estimating is judgment. Estimates that are too short create many additional project problems including severe increases in late-project work and deadline slippage. Excessive optimism stems from a number of causes, but one of the most common is top-down pressure. Far too many projects are undertaken with unrealistically short estimates for project activities because the sponsors and stakeholders impose unrealistic time constraints on the project. These constraints force the project team to create estimates in their plans on the basis of the time available ("schedule to fit"), not based on the reality of the work. Other sources of optimistic estimates are reliance on best-case scenario analysis (each activity is scheduled assuming that everything goes well), assumptions about the amount of time that people will have available to do project work, and overconfidence in the talent and speed of the project team.

A third issue is a lack of information. Initial project estimates are the product of early analysis, when the amount and quality of available project information is still low. Often, scope definition is still changing and incomplete, and significant portions of the work are poorly understood when these estimates are done. Compounding this, on most technical projects there is little (or no) historical information to use in estimating, and there are no defined estimating processes used. One method used far too often is "guessing."

A fourth factor that contributes to poor estimates is the granularity of the work. Early estimates are often done for projects on the basis of descriptions of the work and the deliverables without much detail. Estimates are chronically inaccurate when they are based on high-level project deliverables that lack acceptance criteria. The quality of estimates for long duration project activities is also poor. Guidelines for project planning and decomposing project effort into a WBS recommend activities of roughly two weeks in duration, or in a range of "two to twenty work days" at the activity level. People are generally unable to assess and estimate work with much accuracy when the duration extends beyond a month.

To recap, metrics, well-defined estimating procedures, clear scoping, disciplined planning, and periodic review of the project are all instrumental in improving estimates and decreasing estimation risk.

THE OVERALL ESTIMATING PROCESS

Before you can work on your estimate, you will need many inputs. A comprehensive list of project activities is one input. Another is the resource plan, information about the people and other resources available to the project. The resource plan is part of the "Project Resource Management" segment of the *PMBOK®* Guide, and it is a major topic in Chapter 5. (The resource plan also requires activity duration estimates as an input, so each of these processes is a required input for the other. As with most project planning processes, resource planning and scheduling are iterative; they proceed in parallel and are not actually caught in a loop.)

One key purpose of defining the people and other resources available to the project was mentioned in Chapter 3: identifying owners for the work at the lowest level of the project WBS. Having a single owner for each activity is one way to ensure clear responsibility, and the activity owner is generally responsible for the initial activity duration estimate. The activity owner is also responsible for the planning, execution, and completion of the activity. Whether the owner is the only contributor, is leading a team, or serves as a liaison to another group who will do the work, the estimate is an important determinant of the ultimate success or failure of the work, and that is the owner's responsibility. For larger activities performed by a team, the other contributors should also participate in establishing the initial estimates.

Accurate estimates require clear, specific information about each activity. It is important to document and use any information regarding constraints on activity durations or project assumptions that might affect the estimates. You need to clearly and concisely define the deliverables for each activity. Activities with more than one deliverable may be easier to manage, and have less risk, if they are broken down further, creating a new, smaller activity associated with each deliverable. As part of the documentation for each activity, capture acceptance criteria and any other requirements in unambiguous, measurable terms. If the specifications for any activity deliverables are not defined or are unclear, note this as a risk.

Project time estimates may be measured in duration (work time), in calendar duration (elapsed time), or in effort (a combination of people and time, such as "engineer-days"). Within your project, establish a single standard for the units of each type of estimate to make it easier to compare all the information and to build the schedule. Each of these types of estimate has its value in the planning process. Effort estimates are a large component of project cost. Duration estimates are used for input to computer scheduling tools and for the initial schedule analysis, and calendar durations support accurate tracking.

For each identified activity, the estimating process usually starts with either a duration estimate or an effort estimate and then proceeds to derive the other two types of estimates through a series of logical steps. The final output of the process, actual calendar time, defines the project timeline. Whatever sequence you prefer for developing estimates, only use bottom-up analysis of the project data for your initial estimates. For project planning and preliminary schedule development, avoid "pegged-date" or politically specified arbitrary estimates. Building a plan with unrealistic estimates conceals risks and undermines your ability to negotiate necessary project changes.

Some project leaders prefer to derive duration estimates first and then develop the effort estimates when other planning data, such as activity sequencing information, becomes available. Effort estimates are then used to validate or adjust the duration estimates, based upon the accumulating project information. The approach of starting with effort estimates is usually slightly more efficient and is described here. A graphical summary of the process described appears in Figure 4-2. Whatever sequence you use to develop estimates, the same issues, factors, and risks are involved.

Effort Estimates and Project-Specific Factors

All estimating methods (even guessing) start with information derived in some way from history and experience. The history you use can be anecdotal, stored in a metrics database, built into formulas, jotted down in lab notebooks, or found in myriad other sources. Specific sources and common techniques for obtaining

Figure 4-2. Overall estimation process.

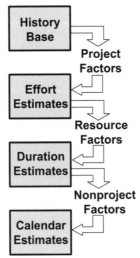

this data follow. On the basis of the initial historical data, effort estimates may be derived by considering project-specific variables. Project-specific information is used to adjust initial historical information, on the basis of specific differences between the current project and earlier work. Project-specific factors include:

❑ Clarity of the project specifications

❑ Likelihood of significant specification change

❑ New resource requirements

❑ Longer expected project duration

❑ Unusual technical complexity

❑ New required technology

❑ Extreme requirements for reliability

❑ Geographic separation and cultural diversity on the project team

❑ Infrastructure and environment differences

❑ Training requirements

Every lowest-level activity in your WBS requires an effort estimate, measured in person-hours (or contributor-days, or some other unit combining people and time). In addition to providing input for adjusting historical data, some of these project-specific factors may also represent significant project risks and should be noted as such.

Effort estimates themselves also reveal risks. Any activities with estimates that no one is very sure of are risky. However, lack of confidence in an estimate is a symptom of risk, not the risk itself. Whenever any of your project estimates seem untrustworthy, probe for why, and note the root cause as the risk. Two common sources of low-confidence estimates are lack of experience with the work and activities that may have several different outcomes, such as an investigation. Also risky are any activities that resist your best efforts to break them down and remain too large to estimate accurately (generally, more than 120 person-hours or twenty days of duration).

Duration Estimates and Resource Factors

Effort estimates, combined with project information on people and teams, provide the basis for duration estimates. Initial resource plans provide information on resource factors, such as:

❑ The amount of time each day each team member has for project work

❑ The number people contributing to each activity

❑ The skills, experience, and productivity of each team member

❑ Training and mentoring requirements

❑ Nonproject responsibilities for each person

❑ Communication lags and other consequences of distributed teams

❑ Expected turnover or attrition of staff during the project

❑ The number and duration for project (and other) meetings

❑ The amount of project communication and reporting

❑ Travel requirements

❑ The number of required people not yet assigned to the project

The first factor in the list, the number of project hours in a day, is a very common cause of underestimation. Not every hour that people work is available for project activities. Meetings, communication (both formal and informal), breaks, meals, and other interruptions take time. Even the common assumption of "five to six" hours per day for project activities is significantly higher than the reality available to many projects. Productivity is also a source of variation. For most types of project work, a ten-to-one difference in productivity between the most and the least competent people is common. All estimates of effort or duration made in advance of assigning the specific people who will do the work are risky. These and other resource-related risks are discussed in greater detail in Chapter 5.

By considering the effort required by each activity in light of the resource factors, you can determine activity durations in workdays (or some other suitable units). Duration estimates are used for most schedule analysis and are required inputs for computer scheduling tools. Computer tools are becoming universal on technical projects, and they are where much of the other project information is stored, including activity names (and the higher levels of the WBS, as well), information about owners and project staffing, activity sequencing information, and even detailed descriptions and project assumptions.

Quite a few terms are used in project management practice to describe a database of project information, including a WBS dictionary, an ETVX (Entry, Task, Validation, eXit) analysis, a project spreadsheet, or simply "the project database." Whatever you call it, for effective risk management this information should be in a format and location easily accessed by the project team members who need to refer to it. Increasingly, network or Internet-enabled software provides timely, current information to the whole project team and all the stakeholders, wherever they are located and whenever they may need it.

Calendar Estimates and Nonproject Factors

The final stage of estimation is to translate duration estimates into calendar estimates. If duration information is entered in a computer scheduling tool, much of this transformation will be done for you. Nonproject factors such as holidays may be put into the calendar database, and the software will do the calculations. To translate workday estimates into elapsed-time estimates, all the days that are not available for project work must be accounted for. Some of the nonproject factors are:

- Holidays
- Weekends
- Vacations and other paid time off
- Other projects

☐ Other nonproject work
☐ Lengthy nonproject meetings
☐ Equipment downtime
☐ Interruptions and shut-downs
☐ Scheduled medical leave

Calendar estimates account for the number of total days between the start and end of each activity. Specific dates for each activity are derived by combining duration estimates, nonproject factors, and the activity sequencing information that is discussed later in this chapter. One particular risk common for global projects is a result of differences in scheduled time off for geographically separate parts of the project team. Frequent loss of some of the project team to various national and religious holidays is disruptive enough, but all too often these interruptions come as a surprise to the project leader, who may be aware only of local holidays. These nonproject factors may differ for each member of the project team, and collecting information about everyone, wherever he or she may be, is an important part of project planning.

ESTIMATING TECHNIQUES

Most of the estimating risks in the PERIL database are categorized as judgment problems. Compared to their plans, the affected projects saw significant delays due to estimates that were unrealistically short. While a few of the cases involved one-time issues that were unlikely to recur, several chronic problems affected project after project. Some projects failed to account for the increasing complexity they encountered as the system components and the number of interfaces grew. Another project always estimated international shipments to take three weeks less than the actual average time they took. Better processes and more attention to performance data will at least identify many of these risks, if not eliminate them.

Effective estimating techniques all rely on history. The best predictor of effort or duration for work on a project is the measurement made of the same (or similar) work done earlier. Project estimating either uses historical data directly or applies processes that have history as a foundation. Sources of appropriate data are essential to estimating well and reducing estimating risk. Discussion of some effective techniques follows.

Finding and Using Historical Data

The simplest technique for estimating is to "look up the answer." For activities that vary little from project to project, this may be the only technique necessary. Even on high-tech projects, many activities are repeated with little variation project after project—things such as creating documentation and conducting standard reviews and tests.

One particularly significant aspect of the extreme programming (XP) methodology, which is increasingly applied to small software projects, is the recognition that the estimates used *must* be based on experience. In XP this principle is called "yesterday's weather," from the observation that today's weather will match yesterday's weather more times than not. Strict use of data collection and application of productivity information to estimate future work is one of the reasons that XP delivers more predictable results than earlier evolutionary software methodologies. Schedules developed for XP projects never commit to deliver more in the next development cycle than was actually completed in the last cycle.

The most useful historical information, for projects of all types, is solid empirical data, collected with discipline and care during earlier work. Unfortunately for most project leaders, project metric databases are still fairly rare for technical projects, so global standards and norms often cannot simply be looked up. While there may be no convenient online database where you can retrieve good estimating information, even for the more routine activities in the project, almost always some usable data are available. For example, potential sources of activity effort and duration information for projects can be found by reviewing data from:

❑ Postproject analysis reports (or lessons learned, or project retrospectives, or postmortems) from earlier projects

❑ Personal notes and status reports from your projects or projects done by peers

❑ Notes from team members on related earlier activities

❑ Engineering or other published technical data (either inside your organization or public) from conference proceedings, papers, or articles

❑ Published reference materials

❑ Engineering or other technical standards

❑ The Web (generally the most plentiful, as well as the least reliable, source)

Anecdotal historical information is all around you; everyone likes to share stories. Your own experiences and memories and the recollections of the rest of the project team are anecdotal history. Other sources are discussions with peers, industry experts, consultants, service suppliers, and anyone else who you think may have experiences that could supplement your team's insight into the work.

Written historical data tends to be more reliable but may be difficult to find. Anecdotal information is relatively easy to get but may not be very trustworthy. (After some time passes, recollections concerning data on activity durations may not be very accurate.) Either source can serve as a good foundation for preliminary estimating and planning, though, especially if the data are recent, relevant, and credible.

Another approach you can use when there are no historical data is to create some. Begin by breaking the activity to be estimated into even smaller pieces of work, and choose a representative portion. Then, perform this part of the work and measure the duration (or effort) required to complete it. Using your assessment of the approximate percentage of the entire activity the completed part represents, you can extrapolate from the measurement and estimate the remainder of the activity. This idea is most easily applied to very repetitive work (to estimate the digging of a one-hundred-meter trench, get out a shovel and time how long it takes to dig the first meter), but it may also be applied to complex, technical projects. By selecting and implementing an average software module or a typical hardware assembly out of a complex system, you can create an estimate of the whole based on factual information, even when the system involves new or changing technology. This technique is basically equivalent to the "yesterday's weather" estimating method used for XP projects. In applying this technique, if you select a portion of the work where you have feasibility issues, it may also assist you in assessing (and managing) scope risk.

In any event, lack of documented history is a problem that is easy to fix. Measurement and productivity analysis are essential to ongoing management of estimation risk, so resolve to begin, or continue, collecting actual activity data at least for your projects. Metrics useful for risk management are covered in detail in Chapter 9.

Experts and Expert Judgment

Historical information need not be personal to be useful. Even when no one on the project has relevant experience or data, there may be others who do, outside your project. One source may be peers, managers, and technical talent elsewhere in your organization. Another possibility is to seek out the opinions of colleagues in professional societies who do similar work for other companies.

Outside consultants in technical or management fields may have useful information that they will share, for a fee. Even quotations and proposals from service suppliers may contain useful data that you can use for estimating project work.

Experience-Based Rules and Parametric Formulas

When a type of work is repeated often, the data collected over time may evolve into useful formulas for effort or for duration. These formulas may be informal "rules of thumb" providing approximate estimates that relate to measurable aspects of activity output, or they may be elaborate, precise (or at least precise-looking) analytical equations derived by regression analysis using data from past projects. In both of these cases, the parameters used as input in the formulas are independent variables relating to the size of the activity deliverables. The outputs of these formulas are dependent variables, calculated to provide estimates for the project plan. Experiential rules include statements such as "It takes one day per page to deliver new documentation (half a day to complete a page of modified documentation)" and "Plan to spend one day developing each hour of training material." These rules can be very accurate if the foundation information is both current and relevant.

Parametric formulas are also widely used, especially where there is a solid base of data and consistency between your project and the projects on which the formulas were derived. There are parametric formulas that use activity outputs at a very low level, such as "noncommented source statements" in software projects or counts of components in hardware projects. For software projects, most low-level parametric formulas are related to the Constructive Cost Model (COCOMO), developed several decades ago by Barry Boehm at TRW, or to the more recent COCOMO II effort undertaken by Boehm and others at the University of Southern California. These formulas relate code size to effort (in "engineering months") and to duration (in "calendar months"). While there are examples where these formulas work well, for many projects it is nearly as difficult to estimate parameters such as lines of code during project planning as it is to estimate activity durations. It has been often observed that the first time you know for sure how many lines of code there are in a software system is the day you deliver it (and sometimes, not even then). The end of the project is a little late to derive project estimates.

There are also formulas that use information at higher levels of abstraction. For hardware projects, you could use system block diagrams or complexity analysis. For software projects, formulas are often based on "function points" or related concepts.

Function points were developed at IBM in the 1970s and have been extended over the years by many others for use with a spectrum of programming languages and in a wide variety of software applications. This higher-level input data may be easier to assess early in your project than low-level "size" data such as components or lines of code, but the formulas tend to have high uncertainty.

There are numerous examples of these size-based estimation methods, and one (or several) may be appropriate for the work in projects of any kind. Even if the initial formulas come from published or borrowed information, you will get the best results if you collect your own, local data and normalize the formulas and experiential rules for your own environment. Every project is different, and someone else's formulas are unlikely to predict what will happen on your project. Reassessment throughout projects, using increasingly more accurate size information, minimizes your estimating risk.

Delphi Group Estimating

The Delphi process was not initially developed to do project estimates. It was first used for a type of estimate where people have historically been even *more* inaccurate—sales forecasts. The process uses inputs from several people (a minimum of four, ranging up to as many as twelve) to establish ranges and stimulate discussion. The Delphi method relies on the fact that, although no one person may be able to confidently provide reliable estimates, the middle range of estimates drawn from a population of stakeholders is frequently a realistic predictor for numeric results.

The process is relatively simple. You begin by selecting a suitable small group that will be the estimating team. Include "experts," project team members, and people from whom you will need buy-in. The process works best when all the people involved have some experience with the project and the activities to be estimated and the group is not so large as to require a lot of overhead or stifle discussions. Ideally, you should gather this team for a face-to-face meeting, but Delphi can also be done with distributed teams through teleconferencing or even by using cycles of electronic mail. Delphi begins with an overview of the process for anyone not familiar with it and a brief description of the project activities that need estimates. The activity descriptions may include any information about the work—expected deliverables, known problems, skills required and people available, assumptions—but *never* any indication concerning the estimate. The point of Delphi is to probe what each individual thinks is the answer to the question, in this case an estimate, and access to other opinions distorts the outcome. For the first cycle, each person on the team quickly provides his or her own estimates, with no help from anyone else.

All the estimates are collected and sorted into three roughly equal groups: shortest, most likely, and longest. The whole group then discusses the merits of the value calculated by averaging the inputs of the middle group, exploring reasons to support or modify it. It is important to hear from those who supplied much higher or lower estimates. The optimists may have insight into better methods, clever shortcuts, or other approaches to the work that realistically justify their shorter estimates. The pessimists are worth hearing from, as they are often the people who have the most experience with the work being considered and know details and requirements that others may be unaware of.

You may repeat this estimation process through one or more additional cycles—collecting estimates, sorting, and discussing—to build consensus. For project activities, Delphi estimates generally converge quickly.

Delphi is a "group intelligence" way to tap into subconscious historical data that would otherwise be unavailable. It is also a collaborative team technique and contributes to group buy-in, ownership, and motivation. Delphi estimates are not seen as imposed by one individual; the estimates belong to the team, and the team will be motivated to do whatever they can to deliver on them.

Further Decomposition

For activities where there are few or no relevant historical data, further decomposition may reveal portions of the work for which you do have data, or which are at least small enough to think through clearly. The same process used to do a WBS for the project may be applied to project activities that are hard to estimate, decomposing the activities into smaller, sequential subactivities (much smaller than would usually be planned or tracked). One approach is to break activities into phases as might be done with the whole project: investigation, analysis, development, documentation, testing. Other ideas are to work using subcomponents of the activity deliverable or from activity completion and acceptance criteria.

PROJECT-LEVEL ESTIMATES

Once every activity in the project WBS has an effort estimate, you can calculate the effort required in each project phase and total project effort. The "shape" of projects is generally consistent over time, so the percentages of effort for each project phase derived from your planning process ought to be consistent with the measured results from earlier projects. Whatever the names and contents of the actual project phases, any significant deviation in the current plan compared with historical norms is good reason for skepticism. Any plan that shows a lower percentage of effort in a given project phase than is normal has either missed some necessary activities or underestimated the activities identified.

Published industry norms may be useful, but the best information to use for comparison is local. How projects run in different environments varies a great deal, even for projects using a common life cycle or methodology. Historical data from peers can be helpful, but data directly from projects that you have run are better. Disciplined collection of project metrics is essential for accurate estimation, better planning, and effective risk management. If you have personal data, use them. If you lack data from past projects, here is yet another good reason to start collecting them.

Not all project phases are as accurately planned as others, because some project work is more familiar and receives more attention. The *middle* phases of most project life cycles contain most of the work that defines "what we do." Programmers program; hardware engineers build things; tech writers write; and, in general, people do what it says on their business card. Whatever the "middle" phases are called (e.g., development, implementation, execution), it is during this portion of the work that project contributors use the skills in which they have the most background and experience. These phases of project work are generally planned in detail, and activity estimates are often quite accurate. The phases that are earlier (e.g., investigation, planning, analysis, proposal generation) and later (e.g., test, roll-out, integration, ramp-up) are generally less accurate. Using the life-cycle norm data, and assuming the "development" portion of the plan is fairly accurate, it is possible to detect whether project work may be missing or underestimated in the other phases. If this analysis shows inadequate effort allocated to the early (or late) phases when compared to historical profiles for effort, it is a good idea to find out why.

Effort profiles for projects also vary with project size. By mapping the data from a large number of projects with various life cycles into a very simple, generic life cycle, you find a significant trend. The simplified project life cycle in Figure 4-3 is far less detailed than any you are likely to use, but all life cycles and methodologies define phases or stages that map into these three broad categories:

❒ *Thinking*—all the initial work on a project, such as planning, analysis, investigation, initial design, proposal generation,

Figure 4-3. Effort by project phase.

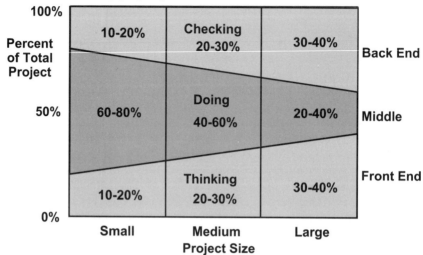

specification, and preparation for the business decision to commit to the project.

❏ *Doing*—the work that generally defines the project, including development. This is where the team rolls up their sleeves and digs into the creation of the project deliverable.

❏ *Checking*—testing the results created by the project, searching for defects in the deliverable(s), correcting problems and omissions, and achieving project closure.

As projects increase in size and complexity, the amount of work grows very rapidly. Project effort tends to expand geometrically as projects increase in time, staffing, specifications, or other parameters. In addition to this overall rise in effort, the effort spent in each phase of the project, as a percentage, also shifts. As projects become larger, longer, and more complex, the percentage of total project effort increases for both early front-end project work and for back-end activities at the end of the project. A graphical summary of this, based on data from a wide range of projects, is in Figure 4-3.

In small projects (less than six months, most work done with a small co-located team), people spend nearly all their effort in "doing"—creating the deliverable. For medium projects (six to twelve months long, with more than one team of people contributing), the team might spend about half of its effort in other work. People on projects that are still larger (one year or longer, with several distributed and/or global teams) spend only about a third of the total effort developing project deliverables. This rise in effort both in the early and the late stages of project work stems from the increased amount of information and coordination required and from the significantly larger number of possible failure modes (and, therefore, statistically expected) in these more difficult projects. Fixing defects in complex systems requires a lot of time and effort. The software consultant Fred Brooks (author of *The Mythical Man-Month*) states that a typical software project is one-third analysis, one-sixth coding, and *one-half* testing.

All this bears on project risk, and failure-prone projects, for at least two reasons. The first is chronic underestimation of late project effort. If a complex project is planned with the expectation that 10 percent of the effort will be in up-front work, followed by 80 percent in development, the final phase will rarely be the expected 10 percent. It will balloon to another 80 percent (or more). This is a primary cause of the all-too-common "late project work bulge." Many entirely possible projects fail to meet their deadline (or fail altogether) due to underinvestment in early analysis and planning.

The second reason that life-cycle norms are valuable is found in the symmetry of Figure 4-3. The total effort required for a project tends to be lower when the initial and final phases of the work are roughly in balance. If the life-cycle norms for typical projects reveal that very little effort is invested up front and a massive (generally unexpected) amount of effort is necessary at the end, then all projects are taking longer and costing more than necessary. Most projects that fail or are late due to end-of-project problems would benefit greatly from additional up-front work and planning.

APPLYING ESTIMATING TECHNIQUES

Figure 4-4 summarizes estimation techniques that are applicable in various situations. For each project activity, either the team has experience or it does not. For the type of work involved, either there are relevant metrics available or there are none.

The worst case is the lower right quadrant: no experience *and* no data. This case is far from unusual; on technical projects, it may be true for a number of activities you need to estimate. The most frequent methods used for estimating involve some sort of guessing, sometimes with arcane rules, and in this situation a guess may be your only option. You can also consider alternatives such as getting someone who does have experience to consult on your project or even replanning the work to use a different approach to the activity where your team does have experience.

Only slightly better than this is the case where you have no

Figure 4-4. Estimation techniques.

	Relevant Metrics Exist	No Data Available
Prior Activity Experience	• Retrospectives • Databases • Parametric Formulas, Experiential Rules ("Size" Methods) • Life-Cycle Norms	• Task Owner Input • Peer Inputs • Inspections • Delphi Analysis • Short Tasks (20-day Maximum) in WBS • Further Decomposition
No Activity Experience	• Published Information • Vendor Quotes • Expert Consultation	• Guess • Get Outside Help • Use Older Technology

experience but you have found some external information. Estimates based on someone else's measurements are better than nothing, but, unless your project is very similar to the project where the measurements were made, the data may not be very relevant. In either of these cases, when a project activity requires work for which you lack experience, estimation risk is high, and your activity duration estimates belong on the project risk list.

The upper right quadrant is for activities that have been done before but for which no data exist. Although this should not happen, it remains fairly common on technical projects. Thorough analysis and estimating methods such as Delphi may provide adequate estimates, but the results of these processes still contain estimation risk. Over time, more disciplined data collection will help you better manage this risk.

The best case is the upper left quadrant. The existence of both experience and measurements should provide credible, reliable estimates for project activities. Eventually, proactive risk management and disciplined application of other project processes will move many, if not most, activities here, even on high-tech projects.

One other significant source of estimation risk arises from the people who are assigned to do the work. "Good" estimates need to be believable, which means that they are derived from data and by methods that make sense. This is a good foundation, but even the best estimating techniques are unreliable unless the project team is involved. To be accurate, estimates also must be *believed*. No matter how many data go into creating estimates, if the people who will do the work have not "bought into" the estimate, it remains a risk. Good estimates are both *believable* and *believed*.

ESTIMATES ADJUSTED FOR UNCERTAINTY

All the techniques just discussed generate deterministic, single-point estimates for project activities. This type of estimate implies a precision that is far from reality. To better deal with uncertainty and risk, the Program Evaluation and Review Technique (PERT) methodology was developed during the late 1950s by the U.S. military. PERT uses an estimate range, using three estimates for each activity: an optimistic estimate, a most likely estimate, and a pessimistic estimate. (PERT may also be used for both time and cost analysis. This discussion concerns only time analysis.) These estimates define a distribution of outcomes similar to Figure 4-5, and they can be used to calculate an *expected* activity duration using the formula:

$$t_e = (t_o + 4t_m + t_p)/6, \text{ where}$$

t_e is the calculated "expected" duration—the mean
t_o is the "optimistic" duration (the "best case")
t_m is the "most likely" duration (the peak of the distribution)
t_p is the "pessimistic" duration (the "worst case")

In addition to the "expected" estimate, PERT also assesses estimation risk quantitatively. For PERT methodology, the range of possible outcomes allows you to calculate the standard deviation for each activity:

$$\text{One standard deviation} = (t_p - t_o)/6$$

Traditionally, PERT assumed a bell-type distribution that could skew toward either the optimistic or pessimistic estimate, similar to the distribution in Figure 4-5. A Beta distribution was most commonly used, but current PERT implementations can use a wide variety of continuous or discrete distributions to model expectations for estimates.

Figure 4-5. Estimates for PERT analysis.

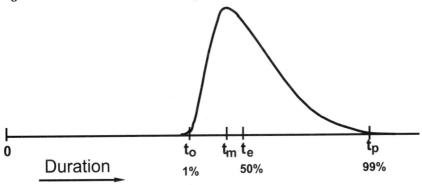

The theory behind PERT is fine, but in practice PERT analysis has not always proved very useful. The three most common problems people have in using PERT are the time and effort required for the analysis, data quality, and misuse of the data collected.

PERT uses computer simulation and Monte Carlo sampling techniques to assess project schedules, and a common criticism in the 1950s, when computers were much slower, was that a typical project analysis took only a little longer than the project itself. Computers today are more than fast enough to simulate project schedules hundreds, or even thousands, of times to create beautiful histograms, and there are dozens of computer tools available. (Some of the tools are listed in Chapter 9, where PERT is covered in more detail.) While the speed required for simulations is no longer an issue, for some project leaders the time required to collect, enter, and interpret PERT output still may still exceed the apparent value of the results.

And the other two problems persist. The data quality problem results from the difficulty of determining the three estimates with any accuracy. The PERT initially defined "optimistic" and "pessimistic" as "1-percent tails," requesting people to imagine doing an activity 100 times and setting the range estimates so that only once would the duration fall below the optimistic estimate and only once would it lie above the pessimistic estimate. For most activities, the estimates were unreliable (or, worse, wild guesses), which was reflected in the output. As the saying goes, "Garbage in, garbage out."

The problem of misusing PERT data is also an ongoing issue, which may be the biggest reason that PERT is not more widely used in technical projects. Many organizations use PERT for a time before they run into this problem. Everything starts out well. Project teams do their best to figure out what the three estimates might be for each activity, using difficult-to-understand definitions involving Beta distributions and 1-percent tails (or 5- or 10-percent tails—there are many variants). PERT analysis of projects proceeds for a while, and some insight into the nondeterministic nature of projects begins to emerge. This continues until some bright mid-level manager starts noticing the optimistic estimates. Because the project teams have admitted that these estimates are not completely impossible, managers begin to insist that schedules be based only on the most aggressive estimates, and these define the project deadlines. The statistical underpinnings of PERT predict that such schedules have essentially no chance of success, and experience invariably proves it. If any interest in PERT remains after all of this, the battered project teams start to use very different definitions for the optimistic estimate in self-defense.

There is a simpler way to apply the concept of PERT to project risk analysis that involves two estimates instead of three—dispensing with the troublesome optimistic estimate. This PERT-like analysis uses the most likely estimate twice, along with the pessimistic estimate, in the PERT formulas. This technique does not cause much distortion, and your initial estimate for each activity will serve as the most likely estimate, so you already have half the data you need.

The PERT formula still requires a pessimistic estimate, and seeking this estimate is an excellent way to identify schedule risk. To collect this data, you do not need to describe complicated scenarios involving doing activities over and over or exotic distributions. Once you have determined the most likely estimate, simply ask, "What might go wrong in this activity that could affect the estimate, and what would the impact be?" The response will provide two pieces of important project risk data. The amount of impact you estimate may be used to determine the pessimistic estimate for PERT analysis. Even more revealing, the *source* of the potential slip is a project schedule risk that should be added to your list of identified risks. The use of worst-case estimates in PERT formulas is a fairly good way to determine "expected" durations, as they will represent a weighted average of the two estimates provided, largely based on the initial estimate but with some adjustment based on the worst case. The inferred distribution is similar to Figure 4-6, where the optimistic and most likely estimates are assumed to be equal, and the formula for expected duration becomes $t_e = (5t_m + t_p)/6$.

While PERT techniques may be used for estimating activities, PERT analysis was created primarily as a tool for *project* risk assessment. This use of PERT and PERT tools is explored in Chapter 9.

Activity Sequencing

Additional scheduling risks become visible as you develop your project schedule by combining sequencing information with

Figure 4-6. "PERT"–like estimating.

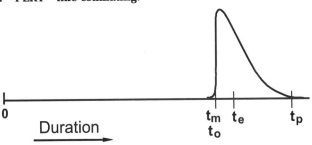

the activity estimates. Activity sequencing requires you to determine the dependencies for each project activity, and these linkages reveal many potential sources of project delay. Delay risks are responsible for most of the scheduling risks in the PERIL database.

One effective method for minimizing schedule risk related to sequencing is to break long, complex projects into a series of much shorter ones. This principle is fundamental to evolutionary, or cyclic, software development methodologies. If the cycles are sufficiently short—two to four weeks are a common cycle in methodologies such as XP—the dependencies either become irrelevant or are sufficiently simple that managing them is trivial. For the most part, XP ignores dependencies except as special cases within each iteration. The same principle applies generally; the shorter the overall arc of a project is, the fewer complications and risks there will be due to dependencies.

In more complex projects, there are many possible types of dependencies that may connect project activities, but most are linked by finish-to-start relationships—once one activity or a collection of activities is complete, other project activities can begin. Occasionally, some activities might need to be synchronized by either starting or finishing at the same time, and the logic of project work may also depend on interruptions and lags of various kinds. Although project plans may include some of these more exotic dependencies, the majority of the dependencies in a typical project network are finish-to-start linkages, and it is these sequential-activity dependencies that are most likely to cause delay risk. In addition to revealing these potential schedule risks, logical project networks also provide the foundation of both critical path and PERT analysis (which is why project activity networks are often referred to as PERT charts).

Project dependencies are a significant source of schedule risks, and discovering them requires construction of a logical network for your project that has *no gaps*. Define the logical flow of work for your project so that all project activities, without exception, have a continuous path backward to your initial project milestone and a continuous path forward the final project deadline. Determine both predecessors and successors for every activity (and milestone) in your project, and inspect the resulting network for missing linkages and logical problems. Project analysis and risk identification will be incomplete (and possibly worthless) if you leave any gaps or dangling connections. For project planning using a computer tool, you should never use features such as "must start on" and "must end on" pegged-date logic. The software will generate a Gantt chart that looks a lot like a project plan, but you will not be able to perform schedule analysis, do proper project tracking, or effectively identify schedule risk.

CRITICAL PATH METHODOLOGY

Critical path methodology (CPM) analysis combines activity estimates with dependency information and calculates the duration for the project on the basis of these data. CPM also identifies schedule risks. You can do this analysis manually for small projects, but CPM calculations for larger networks of activities are extremely tedious. Fortunately, CPM has been automated in computer scheduling tools. Once all your activities, duration estimates, and dependencies are entered into the database of a scheduling tool, the software evaluates the resulting project network and locates the sequence (or sequences) of project activities with the longest total duration. All activities that make up the longest sequence are flagged as "critical," and the entire flow of work from the initial milestone to the project deadline is defined as a project *critical path*. Computer tools helpfully color all the critical activities an appropriately scary red color. Each of these red activities carries schedule risk, because if one is not completed within the time estimated for it, everything that follows it in the project can also be expected to slip, including the project deadline.

CPM also provides information on activities on "noncritical" paths, because the calculations used to find the critical activities determine the earliest and latest schedules for every activity in the project. The difference between the late and the early schedules for an activity is labeled "float" or "slack," and it represents one type of risk associated with each activity. If float is zero (or, even worse, negative—indicating the project must be completed by a date that is earlier than the current plan shows is possible), the activity is risky, colored red, and on a critical path. If float is small—a day or two—the activity is also risky, as it would take only a small slip to make the activity critical. Even project activities that have a large amount of float can be risky if their worst-case estimates exceed the calculated float.

Using computer scheduling tools, it is easy to do "what if" scenarios to identify the activities that represent schedule risk in addition to those on the project critical path. The first step is to make a copy of the database for the project (so that you can manipulate the copy and leave your initial data intact). You can then begin editing the database copy to locate other risks. You can delete all the critical activities in your project (relinking any resulting broken dependencies as you go) to see what the project looks like without them. All activities that are critical in this analysis are also potential schedule risks, especially if the resulting schedule is not significantly shorter than the one you started with. Repeating this analysis by deleting the resulting critical activities through multiple levels may be necessary to identify the riskiest activities on complex projects.

A second way to use a copy of the database to identify schedule risk involves replacing your initial estimates with worst-case estimates to see how these changes will impact the overall schedule. When you do this one activity at a time, you discover how sensitive the overall project is to each individual problem. If you enter all of your worst-case estimates, you get a version of the plan that shows a far longer schedule than is probable, but the end point displays just how bad things might get if *everything* goes wrong. (And, remember, your analysis is based on only *known* risks; if there are significant unknown project risks, even your worst-case schedule might be optimistic.)

In reality, every activity in the project represents at least a small level of schedule risk. Any piece of work in the plan could be the one that causes a project to fail. CPM and related calculations can be used to prioritize the schedule risks to determine which activities have risks that are sufficiently significant to add to your risk list.

MULTIPLE CRITICAL PATHS

Projects can and often do have more than one critical path. Parallel sequences of activities that are equal in duration to the project are all critical, and when this happens, it increases schedule risk even more. If all the estimates used in a project schedule are assumed to be "expected" durations calculated with the weighted-average PERT formula described earlier, the chance of an activity's finishing early (or on time) is the same as the chance of the activity's finishing late. In a project with one critical path, the project as a whole has the same probabilities—50/50. (This assumes that all events and activities are independent—more on this later.) What about the project in Figure 4-7 with two critical paths?

Both paths "A-D-J" and "C-H-L" are critical, and all activities are estimated using "expected" (50 percent) estimates. The expectation for each path is therefore also 50 percent, so each of the two paths is expected to either meet or beat the project estimate half of the time (the infinitesimal probability associated with "exactly on time" is included with "early") and to be late the other half of the time. If the two paths are assumed to be independent, the matrix in Figure 4-8 shows the probabilities for each possible outcome. The project has only one chance in four of finishing early or on

Figure 4-7. Project with two critical paths.

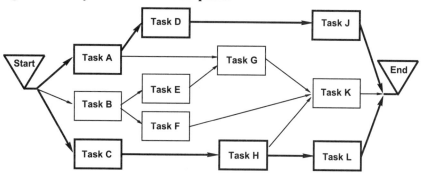

Figure 4-8. Result matrix for project.

<table>
<tr><td colspan="2"></td><td colspan="2" align="center">**A-D-J**</td></tr>
<tr><td colspan="2"></td><td align="center">**Early/ on time**</td><td align="center">**Late**</td></tr>
<tr><td rowspan="4">**C H L**</td><td align="center">**Early/ on time**</td><td align="center">**25%**</td><td align="center">**25%**</td></tr>
<tr><td align="center">**Late**</td><td align="center">**25%**</td><td align="center">**25%**</td></tr>
</table>

time, the same probability as flipping two coins and getting "heads" twice.

Only when both paths complete early or on time will the project complete on time, and three times in four—75 percent of the time—the project will be late. If there are more than two critical paths, the situation gets even worse. With three critical paths, the chances fall to one in eight, and the fraction shrinks by a factor of two with each additional critical path. The more potential failure modes there are, the more likely it is that the project will be late.

Although this picture is bleak, most real technical projects face even larger risks. Few projects are planned using estimates that are equally likely to be slightly early or slightly late. Aggressive estimates are common on technical projects for all the reasons discussed earlier in the chapter, including overconfidence, lack of experience, and political pressure. If the estimates are actually 10 percent likely to be early or on time and 90 percent likely to be late, a matrix similar to Figure 4-8 for two critical paths will calculate only one chance of success in one hundred.

In addition, this analysis assumes statistical independence of all events. The assumption of independence may be valid for some work on projects, but on real projects, all the work is done by a small team of people who have complicated relationships with one another. Assuming that the outcome of one activity will have no effect on succeeding activities is unrealistic. Project problems tend to cascade, and correlation between project activities further decreases the overall likelihood of success. The upshot of all this is that schedule risk increases very significantly when there are multiple parallel possibilities for project slippage.

SCHEDULING RISKY WORK

The timing of activities may also increase project risk. Whenever an activity has high uncertainty, it is human nature to schedule it to start late in the project. If an activity requires the invention of something new, or the specifics of the work are far from obvious, you may be tempted to defer the work until later in the project, reasoning that the delay might give you a chance to figure it out. Also, scheduling risky work toward the end of your project will allow you to write at least a few weekly status reports that are not filled with bad news associated with the more problematic activities.

Tempting though this is, don't do it. Deferring riskier activities until late in the project can lead to increases in both project risk and cost. By scheduling risky activities earlier, you can learn faster, and frequently with less effort, whether there are any "show-stoppers"—activities that make your whole project impossible. When you discover the problems earlier, project decision makers have more options, including shifting the objective, using the time still available to seek alternate ways to proceed with the project, or even abandoning the work altogether. If a risky activity is left until late in the project, it may be impossible or very costly to shift the objective, and there will be little or no time left to find another approach. Perhaps the worst case of all is to discover that the project is not feasible and to cancel it after having spent months (or even years) of money and effort. When risky work is scheduled earlier, a decision to cancel can be made after only a small portion of the project budget has been spent, instead of nearly all of it. In addition to being a waste of money, late cancellation is very demotivating for the project team and will make it difficult to find enthusiastic staff for future projects.

SCHEDULE PATH CONVERGENCE

Another project exposure is "fan-in." Most of the time, the places in a project network that have the largest number of predecessor dependencies are milestones, but any point of convergence in a project network represents schedule risk. Since project work stops at a milestone or activity whenever any of the preceding activities are incomplete, each additional path in the fan-in represents a possible failure mode, and it increases the probability of delay. Milestones, phase exits, stage gates, and other life-cycle checkpoints are often held up in large programs by a single missing requirement; even when all the other work is satisfactorily completed, the work halts to wait for the final dependency.

The largest fan-in exposure for many projects is the final milestone, which usually has a large number of predecessor activities. Even in the very simple project network in Figure 4-7, there are three predecessor dependencies for the finish milestone.

INTERFACES

Dependency risks outside the project are also substantially represented in the PERIL database. Dependencies of all kinds may represent schedule risks, but interfaces—dependencies that connect one or more projects—are particularly problematic; the impact of these risks was the highest for all schedule risks in the PERIL database, averaging more than five weeks per project. Connections between projects are most common for projects that are part of a larger program. As each project team plans its work, dependencies on other projects arise. Dependencies that are wholly within a project carry schedule risk, but interfaces are even riskier. For an interface, each project contains only half of the linkage, the predecessor or the successor. The deliverables can be components, services, information, software, or almost anything that one project creates that is required by another project team. The project that expects to receive the deliverable potentially faces both schedule and scope risk. If the hand-off is late, the dependent project may slip. Even when it is on time, if the deliverable is not acceptable, the project (and the whole program) may be in trouble. Interfaces are particularly important to identify and manage because of the limited visibility of progress in the project responsible for the deliverable.

An interface between projects is depicted graphically in Figure 4-9. The interface is partly in each project and partly in "no man's land." In analyzing these interproject linkages, the terminology of producers and consumers is useful. For linkages that terminate in your project, you are a consumer. For linkages that start in your project, you are the producer.

Interfaces are usually first identified by the consumer project, as part of the planning process. *Inputs* from other projects that

Figure 4-9. Interface connecting two projects.

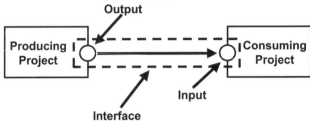

may stop or slow your project represent the greatest risks. It is also useful to start a list of activity *outputs* within your plan that you expect to provide to other projects.

Interface management depends on collecting information in writing on the interfaces—the inputs and the outputs—among all projects in the overall program. Project inputs are generally collected first, as they are the easiest to identify. For the whole program, each input must be matched with a corresponding output. For any required input with no identified output, you must either identify an appropriate producer project or change the scope of the consumer project(s) to resolve the need internally.

The interface planning process seeks agreement and commitments consistent with the overall program plan. The program manager coordinates reconciliation, resolves conflicts, finds owners for outputs not claimed, and eliminates activities that create outputs that are not used. As the process proceeds, the projects involved align both the timing and the specifications of the interfaces. Interfaces are best managed with formality—by treating each agreement as a contract. Even for interfaces entirely within the same organization, you should get *written* agreement between the producer and the consumer(s).

Even when interfaces are documented and well managed, they are risky. Add each project interface where your project is the consumer to your list of project risks.

PLANNING HORIZON

Yet another source of schedule risk relates to the length of the schedule. When you drive an automobile at night on a dark road with no illumination other than your headlights, you can only see a limited distance ahead. The reach of the headlights is several hundred meters, so you must stay alert and frequently reexamine the road ahead to see new things as they come into view.

Similarly, projects have a limited distance of visibility. Projects vary a good deal in how much accurate planning is possible, but all projects have a limit. For some projects, planning even three months in advance is difficult. For others, the planning horizon might be longer, but technical project planning is rarely accurate for work more than six to nine months in the future. The uncertainty inherent in work planned more than a few months in the future is a source of significant schedule risk on any lengthy project. Make specific note of any unusual, novel, or unstaffed activities more than three months into the project. On a regular basis, include explicit activities in the project plan to review estimates, risks, assumptions, and other project data. Risk management relies on periodic recommendations for project plan adjustments based on the results of these reviews.

Project reviews are most useful at natural project transitions: the end of a life-cycle phase, a major milestone or checkpoint, a significant change to the project objective, whenever key contributors leave or are added to the project team, or following business reorganizations. At a minimum, schedule reviews for longer projects at least every three to six months. A process for project review is detailed in Chapter 11.

Document the Risks

Schedule risks become visible throughout the planning and scheduling processes. The specific instances discussed in this chapter are all project risks:

- ❐ Long-duration activities
- ❐ Significant worst-case (or pessimistic "PERT") estimates
- ❐ High-uncertainty estimates
- ❐ Overly optimistic estimates
- ❐ All critical path (and near-critical path) activities
- ❐ Multiple critical paths
- ❐ Convergence points in the logical network
- ❐ External dependencies and interfaces
- ❐ Deadlines further out than the planning horizon
- ❐ Cross-functional and subcontracted work

Augment the list of project scope risks, adding each schedule risk identified with a clear description of the risk situation. The list of risks continues to expand throughout the project planning process and serves as the foundation for project risk analysis and management.

Key Ideas for Identifying Schedule Risks

☐ Determine the root causes of all uncertain estimates.

☐ Identify all estimates not based on historical data.

☐ Note dependencies that pose delay risks, including all interfaces.

☐ Find any differences between project effort requirements and life-cycle norms.

☐ Identify risky activities and schedule them early in the project.

☐ Ascertain risks associated with multiple critical (or near-critical) paths.

☐ Note risks associated with lengthy projects.

Panama Canal: Planning (1905–1907)

Early in his work in Panama, John Stevens spent virtually all of his time among the workers, asking questions. His single-minded pursuit was planning the project well and thoroughly. Stevens put all he learned into the plans, setting the foundation required to get the project moving forward.

The primary tool for construction was one Stevens was very familiar with: the railroad. He recognized that digging enormous trenches was only part of the job. Excavated soil had to be moved out of the cut in central Panama where someday ships would pass, and it had to be deposited near the coasts to construct the required massive earthen dams. In the rain forests of Panama at the turn of the twentieth century, the railroad was not only the best way to do this; it was also the only practical way. Much of the planning that Stevens did centered on using the railroad, and, by early in 1906, he had documented exactly how this was to be done. When excavation resumed, his elaborate, "ingeniously elastic" use of the railroad enabled work to progress at a vigorous pace, and it continued virtually nonstop through project completion.

Once Stevens had broken the work down into smaller, easily understood activities, the canal project began to look possible. Each part of the job was now understood to be something that had been done, somewhere, before. It became a matter of getting it all done, one activity at a time.

For all his talents and capabilities, John Stevens never considered himself fully qualified to manage the entire project. His experience was with surveying and building railroads. The canal project involved building massive concrete locks (like enormous bathtubs with doors on each end) that would raise ships nearly thirty meters from sea level and then lower them back again—twelve structures in all. The project also required a great deal of knowledge of hydraulics; moving enormous amounts of water quickly was essential to efficient canal operation. Stevens had no experience with either of these types of engineering. These gaps in his background, coupled with his dislike of the hot, humid climate and the omnipresent (and still dangerous) insects, led him to resign as chief engineer after two years, in 1907.

This did not sit well with Theodore Roosevelt. Losing such a competent project leader was a huge risk to the schedule. Both of his project leaders had resigned before completing his most important project, and Roosevelt was determined that this would not happen again. To replace John Stevens, Roosevelt selected George Washington Goethals, an immensely qualified engineer. Goethals had been seriously considered for the job twice previously and was ideally qualified to build the Panama Canal. He had completed a number of similar, smaller projects, and he had a great deal of experience with nearly all the work required at Panama.

Theodore Roosevelt wanted more than competence, however. For this project, he wanted "men who will stay on the job until I get tired of having them there, or until I say they may abandon it." His new chief engineer and project leader could not resign; George Goethals was a major (soon to be lieutenant colonel) in the U.S. Army Corps of Engineers. If Goethals tried to resign, he could be court-martialed and sent to jail.

CHAPTER 5

IDENTIFYING PROJECT RESOURCE RISK

"If you want a track team to win the high jump, you find one person who can jump seven feet, not several people who can jump six feet."

—FREDERICK TERMAN, Stanford University Dean and Professor of Engineering

Fred Terman is probably best known as the "Father of Silicon Valley." He encouraged Bill Hewlett and Dave Packard, the Varian brothers, and hundreds of others to start businesses near Stanford University. Starting in the 1930s, alarmed at the paucity of job opportunities in the area, he helped his students start companies, set up the Stanford Industrial Park, and generally was responsible for the establishment of the world's largest high-tech center. He was very good at identifying and nurturing technical talent, and he understood how critical it is in any undertaking.

A lack of technical skills or access to appropriate staff is a large source of project risk for complex, technical projects. Risk management on these projects requires careful assessment of needed skills and commitment of capable staff.

Much of the content of this chapter falls into the "Project Human Resource Management," "Project Procurement Management," and "Project Cost Management" segments of the *PMBOK®* *Guide.* In particular, the principal project resource risk ideas covered in this chapter include:

❏ Sources of resource risk
❏ Resource planning

❐ Staff acquisition

❐ Procurement planning and source selection

❐ Cost estimating

❐ Cost budgeting

Sources of Resource Risk

Resource risks represent less than one-third of the records in the PERIL database. There are three categories of resource risk: *people, outsourcing,* and *money.* People risks arise within the project team. Outsourcing risks result from the use of people and services outside the project team to perform critical project work. The third category, money, is something of an anomaly in the data, as very few of the problems reported were *primarily* about funding. Money is, however, a key factor in many of the people and outsourcing problems, and the effect of insufficient funding on projects has substantial impact on a project in many other ways. The summary shows:

RESOURCE RISKS	COUNT	CUMULATIVE IMPACT (WEEKS)	AVERAGE IMPACT (WEEKS)
People	45	194	4.3
Outsourcing	17	109	6.9
Money	2	58	29.0

The root causes of people and outsourcing risk are further characterized by type, and a Pareto chart of overall impact by type of risk is summarized in Figure 5-1. Although risks related to internal staffing dominate the resource risk data, the single most damaging factor is delay associated with outsourced work.

PEOPLE RISKS

Risks related to people represent the most numerous resource risks, accounting for more than two-thirds of the incidents. Availability of people was the primary issue, with four subcategories:

Figure 5-1. Resource risks in the PERIL database.

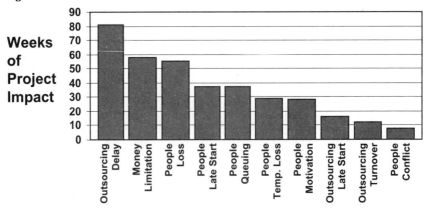

❐ Staff leaving the project permanently

❐ Staff leaving the project temporarily

❐ Staff joining the project late

❐ Queuing issues involving people not dedicated to the project

There were a few risks associated with conflict among staff members and some related to motivation.

Losing people midproject, permanently or temporarily, was the most common people risk, with permanent loss leading to an average slip of more than five weeks and temporary loss causing a typical slip of just over two weeks. The reasons for permanent staff loss included resignations, reassignments to other work or different projects, and staffing cutbacks. Discovering these risks in advance is difficult, but good record-keeping and trend analysis are useful in setting realistic project expectations. The total impact due to permanent staff loss dominated the people risks. Although its overall impact was lower, temporary loss of project staff was the most common people-related risk. The most frequently reported reason for short-term staff loss was a customer problem (a "hot site") related to the deliverable from an earlier project. Other reasons for short-term staff loss included illness, earthquakes, travel nightmares, and organizational reorganization.

There were also a number of projects that missed the deadline at the end because required staff was not available at the beginning. There were a number of root causes for staff joining the project late, but the most common was a situation described by one project leader as the "rolling sledgehammer." Whenever a prior project is late, some, perhaps even all, of the staff for the new project is still busy working to complete it. As a consequence, the next project gets a ragged start, with key people beginning their contributions to the new project only after they break free of the older one. Even when these people do become available, there can be additional delay. Staff members coming from a late project are often exhausted from the bulge of work and long hours typical of a project that runs beyond its deadline. The "rolling sledgehammer" creates a cycle that self-perpetuates and is very difficult to break. Each late project causes the projects that follow to be late.

Other reasons that can delay engagement of project staff include scarcity of certain skills, which is the root cause of the fourth risk related to people availability: queuing. Specialized expertise is often expensive, and it is common for businesses to minimize the cost of these skills by investing as little as possible. Most technical projects rely on at least some special expertise that they share with other projects, such as system architects needed at the start, testing personnel needed at the end, and other specialists needed throughout the project. If an expert happens to be free when a project is ready for him or her to start work, there is no problem. If the expert has activities for five other projects queued up already when your project activity needs attention, your activity will enter the queue, and any following work will slip while the queued activity waits. Queuing analysis is well understood, and it is used to optimize manufacturing, engineering, system design, computer networks, and many other business systems. Any system subject to queues requires some excess capacity to maximize throughput. Optimizing project resources based only on cost drives out any spare capacity and causes project delay.

Thorough planning and credible scheduling of the work well in advance will reveal some of the most serious potential exposures regarding people. Histogram analysis of resource requirements may also provide insight into staffing exposures a project will face, but, unless analysis of project resources is credibly integrated with comprehensive resource data for other projects and all the non-project demands within the business, the results will not be very useful. Aligning staffing capacity with project requirements requires ongoing attention. One significant root cause for understaffed projects is a failure to use project planning information to make or revise project selection decisions at the organization level, triggering the "too many projects" problem. Retrospective analysis of projects over time is also a powerful way to detect and measure the consequences of inadequate staffing, especially when the problems are chronic.

Other people-related risks in the PERIL database involved conflict, where two simultaneous projects had essentially the same objective and each interfered with the progress of the other. Low motivation also contributed to delay on several long projects. Falling morale is one risk (among many) for lengthy projects.

OUTSOURCING RISKS

Outsourcing accounts for more than a quarter of the resource risks. Though the frequency of this risk in the PERIL database is lower than that for people risks, the impact of outsourcing risk was nearly six and a half weeks, well above the database average. The risks related to outsourcing are similar to the people risks: delays, late starts, and turnover.

Delays, such as when a supplier fails to complete assigned work on schedule, are the most common outsourcing risk and represent the largest total impact for the projects in the PERIL database. Delays result from queuing problems and other people availability issues, but often a precise cause is not known. Outsourced work is generally done somewhere else, so the project team may not be able to observe it and assess the cause of problems. Compounding the impact of late delivery is the added element of surprise; the problem may be invisible until the day of the default, when it is too late to do much about it. Lateness of the deliverable was exacerbated in several examples in the PERIL database by work that did not meet stated specifications and caused even more delay.

Late starts are also fairly common with outsourced work. Contracts need to be negotiated, approved, and signed, all processes that can be very time-consuming. Beginning a new, complex relationship with outside people you have never worked with before can require more time than is expected. For projects with particularly unusual needs, just locating an appropriate supplier may cause significant delays.

The third risk, turnover, can also lead to project delay because of the ongoing need to redo training, conduct additional project plan and specification reviews, and rebuild working relationships.

Outsourcing risks are detected through planning processes and through careful analysis and thorough understanding of all the terms of the contract. Both the project team and the outsourcing partner must understand the terms and conditions of the contract, especially the scope of work and the business relationship.

MONEY RISKS

The third category, money, is not very common in the PERIL database. The two data points include the single largest delay in the database (for a project that was subject to such severe funding cutbacks that it was nearly a year late), so the average for this subcategory, twenty-nine weeks, is skewed. As with any other resource needed by a project, however, if there are limits on money that create bottlenecks, the result will be impeded progress and project delay.

Resource Planning

Resource planning is a useful tool for anticipating many of the people, outsourcing, and money risks. Inputs to the resource planning process include the project work breakdown structure (WBS), scope definition, activity descriptions, preliminary duration estimates, and the project schedule. Resource requirements planning can be done in a number of ways, using manual methods, histogram analysis, or computer tools.

RESOURCE REQUIREMENTS

On the basis of the preliminary schedule and assumptions about each project activity, you will need to determine the skills and staffing required for each activity. It is increasingly common, even for relatively small projects, to load this data into a computer scheduling tool. As early as possible, identify staffing for each activity *using the names of each individual.* While preliminary resource planning can be done with functions or roles, resource analysis based on names makes it more likely that estimates will be accurate and that staffing will be committed to the project as planned. Identify as a risk any required project staff members who cannot be named during project planning.

For the project as a whole, also identify all holidays, scheduled time off, significant nonproject meetings, and other time that will not be available to the project. Do this for each person, as well, and identify any scheduling differences for different regions, countries, and companies involved in the project. A computer scheduling tool is a good place to store calendar information, such as holidays, vacations, and any other important dates. If you do use a computer tool, enter all the calendar data into the database *before* you begin resource analysis.

You also need to determine the amount of effort available from each contributor. Even for "full-time" contributors, it is difficult to get more than five to six hours of project activity work per day, and "part-time" staff will contribute much less.

Particularly for project activities that are already identified as potential risks, such as those on the critical path, you need to determine and verify the total effort required and ascertain who will be involved with each activity. There are a number of effective approaches for doing this.

MANUAL METHODS

For smaller projects, resource analysis need not be overly complex. The primary objective of resource analysis is to identify portions of the project where the resources available do not support the project work planned. It may be easy to inspect the project timeline to see where the hours needed from an individual on a week-by-week basis exceed what will be available. Even on more complex projects, inspecting the overall plan is a quick way to identify resource problems such as obvious resource shortfalls or significant project milestones that align with holidays or other conflicts.

TABULAR ANALYSIS USING COMPUTER TOOLS

While inspections of the plan and manual resource analysis provide a good starting point, computer tools offer some benefits for more detailed analysis. They facilitate tabular resource reporting, and they may be used to easily identify resource overcommitments and undercommitments. Computer tools also help in managing important calendar information. In addition to this, computer-based project management software also is an effective tool for "what if?" analysis and can make project tracking and collection of metrics much easier. There are dozens of applications to choose from: Microsoft Project, CA SuperProject, Autoplan, Project Scheduler, Primavera, and Project Workbench are just a few. It is even possible to use computer spreadsheet applications to perform project resource analysis.

Whatever tool you choose, planning data may be used to do tabular analysis for individuals, as well as for entire projects. Scheduling tools also permit the resource plan to be updated easily following schedule or other project changes. Keep in mind, however, that a scheduling tool is primarily a database with specialized output reporting capability. The quality of the information the tool provides will never be any better than the quality of the data that you put in. *You* and the project team must still do the thinking; a computer tool cannot plan your project or identify its risks.

HISTOGRAM ANALYSIS USING COMPUTER TOOLS

For more complicated projects, graphical resource analysis is also useful. Loading each person's effort allocation into a computer scheduling tool allows aggregate workload analysis in several formats, in addition to tabular reports. Resource histograms show graphically where the staffing of the project is inadequate on an individual-by-individual or an overall project basis. The graphical format provides a visible way to identify places in the preliminary schedule where project staffing and the logical sequencing of the work are in conflict, as shown in the example in Figure 5-2. In this case, the effort profile for a project team member who is expected to contribute to all these activities demonstrates that, when the activities overlap, he or she would need to work a double shift.

The benefits of entering resource data into a computer scheduling tool include:

❐ Identifying resource risks

❐ Improving the precision of the schedule

❐ Building compelling evidence for negotiating budgets and schedules

❐ Focusing more attention on project estimates

These benefits require some investment on your part. Histogram analysis adds complexity to the planning process, and it increases the effort for both planning and tracking. In your resource analysis, allocate sufficient effort for this into your overall project workload.

Histograms for the overall project display the effort profile of the entire project as forecast by the project plan. Different sorts of projects have different sorts of profiles, such as front-loaded, back-loaded, bimodal, flat, and the Rayleigh curve, shown in Figure 5-3.

Aggregated effort curves for projects may take any possible

Figure 5-2. Histogram analysis for an individual.

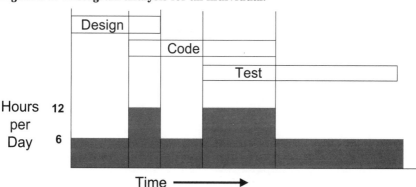

shape. The resource profile in Figure 5-3 is fairly common for projects of many types, but measurement and planning may reveal that the effort profiles for projects common to your environment are quite different. One useful technique for a quick plan review is to compare the effort profile from your plan with a profile created using historical project data. Most significant deviations between the two profiles are probably a result of omissions or errors in your plan.

Whatever the shape of the work profile, there is generally a lag between the formal start of a project and the beginning of substantial effort, as in Figure 5-3. As a new project begins, effort consumed builds gradually, not necessarily due to lack of staff (although the PERIL database shows that this is a factor), but because at the start of most projects no one knows exactly what to do. Until planning has begun and the identification and delegation of work is under way, there are few defined activities to work on. This generates two opportunities that relate directly to resource risk: people development and infrastructure upgrades.

Even in the opening days of a new project, a few requirements for training will likely emerge. Even a quick assessment of the project scope will probably reveal new skills and knowledge gaps in the organization, and the early days of a project are an excellent time to address these needs. Waiting until the moment in the project when these new capabilities are required increases two risks: that the time or money required for training may be unavailable and that the "ramp time" to competence may exceed what you planned. Investment in people development early in a project can also be a powerful motivator and team builder—both of which can reduce risk for any project.

The second opportunity in the early part of a project starts with a quick assessment of your project infrastructure: the equip-

Figure 5-3. Typical effort loading on projects.

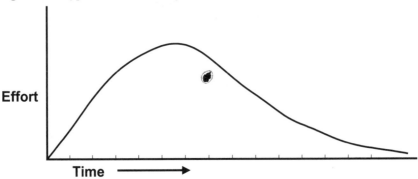

ment, software, and any other project assets. If required computers, software applications, test gear, instruments, communications and networking equipment, or other hardware available are not up to date, replacement or upgrade might greatly improve the efficiency and speed of your project. The effort and money to do this tends to be easiest to obtain during the planning and start-up of a new project. Getting familiar with new hardware and software is less disruptive early on than it will be in midproject, and the effort needed to install and check the new systems is not as likely to delay high-priority project activities (since many of these are not yet identified).

One of the best reasons to jump on these opportunities at the outset is that project budgets tend to be set early, and, unless these needs are identified right away and integrated into the project finances, it may prove impossible to get approval for them at all. Of course, getting such requests approved early on is not a sure thing, but the odds are better, and it never hurts to ask. Even if you fail to get approval, your written proposal coupled with any project problems related to older equipment will make similar requests on subsequent projects more successful.

The most significant project exposures that an overall project resource histogram, spreadsheet table, or other assessment will reveal are the portions of the project timeline where the human resources required by the preliminary plan exceed what is expected to be available. Unless these issues are resolved through additional staff acquisition or procurement of outside services (discussed later in this chapter), replanning (discussed in Chapter 6), or by some other means, the risk to the project is high. Project risks due to insufficient staffing are most significant near the scheduled project completion, as the likelihood of deadline slippage grows and the options for response dwindle.

Another source of project resource risk is the assumption that resources will scale with other project factors. Increases in project duration, the number and complexity of the deliverables, and the number of contributors (or locations) involved will all increase required project effort more than a simple linear extrapolation would predict. Due to communication, overhead, and many other factors, the effort required by a "larger" project expands geometrically.

An example of this is seen in two otherwise similar projects undertaken recently in Europe. These were staffed differently as an experiment. One project team was at a single site. The other project team was distributed among half a dozen locations, though all still within the same time zone. The assessment of effort following project completion was striking; the distributed team spent about 60 percent more effort getting its work completed, compared with the co-located team. Differences in project factors as low as 20 percent (for example, in team size) start to reveal the nonlinear expansion of required effort. As project factors that complicate the work grow, reflect this appropriately in your effort estimates. Whenever resource analysis indicates requirements that exceed what typical, successful projects have used in the past, record it as a project risk.

Staff Acquisition

Histograms and other project analysis are necessary, but rarely sufficient, to determine whether the project has the staffing and skills required to do the work. Particularly for the riskiest project activities, revalidate both the skills needed and your effort estimates.

Skill Requirements

Through project scope definition and preliminary planning, you can identify specific skills and other needs required by your project. Your initial project staffing will often include adequate coverage for some or even most of these, but on many projects there are substantial gaps. These gaps are project resource risks until they are resolved.

Specific skills that are not available on the project team may be acquired by negotiating for additional staff or through training or mentoring. In some cases, needed skills may be added though outsourcing. These options are most possible when the need is made known early and supported with credible planning data. You may also be able to replan the parts of the project that require unavailable skills to use methods that require only the skills that you already have on the project team.

The goal of staff acquisition is to align the work required for each project activity with specific individuals who can and will get it done. The names of all these people are listed on a roster, or team directory, along with each person's assigned role, contact information, and other relevant data.

Two significant resource risks related to staff acquisition are unknown staff members and contributors with unique skills. Having your project roster remain incomplete late in the planning process is risky. Every identified staffing need that is still blank, identified only with a function, or marked "to-be-hired" is a risk. Even if these people are later named, their productivity may not be consistent with the estimates and assumptions in your project plan. It is also possible that the names will *still* be missing even after work is scheduled to begin—and some assignments may never be made. The quality of a plan with unassigned staffing is suspect, and every project staffing requirement that lacks a credible commitment by an actual person is a project risk.

Unique skills pose a problem as well. When project work can be assigned to one of several competent contributors, there is a good chance that it will be done adequately and on schedule. When only a single person knows how to do the work, the project faces risk. There are many reasons why a necessary person may not be available to the project when needed, including illness, resignation, injury, or reassignment to other, higher-priority work. There are no alternatives for the project when this happens; work on a key part of the project will halt. Whenever a key part of your project depends on access to a single specific individual, note it as a risk.

REVISITING ESTIMATES

As noted in Chapter 4, resource planning and activity estimating are interrelated. As the staffing plan for the project comes together, additional resource risks become apparent through review of the assumptions you used for estimating. Project resource risks are usually most severe for activities that are most likely to impact the project schedule—activities that are on the critical path, or have little float, or have worst-case estimates that could put them on the critical path. Reviewing the effort estimates for these and other project activities reveals resource risks related to staff ability, staff availability, and the work environment.

Staff Ability

Individual productivity varies a great deal, so it matters who will be involved with each project activity. Even for very simple tasks, there can be very great differences in performance. Cooks often encounter the requirement for "one onion, chopped." The amount of time this task takes depends greatly on the person undertaking it. For a home cook, it might take two or three minutes (assuming that the majority of the chopping is restricted to the onion). A trained professional chef, as watchers of television cooking shows know, dispatches this task in seconds. On the other extreme one finds the perfectionist, who could make an evening out of ensuring that each fragment of onion is identical in size and shape.

Productivity measurements for "knowledge" work of most kinds show a similar wide spectrum. From research on productivity, people who are among the best at what they do typically work two to three times as fast as the average, and they are more than *ten times* as productive as the slowest. In addition to being faster, the best performers also make fewer errors and do much less rework.

If a programming activity given to a "world-class" software engineer takes one day, the same activity given to an "average" coder will take three days. If the project is unlucky enough to hand the work to one of the least productive programmers, it could take two weeks. Knowing the skills and historical performance of project team members is critical to accurate estimates of effort and duration.

Differences due to variations in productivity are a frequent source of inaccurate project estimates. Project leaders often plan the project using data from their own experience and then delegate the work to others who may not be as skilled or as fast as they are. It is not uncommon on technical projects to select the most talented team member from the last project to take over and lead the next project. Selecting new project leaders this way leads to several potential problems, starting with inappropriately aggressive activity estimates. This tactic also tends to deprive the project of the best technical talent available (or, even worse, to leave the project effectively leaderless because the project leader continues doing technical work). Yet another issue results from taking away responsibilities that a person likes and is good at in exchange for a role that he or she is ill prepared for and may not like. The "accidental" project manager creates a wide range of project resource and other risks.

When there are historical metrics that draw on a large population, you can accurately predict how fast an *average* person will be able to accomplish similar work. If your project contributors are significantly more (or less) productive than the average, your effort and duration estimates will be accurate only if they are adjusted accordingly. When you have no specifics on who will be involved in the work, accurate estimates are unlikely and risks are significant.

Staff Availability

No one can ever actually work on project activities "full time." Every project contributor has commitments even within the project that are above and beyond the scheduled project work, such as communications. Further, some team members are usually responsible for significant work outside the project. Studying computer and medical electronics firms, Wheelwright and Clark (in *Revolutionizing Product Development*) reported the effect of assigning work on parallel projects to engineers. For engineers assigned to a single project, roughly 70 percent of the time spent went into project activities. This is equivalent to the often-quoted "five or six" hours of project work per day and reflects the reality that even someone working on only one project still has other responsibilities, such as meetings, telephone calls, e-mail, and voice mail.

The study reported that, with the addition of a second project, the time spent doing project work rose a little bit, to about 80 percent. The reason for the rise was not included, but it likely relates to queuing effects—an engineer on a single project sometimes will complete an activity before the next assignment is available, but with two projects there is nearly always more work pending. With three and more projects, useful time plummets precipitously. An engineer with three projects uses 60 percent of his or her time on project work, and with four or five the rates fall to 45 percent and 30 percent, respectively.

An engineer working a nominal fifty-hour week on five projects will be available only *fifteen* hours each week to do project work. The rest of the time will be spent attending five weekly project meetings, communicating with the leaders and others on all five projects, reading five project status reports, and in related activities.

Splitting the fifteen available hours among the five projects gives an average of three hours per project per week (assuming the projects all have equal priority, which they probably do not). At this rate, it will take many weeks to accomplish much. The "too many projects" problem takes a heavy toll on project progress, and estimates of duration or effort that fail to account for the impact of competing priorities are often absurdly optimistic.

PROJECT ENVIRONMENT

The project environment is yet another factor that has an impact on the quality of project estimates. Noise, interruptions, the workspace, and other factors may erode productivity significantly.

When people can work undistracted, a lot gets done. Realistically, frequent disturbances are commonplace for technical projects, particularly those done in an "open office" environment. The background noise level, nearby conversations, colleagues who drop by to chat, loudspeaker announcements, and other interruptions may be much more disruptive than assumed in project estimates. People cannot shift from one activity to a different one instantaneously. Studies of knowledge workers indicate that it takes twenty minutes, typically, for the human brain to come back to full concentration following an interruption as short as a few seconds. A programmer who gets three telephone calls, even wrong numbers, or "quick questions" from a peer each hour cannot accomplish much. Validate your productivity assumptions periodically with measurements, especially for work that must be done in chaotic conditions. Reflect the effects of "context shifting" in your estimates, and note the risks associated with work subject to frequent interruptions.

Other aspects of the working environment that affect productivity include the size of the workspace, access to services such as printing and copying, the ergonomics and comfort of office furniture, and access to quiet places to get away from telephones for project discussions. While managing risks associated with these factors may be beyond your control as a project leader, you can at least assess the impact, note the risks, and make necessary adjustments to your estimates. The trend in recent years has been toward modular office furniture, which is more compact than traditional desks, credenzas, file cabinets, and bookcases. The primary motivation behind this is to get more people into less space, minimizing office costs. It does not necessarily make workers more productive. While a more compact office can reduce reaching and walking around, which can improve efficiency, the amount of workspace available to spread out books, documents, plans, drawings, and other materials can be significantly less than optimal. The reduction in filing space using modular setups also often results in large piles of paper (which technical people are always reluctant to discard and has to go *somewhere*), which further cuts down on working space. Without adequate flat, clear space, project activities are more frustrating and require more time and effort. Modular furniture also results in closer neighbors, so the noise and interruptions also increase. All of these factors affect productivity and impact the accuracy of your project estimates.

Adequate lighting and access to adequate tools and other resources are also critical in establishing a realistic basis for aggressive duration estimates. During the power shortage in California throughout much of 2001, many companies cut out some (and, in selected cases, all) of the office lighting to save power and money. Working in a dark office is not conducive to productivity. Replacing printers and copiers with cheaper equipment may seem to save money, but if they are usually out of service and people have to hunt down equipment that works, the change will impede project progress significantly.

Whenever these or other environmental factors seem likely to cause project problems, note them as risks, adjust project plans to reflect the environment, and, whenever it is practical, propose improvements and work toward resolution of problems to minimize the impact of future projects.

Distance is another factor that can invalidate estimating assumptions. New teams go through the "phases" of team development—forming, storming, norming, and performing. Many project teams never get out of the "storming" phase, especially if they are a distributed or "virtual" team where none of the people have ever met each other. People tend to like and trust other people that they have met face-to-face, and they generally mistrust strangers. On a complex project, team members need to trust and depend on one another, and, until there is a basis for this relationship, they don't. Every question someone asks is a challenge. Every project issue is presumed to be "those people over there, out to get us again," instead of a legitimate technical problem. When teamwork is weak or lacking, a great deal of time may be lost to miscommunication, confusion, fighting, and disagreement. Without adequate mutual trust, even conservative project estimates may prove to be too optimistic.

A final source of resource risk relates to project team members who are responsible for other work outside your project. The quality of the estimates and plans for work delegated to "multiproject" resources depends on how these individuals perceive the priorities of their activities. To assess this, ask each part-time contributor about both the *importance* and the *urgency* of the work he or she is responsible for on your project. Whenever contributors see the priority of your project's work as low, it is a risk. You may be able to minimize the risks through effective communication, involving and motivating the people, escalating the discussion to their management, or otherwise raising the priority of your project work. In some cases, you may need to consider alternative resources or other methods to do the project work.

Once the staffing for your project is set, consider all these factors, particularly the talent, the proportion of time dedicated to your project, and the effect of the environment on the estimates in your project plan, and make adjustments as necessary. Also, as you consider these factors, identify the resource risks that emerge, and add them to the project risk list.

Procurement Planning and Source Selection

Outsourcing risk is not only a significant source of resource risk in the PERIL database; it also caused an average project slip of nearly seven weeks, well above the database average. Better management of outsourcing and procurement can uncover many of these problems in advance.

Not all project staffing needs can be met with internal people. More and more work on technical projects is done using outside services. It is increasingly difficult (not to mention expensive) to maintain competence in all the fields of expertise that might be required, especially for skills needed only infrequently. A growing need for specialization underlies the trend toward increased dependence on project contributors outside the organization. Other reasons for this trend are attempts to lower costs and a desire in many organizations to reduce the amount of permanent staff. In the *PMBOK® Guide*, Project Procurement Management has six components:

❐ Procurement planning

❐ Solicitation planning

❐ Solicitation

❐ Source selection

❐ Contract administration

❐ Contract closeout

The first four of these provide significant opportunities for risk identification.

PROCUREMENT PLANNING

Outsourcing project work is most successful when the appropriate details and specifics are thoroughly incorporated into all the legal and other documentation used. Outsourced work must be specified in detail both in the initial request and in the contract so that both parties have a clear definition for the work required and how it will be evaluated. The planning required to do this effectively is difficult, and it takes more effort and specificity than might otherwise be applied to project planning.

Specific risks permeate all aspects of the procurement process, starting even before any work directly related to outsourcing formally starts. The process generally begins with identification of any requirements that the project expects to have difficulty meeting with the existing staff. Procurement planning involves investigation of possible options and requires a "make-or-buy" analysis to determine whether there are any reasons that using outside services may be undesirable or inappropriate. From the perspective of project risk, delegating work to dedicated staff whenever possible is almost always preferable. Communication, visibility, continuity, motivation, and project control are all easier and better for nonoutsourced work. Other reasons to avoid outsourcing may include higher costs, potential loss of confidential information, an ongoing significant need to maintain core skills (on future projects or for required support), and lack of confidence in the available service providers. Some outsourcing decisions are made because all the current staff is busy and there is no one available to do needed project work. These decisions seem to be based on the erroneous assumption that project outsourcing can be done successfully with no effort. Ignoring the substantial and very real effort required to find, evaluate, negotiate and contract with, routinely communicate with, monitor, and pay a supplier is quite a serious risk.

While it may be desirable to avoid outsourcing, project realities may require it. Whenever the "make versus buy" decision comes out "buy," there are significant risks to manage.

SOLICITATION PLANNING

The next step in the outsourcing process is to develop a Request for Proposal (RFP). There are other names for this document, such as Request for Bid, Invitation to Bid, and Request for Quotation; they all serve a similar purpose. In organizations that outsource project work on a regular basis, there are usually standard forms and procedures to be used for this, so the steps in assembling, distributing, and later analyzing the RFP responses are generally not up to the project team. This is fortunate, because using well-established processes, preprinted forms, and professionals in your organization who do this work regularly are all essential to minimizing risk. If you lack templates and processes for this, consult colleagues who are experienced with outsourcing, and borrow theirs, customizing as necessary. Outsourcing is one aspect of project management where figuring things out as you proceed will waste a lot of time and money and result in very significant project risk.

Risk management also requires that at least one member of the project team be involved with planning and contracting for outside services so that the interests of the project are represented throughout the procurement process.

Ensure that each RFP includes a very clear, unambiguous definition of the scope of project work, with the terms and conditions for evaluation and payment. While it is always risky for any project work to remain poorly defined, outsourced work deserves particular attention. Inadequate definition of outsourced work leads to all the usual project problems, but it may also lead to even higher schedule and resource risk. Problems with outsourced deliverables often surface late in the project with no advance warning (generally, following a long series of "we are doing just fine" status reports) and frequently delay the project deadline, as is evident in the PERIL database. There may also be significant increased cost due to required changes and late-project expedited work. Minimize outsourcing risks through scrupulous definition of all deliverables involved, along with all measurements and performance criteria to be used for their evaluation.

As part of solicitation planning, establish the criteria that you will use to evaluate the responses. Determine what is most important to your project and ensure that these aspects are clearly spelled out in the RFP, with guidance for the responders on how to supply the information that you require. Because the specific work on technical projects tends to evolve and change quickly, there is a good chance that well-established criteria for selecting suppliers will, sooner or later, be out of date. In light of your emerging planning data for the project, review the proposed criteria to validate that they are still appropriate. If the list of criteria used in the past seems in need of updating, do it *before* sending out the RFP. Establish priorities and relative weights for each evaluation criterion, as well as how you will assess the responses you receive. Communicating your priorities and expectations clearly in the RFP will help responders to self-qualify (or disqualify themselves) and will better provide the data you need to make a sound outsourcing decision.

Relevant past experience is also important to avoiding outsourcing risk. In the RFP, request specifics from responders on similar prior efforts that were successful, and ask for contact information so that you can follow up and verify. Even for work that is novel, ask for reference information from potential suppliers that will at least allow you to investigate past working relationships. While it may be difficult to get useful reference information, it never hurts to request it.

Before finalizing the RFP, determine when any bidder conferences or other meetings will be scheduled and to whom the responders should address any questions or other feedback. Also, determine and clearly specify when responses must be submitted, and establish a deadline for making your decision.

SOLICITATION

Once you have established the specifics of the work to be outsourced, as well as the processes and documents you plan to use, the next step is to find potential suppliers and encourage them to respond. One of the biggest risks in this step is failure to contact enough suppliers. For some project work, networking and informal communications may be sufficient, but sending the RFP to lists of known suppliers, putting information on public Web sites, and even advertising may be useful in letting potential responders know of your needs. If too few responses are generated, the quality and cost of the choices available may not serve the project well.

Communication throughout the process is also essential. Anything that one potential supplier finds unclear in the RFP needs to be addressed, and any clarifications should be provided to all the others who have the RFP. The questions asked by responders are often good early indicators of the working relationship that will develop. Bidders who ask lots of trivial questions or who request information already provided in the RFP will probably not be very thorough and may be a great deal of trouble to work with. Less risky partners are suppliers who provide insightful feedback, ask about things that probably should have been in your RFP but were left out, or otherwise demonstrate in discussions that they really know what they are doing.

SOURCE SELECTION

Bringing the solicitation to closure is also a substantial source of risk. There are potential risks in decision making, negotiation, and the contracting process.

Decision Making

Decision-making risks include not doing adequate analysis to assess each potential supplier and making a selection based on something other than the needs of the project.

Inadequate analysis can be a significant source of risk. It is fairly common for the decisions on outsourcing to coincide with many other project activities, and writing and getting responses to an RFP often takes more time than expected. As a result, you may be left with very little time to evaluate the proposals on their technical merit. Judging proposals by weight, appearance, or some other superficial criteria may save time but is not likely to result in the best selection. Evaluating and comparing multiple complex proposals thoroughly takes time and effort. Before you make a decision, spend the time necessary to ensure a thorough evaluation. It's like the old saying, "Act in haste; repent at leisure," except that, in your case, you will be repenting when you are *very* busy.

Another potential risk in the selection process is pressure from outside your project to make a choice for reasons unrelated to your project. Influences from other parts of the organization may come to bear during the decision process—to favor friends, to avoid some suppliers, to align with "strategic" partners of some other internal group, or to use a global (or a local) supplier. Since the decision will normally be signed and approved by someone higher in the organization, sometimes the project team may not even be aware of these factors until very late in the process. Documenting the process and validating your criteria for supplier selection with your management can reduce this problem, but use of outside suppliers not selected by the project team represents significant, and sometimes disastrous, project risk.

Overall, you must diligently stay on top of the process to ensure that the selections made for each RFP are as consistent with your project requirements as possible.

Negotiation

After you select a supplier, the next step in the procurement process is to finalize the details of the work and finances. Once a selection is made, the balance of power begins to shift from the purchaser to the supplier, which raises additional risks. When the work begins, the project becomes dependent on the supplier for crucial, time-sensitive project deliverables. The supplier is dependent on the project primarily for money, which in the short run is neither crucial nor urgent. To a lesser extent, suppliers are also dependent on future recommendations from you (which can be important for ongoing risk management), but, from the supplier's perspective, the relationship is based mainly on cash.

Effective and thorough negotiation is the last opportunity available to the project to identify (and manage) risks without high potential costs. All relevant details of the work and deliverables need to be discussed and clearly understood so that the ultimate contract will unambiguously contain a scope of work that both parties see the same way. Details concerning tests, inspections, prototypes, and other interim deliverables must also be clarified. Specifics concerning partial and final payments, as well as the process and cost for any required changes or modifications, are also essential aspects of the negotiation process. Failure to conduct thorough, principled negotiation with a future supplier is a potential source of massive risk. Shortening a negotiation process to save time is never a good idea.

Since the primary consideration on the supplier side is financial, the best tactic for risk management in negotiation is to strongly align payments with achievement of specific results. Payment for time, effort, or other less tangible criteria may allow suppliers to bill the project even when they fail to produce what your project requires. Contracts based on "time and materials" can also make it difficult to determine whether the people involved are being treated as outside contractors or as employees of your organization, which creates additional risk. When negotiating the work and payment terms, the least risky option for you as the purchaser is to establish a "payment for result" contract.

Outsourcing risk can also be lowered by negotiating contract terms that align with specific project goals. While a contract must include consequences for supplier nonperformance, such as nonpayment, legal action, or other remedies, these terms do little to ensure project success. If the supplier fails to perform, your project will still be in trouble. Lack of a key deliverable will lead to project failure, so it is also useful to negotiate terms that more directly support your project objectives. If there is value in getting work done early, incentive payments are worth considering. If there are specific additional costs associated with late delivery, establish penalties that reduce payments proportionate to the delay. For some projects, more complex financial arrangements than the simple "fee for result," such as arrangements in which percentages of favorable variances in time or cost are shared with the supplier and portions of unfavorable ones may be deducted from their fees, may be appropriate. Negotiating terms that more directly support the project objectives and involve suppliers more deeply in the project can significantly reduce outsourcing risks.

If the negotiation process, despite your best efforts, results in terms that represent potential project problems, note these as risks. In extreme cases, you may need to reconsider your selection decision, or even the decision to outsource the project work at all.

Contracting

Once the terms and conditions for the work have been agreed to by both parties, they must be documented in a contract, signed, and put into force. One effective tool for minimizing risk is to use a well-established, preprinted contract format to document the relationship. This should include all of the information that a complete, prudent contract must contain so that the chances of leaving out something critical, such as protection of confidential information or proprietary intellectual property, will be reduced. For this reason, you can reduce project risk by using a standard contract form with no significant modifications or deletions. In addition, using standard formats will reduce the time and effort needed for contract approval. In large companies, contracts that vary from the standard may take an additional month (or even more) for review, approval, and processing. Adding data to a contract is also generally a poor idea, with one big exception. Every contract needs to include a very clear, unambiguous definition of the scope of work that specifies measurable deliverables and payment terms. A good contract also provides an explicit description of the process to be used if any changes are necessary.

One other source of risk in contracting is also fairly common for technical projects. The statement of work must be clear not only in defining the results expected but also in specifying who will be responsible. It turns out that this is quite a challenge for engineers and other analytical people. Most engineering and other technical writing is filled with passive-voice sentences such as: "It is important that the device be tested using an input voltage varying between 105 and 250 volts AC, down to a temperature of minus 40 degrees Celsius." In a contract, there is no place for the passive voice. If the responsible party is not clearly specified, the sentence has no legal meaning. It fails to make clear who will do the testing and what, if any, consequences there may be should the testing fail. To minimize risks in contracts, write requirements in the active voice, spelling out all responsibilities in clear terms and *by name*.

Finally, when setting up a contract, minimize the resource risk by establishing a "not to exceed" limitation to avoid runaway costs. Set this limit somewhat higher than the expected cost to provide some reserve for changes and unforeseen problems, but not a great deal higher. Many technical projects provide a reserve of about 10 percent to handle small adjustments. If problems or changes arise that require more than this, they will trigger review of the project, which is prudent risk management.

OUTSOURCING RISKS

There are a variety of other risks that arise from outsourcing. One of the largest is cost, even if the work seems to be thoroughly defined. Unforeseen aspects of the work, which are never possible to eliminate completely, may require expensive fees for change.

Continuity and turnover of contract staff is a risk. While people who work for another company may be loyal to your project and stay with it through the end, the probabilities are lower than for the permanent staff on your project. Particularly with longer projects, turnover and retraining can represent major risks.

Outsourcing may increase the likelihood of turnover and demotivation of your permanent staff. If it becomes standard procedure to outsource all the new, "bleeding edge" project work, your permanent staff gets stuck doing the same old things, project after project, never learning anything new. It becomes harder to motivate and hold on to people who have no opportunity for development.

There may also be hidden effort for the project due to outsourcing that is not visible in the plan. Someone must maintain the relationship, communicate regularly, deal with payments and other paperwork, and carry the other overhead of outsourcing. While this may all run smoothly, if there are any problems it can become a major time sink. The time and effort this overhead requires is routinely overlooked or underestimated.

Finally, the nature of work at a distance requires significant additional effort. Getting useful status information is a lot of work. You will not get responses to initial requests every time, and verifying what is reported may be difficult. You can expect to provide much more information than you receive, and interpreting what you do get can be difficult. Even if the information is timely, it may not be completely accurate, and you may get little or no advance warning of project problems. Working to establish and maintain a solid working relationship with outsourcing partners can be a major undertaking, but it is prudent risk management.

Cost Estimating

Project cost estimates are generally dominated by staffing and outsourcing costs but also include expenses for equipment, services, travel, communications, and other project needs.

STAFFING AND OUTSOURCING COSTS

Staffing costs can be calculated using the activity effort estimates or on the basis of your histograms, spreadsheets, or other resource planning information. Using standard hourly rates for the project staff and your effort estimates, you can convert effort into project costs. For longer projects, you may also need to consider factors such as salary changes and the effect of inflation.

Estimate any outsourcing costs using the contracts negotiated for the services, working with figures about halfway between the minimum you can expect and the "not to exceed" amounts.

EQUIPMENT AND SOFTWARE COSTS

The best time to request new equipment or upgrade older hardware, systems, and applications for a project is at the outset. You should assess the project's needs and research the options that are available. Inspect all equipment and software applications already in place to determine any opportunities for replacement or upgrade. Document the project's needs, and assemble a proposal including all potential purchases. As discussed earlier in the chapter, proposing the purchase and installation of new equipment at the start of the project has two benefits: getting approval from management when it is most likely, and allowing for installation when there is little other project work to conflict with it. Propose purchase of the best equipment available so that, if purchase is approved, you will be able to work as fast and as efficiently as possible. If you propose the best options and only some of the budget is approved, you still may be able to find alternative hardware or systems that will enable you to complete your project. Estimate the overall project equipment expense by summing the cost of any approved proposals with other expected hardware and software costs.

TRAVEL

Midproject travel requests are often refused; the best time to get travel money for your project is at the beginning. As you plan the project work, determine when travel will be necessary, and decide who will be involved. Travel planned and approved in advance is easier to arrange, less costly, and less disruptive for the project and the team members than last-minute, emergency trips. Request and justify face-to-face meetings with distant team members, getting team members from each site together at the project start and, for longer projects, at least every six months thereafter. Also, budget for appropriate travel to interact with users, customers, and other stakeholders.

There are no guarantees that travel requested at the beginning of the project will be approved or that it might not be cut back later, but if you do not estimate and request travel funds early, the chances get a lot worse.

OTHER COSTS

Communication is essential on technical projects, and, for distributed teams, it may be quite costly. Video (and even audio) conferencing technology may require up-front investments, as well as usage fees. Schedule and budget for frequent status meetings, using the most appropriate technology you can find.

Projects that include team members outside a single company may need to budget for setup and maintenance of a public-domain secure Web site outside corporate fire walls for project information that will be available to everyone. Other services such as shipping, couriers, and photocopying may also represent significant expenses for your project.

Cost Budgeting

Cost budgeting is the accumulation of all the cost estimates for the project. For most technical projects, the majority of the cost is for people, either permanent staff or workers under some kind of contract. The project cost baseline also includes estimated expenses for equipment, software and services, travel, communications, and other requirements. Whenever your preliminary project budget analysis exceeds the project cost objectives, the difference represents a significant project risk. Unless you are able either to devise a credible lower-cost plan or to negotiate a larger project budget, your project may fail due to lack of resources.

Document the Risks

Resource risks become visible throughout the planning and scheduling processes. Resource risks discussed in this chapter include:

- Activities with unknown staffing
- Understaffed activities
- Work that is outsourced
- Contract risks
- Activities requiring a unique resource
- Part-time team members
- Remote team members
- The impact of the work environment
- Budget requirements exceed the project objectives

Add each specific risk discovered to the list of scope and schedule risks, with a clear description of the risk situation. This growing risk list provides the foundation for project risk analysis and management.

Key Ideas for Identifying Resource Risks

❏ Identify all required skills you need for which you lack named, committed staffing.

❏ Determine all situations in the project plan where people or other resources are overcommitted.

❏ Find all activities with insufficient resources.

❏ Identify uncertain activity effort estimates.

❏ Note outsourcing risks.

❏ Gain funding approval early for needed training, equipment purchases, and travel.

❏ Ascertain all expected project costs.

Panama Canal: Resources (1905–1907)

Project resource risk arises primarily from people factors, as demonstrated in the PERIL database, and this was certainly true on the Panama Canal project. On the basis of the experiences of the French during the first attempt, John Stevens realized that project success required a healthy, productive, motivated workforce. For his project, money was never an issue, but retaining people to do difficult and dangerous work in the hot, humid tropics certainly was. Stevens invested heavily, through Dr. Gorgas, in insect control and other public health measures. He also built an infrastructure at Panama that supported the productive, efficient progress he required. At the time of his departure from the project, Stevens had established a well-fed, well-equipped, well-housed, well-organized workforce with an excellent plan of attack.

This boosted productivity, but George Goethals realized that success also relied on continuity and motivation. He wanted loyalty, not to him but to the project. The work was important, and Goethals used any opportunity he had to point this out. He worked hard to keep the workers engaged, and much of what he did remains good resource management practice today.

Goethals took a number of important steps to build morale. He started a weekly newspaper, the *Canal Record*. The paper gave an accurate, up-to-date picture of progress, unlike the *Canal Bulletin* that had been issued periodically during the French project. In many ways, it served as the project's status report, making note of significant accomplishments and naming those involved to build morale. The paper also provided feedback on productivity. Publishing these statistics led to healthy rivalries, as workers strove to better last week's record for various types of work so that they could see their names in print.

It was crucial, Goethals believed, to recognize and reward service. Medals were struck at the Philadelphia Mint, using metal salvaged from the abandoned French equipment. Everyone who worked on the project for at least two years was publicly recognized and presented with a medal in a formal ceremony. People wore these proudly. In a documentary made many years after the project, Robert Dill, a former canal worker interviewed at age 104, was still wearing his medal, number 6726.

Goethals also sponsored weekly open-door sessions on Sundays when anyone could come with questions. Some weeks more than one hundred people came to see him. If he could quickly answer a question or solve a problem, he did it then. If a request or suggestion was not something that would work, he explained why. If there were any open questions or issues, he committed to getting an answer, and he followed up. Goethals treated workers like humans, not brutes, and this engendered fierce loyalty.

While all this contributed to ensuring a loyal, motivated, productive workforce, the most significant morale builder came early on, from the project sponsor. In 1906, Theodore Roosevelt sailed to Panama to visit his project. Roosevelt's trip was without precedent; never before had a sitting U.S. president left the country. The results of the trip were so noteworthy that one newspaper at the time conjectured that, someday, a president "might undertake European journeys."

Roosevelt chose to travel in the rainy season, and the conditions in Panama were dreadful. This hardly slowed him down at all; he was in the swamps, walking the railroad ties, charging up the slopes, even operating one of the ninety-seven-ton Bucyrus steam shovels. He went everywhere the workers were. The reporters who came along were exhausted, but the workers were hugely excited and motivated.

On Roosevelt's return to Washington, so much was written about the magnitude and importance of the project that interest and support for the canal spread quickly throughout the United States. People believed that "with Teddy Roosevelt, anything is possible."

CHAPTER 6

MANAGING PROJECT CONSTRAINTS AND DOCUMENTING RISKS

"A good plan, violently executed right now, is
better than the perfect plan executed next week."

—GENERAL GEORGE S. PATTON

Reviewing a plan to detect problems and make improvements generally ought to be a brief exercise done toward the end of initial project planning. This chapter is not about obsessive application of every single project management practice in an endless quest for the flawless plan (sometimes called "analysis-paralysis"). The topic here is realistic, common-sense project analysis. The principal objective of reviewing the plan is to find defects and omissions, to deal with unmet constraints, and to seek an improved plan, *quickly*. You are not after a perfect plan, just the best one possible using what you currently know about your project.

This part of the planning process relates to risk management in several ways, but two aspects are particularly important. First, the process of replanning to deal with constraints nearly always *creates* project risk, as minimizing one parameter of a project often leads to more pressure on other aspects of the work, creating additional exposures, failure modes, and potential problems. These new risks result from trade-offs made by the project team, and they need to be recognized, documented, and added to the project risk list. A second type of project risk is that of not taking on the "right" project. All projects have alternatives, and examining at least some of these options is key to *opportunity* management, also discussed in this chapter.

Much of the content of this chapter falls into the "Project Time Management," "Project Risk Management," and "Project Integration Management" segments of the *PMBOK® Guide*. The key risk management concepts covered in this chapter are:

❐ Constraint analysis

❐ Scope options and opportunity management

❐ Resource options

❐ Schedule options

❐ Assessment of plan alternatives

❐ Additional project risks

Analyze Constraints

As you proceed through preliminary project definition and planning, a coherent picture of your project starts to emerge. Although your project plan is still incomplete at this point, it does begin to provide insight into whether the project objective is most likely possible or impossible. Often, it reveals the unpleasant fact that the project (at least as defined so far) *is* impossible; the result of your bottom-up plan leaves at least part of the project objective unmet. Your preliminary analysis might reveal a schedule that extends beyond the deadline, resource requirements that exceed initial budgets, or other significant issues. Your planning process reveals just how much trouble you are in.

Failure of the preliminary plan to meet the overall project objective is not the only issue that emerges at this stage of planning. Above and beyond the high-level constraints, most projects also have other constraints that you must manage. Timing requirements for intermediate documents, prototypes, and other midproject deliverables may mandate fixed-date milestones within the project plan. The profile of available resources may be interrupted at specific times by the business cycle, by holidays and vacations, or by higher-priority projects. In addition, projects undertaken in lean organizations (where keeping everyone busy all the time in the name of efficiency is a top priority) will frequently run into a queue when access to a critical, unique resource is required. Delays for contract approvals, management sign-off, and other decisions are common. Identifying and managing risks from these other constraints is also part of risk management on high-tech projects.

Your primary goal in managing project constraints is to remove, or at least minimize, the differences between the project objective and your project plan, in terms of scope, schedule, and resources. The standard triangle diagram for examining project trade-offs is one way to show these differences, as in Figure 6-1. The plan, represented by the triangle with the dashed-line edges, is quite a bit larger than the objective, shown as the solid-edged triangle.

For this project, the initial plan suggests that the deliverable is probably feasible, so this project is not *literally* impossible—its scope is within your capabilities. However, as shown, the project will require both more time and more resources (e.g., people, money) than requested in the project objective, so, on the basis of the current plan, it is infeasible because of its *constraints*. For projects where the scope is plausible, the situation in Figure 6-1 is fairly common. Bottom-up project planning begins with a work breakdown structure (WBS) that is consistent with the desired scope, but the initial schedule and resource plans fall wherever the WBS leads them—often at significant variance with the project objective.

For some projects, the objective is firm, based on hard limits that cannot be modified. For other projects, the objective may be based on softer constraints, goals that are desirable but not absolutely necessary. Each project is unique, so determining how to approach trade-off analysis for your project requires you to understand what the constraints and priorities are and how they were determined. In the simplest form, project priorities boil down to

Figure 6-1. Objective versus plan.

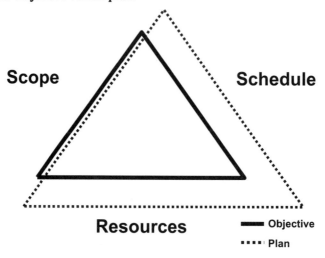

the old saying, "Good, fast, cheap: pick two." Every project requires at least one degree of freedom; it is never realistic to nail down all aspects of a project, especially prior to completing a thorough analysis of the required work. Any of the three parameters *could* be most flexible, but one of them *must* be. While you can get a deliverable out of a project quickly and cheaply, it is unlikely to be very good. This lesson was relearned quite often in the late 1990s by projects executed in Internet time, as well as by NASA on several failed Mars missions. Similarly, excellent results are often possible in very short time frames, but the cost of this compression is high and may not be justified by the result ("crashing" project activities in the project schedule is covered later in this chapter). You may even be able to deliver good results at very low cost in projects where time is not at issue (though this scenario could result in the "analysis-paralysis" mentioned earlier).

A slightly more sophisticated analysis rests on prioritizing the triple constraint, by rank-ordering scope, schedule, and resources to show which of the three is most important to your project. A simple three-by-three grid is often used to show this, as in Figure 6-2.

The project priorities shown here are common for high-tech projects, as timing dominates more and more of the work. In contract work, deadlines with financial penalties are often looming. In product development, pressure from competitors, trade show schedules, and other real constraints on timing are often at issue. Even in application development, timing often dominates because of the need to synchronize with fiscal accounting periods, the release (or obsolescence) of software or hardware, and other time-critical requirements. Schedule in all these cases is the dominant priority, and failure to meet the project deadline will have significant, possibly dire consequences. Schedule is the parameter such projects *constrain*.

In Figure 6-2, the second priority is resources. This is also

Figure 6-2. Project priority matrix.

	Schedule	Scope	Resources
Constrain Least Flexible	●		
Optimize Somewhat Flexible			●
Accept Most Flexible		●	

common, as the desire to minimize resources and execute as efficiently as possible is a key goal for many projects. In fact, many projects face significant limits on competent, available staff. In the time frame of many technical projects, the number of available people who are familiar with new or evolving technologies is fixed and can increase gradually over time only through training, mentoring, and other time-honored methods for hauling people up the learning curve. Projects such as this must do the best they can to *optimize* their resources.

The largest degree of freedom for the project in Figure 6-2 is for scope, indicating that there may be aspects or specifications set in the objective that, while desirable, may not be absolutely required. The project will *accept* small changes to the deliverable, particularly if not making the changes would necessitate using more time, more resources, or both.

This prioritization is one of six possibilities, and examples for each of the other five are easily imagined. This particular example is sometimes referred to as the "Sunday newspaper" model, and projects with these priorities may be approached much the same way a newspaper editor manages the weekly project of publishing the Sunday edition. The top priority is time; the paper must be available on Sunday, the only day of the week for most people where such a large quantity of newsprint makes any sense. The next priority is resources; the permanent staff available to put out the paper varies little over short periods of time, and adding extra temporary staff involves high costs and may be unsatisfactory in any case. The highest degree of freedom is with scope, in this case content. If some planned article or feature is not ready when the paper is "put to bed" late on Saturday, as required by the printing and distribution processes, the choices are clear. Holding the paper or pouring on more resources to finish the work cannot be done. In some cases, an unfinished story is simply thrown away. In others, work continues so that it can be used when complete in a future edition, on Monday, or perhaps the following Sunday.

Increasingly, high-tech projects are adopting similar methods. Features are dropped from products being developed. Additional features and capabilities are phased into planned (and frequently adjusted) releases for system software products and for custom application solutions. Even major platform development programs are broken down into a sequence of smaller, evolutionary stages. This philosophy underpins many of the current "agile" software project methodologies, such as extreme programming (XP). Adjustments and adaptations in XP are made frequently, treating each development cycle as a small project with fixed timing and staffing.

While the stated highest priority for high-technology projects is generally schedule, resources are often equally, if not more, constrained. Lack of qualified staff may actually represent a more significant constraint for the project than the deadline. In any case, the point of setting priorities is to understand what matters to the project, and why.

In the example from Figure 6-1, the initial plan failed to meet the deadline and also was not within the budget. Doing some "what if?" analysis, you may discover a way to use a top-notch group of consultants (with a credible track record) to perform more work in parallel, shortening the overall project. This approach is not inexpensive; it makes the budget problem even bigger and results in the shift shown in Figure 6-3. In this figure, the schedule has been compressed, bringing it in line with the objective, but the resources required for the project, which already exceeded the objective, are *even farther* out of line with the project expectations.

For projects where resources are the lowest priority, this tactic may be a good alternative. For projects with priorities like those of the Sunday newspaper, however, it is not likely to be the best plan. It may be better to reevaluate the specifications and to propose a plan that achieves its deadline within budget but falls slightly short on scope. Some projects may find requested requirements that are not actually needed. Other projects may propose delivering the most valuable functionality on time and delivering the rest in a follow-on project somewhat later. The analysis for such a scope reduction might result in a shift similar to Figure 6-4.

In this case, changes proposed to the initial plan affect all

Figure 6-3. Plan trade-offs.

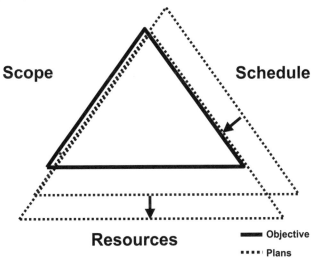

Figure 6-4. Seeking the "best" plan.

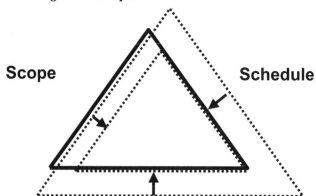

three of the project parameters, with the most significant difference between the objective and the plan being a small reduction in
the feature set for the deliverable.

The overall objective of the plan review and "what if?" analysis is to discover the options available as alternatives to the initial
plan and to see whether it might be desirable, or even necessary,
to revisit the project objective and change the project definition.
This triangle model can be thought of as a representation of projects in a two-dimensional state space, and the exploration of plan
alternatives will reveal where in this space you can find realistic,
feasible projects. For particularly ill-conceived projects, the analysis may fail to turn up any options close to the original objective.
For a project such as this, you need to negotiate a major change to
the objective, abandon the project, or at least think about updating
your resume.

In most cases, though, reasonable alternatives for your
project are not difficult to find. Start your analysis of the project
plan with the parameter that has the lowest priority, and explore
possible changes related to that aspect of the project. These modifications are generally the easiest to negotiate, so it makes sense to
focus first on that side of the triangle. For most projects, you will
also want to examine alternatives for the other two parameters.
The next three sections describe options for scope, then resources,
and finally schedule (following the prioritization in Figure 6-2).

Scope Options and Opportunity Management

Proposed changes to the project deliverable may be easily
accepted, absolutely nonnegotiable, or anything in between. This

depends on the project, the sponsors and users, and the type and magnitude of the change. Whatever the circumstances, a conscientious project team will spend at least a little time examining the effect on the project of adjusting the project deliverable, by both adding to the functionality and reducing it. This "what if" exercise helps your team understand the work better and provides you with valuable information for decision making.

Opportunity Management

When the preliminary plan falls short of the project objective, it may seem unnecessary to explore the effect of *increasing* the scope of the project. The reasons for examining more aggressive project options stem from *opportunity* management, which is closely related to, and supports, risk management. Where risk management seeks to understand what might go badly in a project, opportunity management looks for what might go better. In particular, opportunity management asks what similar, but superior, projects might be possible. Halfway through the work, realizing that you could have achieved a more valuable result is not very useful, because it is too late at that point on most projects to do anything about it.

Deliverables for high-tech projects are set using two kinds of input: user/market demand and technological possibilities. The source for most kinds of project work is the first. The sponsors, economic buyers, managers, and others who get projects started are generally doing so to meet a need, solve a problem, or respond to some specific request. While this may be sufficient for some kinds of projects, the requested deliverables in high-tech projects may fall well short of what is possible. Technology moves fairly quickly, so the demand for project deliverables may represent continued use of an older technology even after emerging new ideas and approaches are available. If you requested specifications for a project deliverable from people sitting on a river bank washing their clothes with two large stones, their answer would probably involve developing lighter-weight rocks. The concept of a washing machine may not occur to them, as the technology is not part of their experience. Similarly, the project team may be able to see possibilities based on technology unknown to the users that would solve the problem or meet the need much more effectively than the original request. Opportunity management is about merging a deep understanding of user needs with the technical capabilities available to create the best deliverable—not necessarily the one initially envisioned.

Opportunity management on projects includes two types of potential changes: to scope or to process. Scope opportunities involve adjustment to the features of the deliverable that are visible to anyone (a washing machine, for example, instead of two extremely light rocks). Process opportunities are not as visible, and they may have no impact on the feature set of the deliverable at all. Scope changes affect everyone, where process opportunities affect primarily the project team.

Scope opportunity management often requires a counterproposal to the original objective and may involve negotiation. Some project leaders and teams on high-tech projects go to great effort to avoid this sort of confrontation, viewing it as unpleasant and usually unproductive. This is unfortunate, because this process represents one of the real sources of power and influence that the team has. There is an old saying, "If you are going to lose an argument, change the subject." Proposing an alternative that is demonstrably superior to the requested deliverable can effectively "change the subject," avoiding a potentially doomed project by substituting a better, more realistic one. The new project may also be more motivating for the team and more fun to work on.

The main motivation for opportunity management, though, is to increase the business value of the project. There are a number of ways to approach this. Surveying the current state of relevant and closely related technologies is a typical starting point. It may be that a new generation of hardware is available, or expected during the project, that could effectively be incorporated into a system being developed. New technologies methods may provide greater speed or reliability. New or existing standards may have application to your work, which may extend the possible uses of the deliverable, both in the current project and for future applications. It might be possible to develop a deliverable with capabilities that solve a whole class of problems instead of the single one that triggered the project. Conversely, it may be possible to break up an ambitious project into shorter stages, developing something that provides tangible value (perhaps much of what is desired from the project) in a fraction of the time the entire project would require.

This approach may even provide new significant business opportunity to the project team. Some years ago, a team I was part of received a particularly incoherent Request for Proposal (RFP) from a large telecommunications company. Our initial reaction was to "no bid," as none of us could figure out what the customer was really asking for. Instead, we decided to counterpropose working with the customer (for a fee) to clean up the RFP and develop a specification that we, and others, could bid on. The company was highly offended by this counterproposal and told us so. As time went on, however, every company to whom it sent the RFP also declined to bid, and it did end up hiring us to structure a new RFP.

The new RFP made a lot more sense (and it also included a few things that we could do better than most of our competitors).

REUSE AND LEVERAGE

Process opportunities are less visible on a project. Project teams can identify opportunities to develop methods or tools that will make work on the current, as well as future, projects faster and easier. Adopting new methods, current versions of computer-aided design and development tools, or industry standards may also lead to more efficient execution. Reuse and leverage also represent process opportunities.

The tactics of reuse (employing available components) and leverage (modifying available components) are both potentially effective ways to get project work done faster. Unfortunately, the approach used most of the time is *retrospective*, sifting through all the bits and pieces developed on earlier projects looking for things that might be used again. Usually, most of the code written, or hardware components built, has been quickly developed for a specific project, and it is not easily adapted to new work.

Reuse and leverage are most effective when viewed *prospectively*, looking forward from the current project to envision places where work can be made easier or more efficient on future projects. Examples of this include parts libraries, software objects, standard component modules, Web style sheets, and a wide range of other resources that can be readily employed to expedite work that is similar, or identical, on successive projects.

Opportunities for reuse and leverage are not limited to components and other deliverables produced by the project; other benefits come from by-products of project activities, such as tools, new techniques, or more efficient methodologies. If work can be reused or leveraged at least three times, the effort invested in generalizing (and documenting) it is probably justified. One opportunity for leverage specific to project management is development of plan templates. Project planning is much faster and more thorough when it starts with all the typical and required project activities already defined. Templates also save data entry time with computer tools. Your planning process still needs to define and list the activities unique to your project, but a template allows you to focus on what is different and saves a lot of time and effort.

Of course, prospective reuse and leverage opportunities are not free, and establishing them usually requires a *larger* investment in the current project, an investment that you expect will make future work easier and faster. In some cases, the resources and time required for these process investments may be easily incorporated into the project without significant change to the objective. In other cases, necessary changes to the project budget or timeline may require discussion and negotiation. Because the benefits of process opportunities are harder to measure and accrue mainly on future projects, selling your management on process improvement opportunities with significant costs will require extra effort.

Not all opportunities are worth pursuing. Before either accepting a small process opportunity or deciding to propose changes to scope or significant process opportunities, you should do some cost-benefit analysis. Estimate the expected value derived from the proposed changes, and then deduct the estimated incremental cost for those changes to the project. If an idea has a credible positive net value, it is probably worth considering. Even when the cost impact is too high, you will still know a lot more about the project as a result of the analysis, and you will also gain confidence that the objective you are working toward is likely the best available.

TRIMMING SCOPE

While opportunity analysis is useful and may reveal superior projects, for many projects the scope will end up shifting in the other direction. Before deciding what features or aspects of the project deliverable to drop or change, determine which requirements are absolute "must have" features and which (if any) are more expendable. There are several techniques for prioritizing requirements. The simplest is to list the requirements and sort them into a sequence where the most essential ones are at the top of the list and the least important ones fall to the bottom. More analytical tools for ranking and valuing release criteria and other requirements can be found in tools such as quality function deployment (QFD).

The purpose of the exercise, however you approach it, is to capture and document the specifications that you *must* deliver, separating them from the portions of the requested deliverable that are desirable but not absolutely necessary. Accepting small decreases in reliability or performance may result in significant reduction in time and cost for the project, and such trade-offs may result in a project that better meets its overall goals. Other tactics to consider include using older technologies or methods to achieve functionality similar to the requested deliverable or avoiding custom-developed components in favor of purchased ones. These ideas might protect all or most of the specified scope while lowering cost and reducing the planned schedule, but each trade-off potentially introduces new risks to the project that you must note and manage.

Project scope requirements are easiest to change early. Late changes are often painful and expensive, resulting in work that would have been unnecessary had the change been made earlier. From a risk management standpoint, the "is/is not" technique, discussed in Chapter 3, is the most effective technique. Determining what portions of scope can be demoted to the "is not" list effectively limits scope. This is particularly useful for projects that have hard limits on timing and budget; the "is/is not" technique establishes a firm boundary for scope that is consistent with the other limits.

Defining scope using "is" and "is not" lists does not mean that project scope will never shift; it just means that any modifications will be subject to analysis and change control before being accepted. Determining the lowest-value features and requirements allows you to intelligently determine what to exclude (either permanently or to be part of a follow-on project). It also provides you with limits on project deliverables early enough to support thorough planning and risk analysis.

Resource Options

Revisiting the resource plan also can lead to an overall plan that better fits the objective. Alternative approaches to staffing, cross-training, outsourcing, and other elements of the resource plan are all potentially useful options.

RESOURCE ANALYSIS

For some projects, there may be ways to get work done faster without increasing the overall required resources. One possibility is to identify any portions of the plan where project team members are not busy, rearranging the work to use their time more fully and effectively. Schedules may be too long due to nonproject commitments by your project staff. If the external work can be postponed or eliminated, it could have a significant impact on your schedule. You may also be able to find ways to improve the effectiveness of the project team by simply asking individuals what they need in order to work faster. Many people get more work done through telecommuting, working at times when they are more efficient or in an atypical work environment. Unless you ask, these possibilities will remain hidden. You may even be able to minimize distractions and noise during some or most of the project through moving work off-site, co-locating the team in a closed-off area, or relocating to space that is out of normal foot-traffic areas. One project team I worked with attributed much of its on-schedule performance to its location in a trailer (while new buildings were being completed) where it was quiet and no one dropped by to visit.

TRAINING ADDITIONAL STAFF

Another tactic that can potentially help the schedule as well as mitigate a source of project risk is mentoring and cross-training. Project timelines are often longer than theoretically necessary on high-tech projects because only one person knows how to do some of the required activities. The work must be scheduled in sequence, queued up for the expert to do it. Work can be speeded up if others on the staff have an interest in this area of expertise and can be trained to take on activities in parallel. Of course, people new to a discipline will rarely work as fast as experienced staff, and duration estimates for activities assigned to them will generally be longer, due to training requirements and lower work efficiency. Activities assigned to the current expert will also take somewhat longer, because of the required mentoring. Despite this, the benefits to the schedule in getting the work done concurrently can be substantial. In addition, the project risk profile will improve, as the project will no longer be as dependent on access to a single person. If the expert becomes unavailable to your project (due to illness, higher-priority work, resignation, or any other reason), your project will not grind to a halt but can continue (although more slowly) using the newly trained staff.

STAFFING ALTERNATIVES

For projects where schedule is much more important than budget, subcontracting work to outside service providers can speed things up whenever a larger effective staff can work in parallel on activities that are currently planned in sequence. If the project priority is high, adding staff from within the organization may be an option. Some projects cannot run as quickly as theoretically possible because the experience and talent available on the original project team are low, so it is useful to explore the possibility of finding staff who are more efficient or who do not require any training before taking on project activities. If adding these people is not possible, propose exchanging staff with projects that the more capable people are working on, especially if your project has higher priority. Additional resources of other types can also potentially help to compress the project, such as faster computers, newer equipment for tests and other work, or systems to automate manual activities. New work methods require training and practice but may still represent options for saving time. All of this will raise the resource cost of the project, but for some projects this trade-off may be justified.

Schedule Options

Reexamining the schedule also provides alternative projects. Some ideas to consider include using float, revising activity dependencies, and "crashing" the schedule.

USING FLOAT

One simple approach for shortening your project involves reducing the amount of float on noncritical activities. Float (or slack) is derived from the critical path analysis of the schedule (discussed in Chapter 4), and it measures how much an activity can slip without impact to the project deadline.

To shorten your project using float, you shift some of the work on critical path activities to staff assigned to noncritical activities. These staffing shifts will cause changes to noncritical activities (such as delaying the start, interrupting the activity, or reducing productivity), but, as long as the activities retain some float, the additional effort on the critical activities can shorten the project. Bear in mind that this sort of schedule compression comes with a price. Using all (or nearly all) of the float for an activity makes it more critical. This increases project risk by creating new failure modes.

REVISING ACTIVITY DEPENDENCIES

A second, more elaborate idea involves revising activity dependencies. Here, the schedule is shortened through rearranging or redefining the work. The simplest possibility is to inspect the dependencies linking critical path activities, looking for opportunities to shorten the schedule using a more compact logical work flow.

If revising activity sequences is ineffective, you can reexamine the activities and brainstorm alternate ways to approach longer activities on the critical path by using a different breakdown or a completely new approach. This second method often involves breaking critical path activities down further to create smaller activities that can be executed in parallel, as in Figure 6-5.

This concept has a variety of names, including concurrent engineering, "fast tracking," and simultaneous development. For

Figure 6-5. Converting activities to parallel execution.

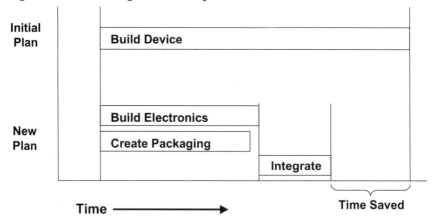

parallel execution to be effective, there are at least two require-ments. First, you need to allow integration time in the estimates for the parallel activities or define a new activity (as in Figure 6-5) dur-ing which all the separately developed components are assembled. The second requirement is often less visible, but it is even more important. Detailed up-front analysis is essential to ensure that the integration works. All the connections, interfaces, and relation-ships between the independently developed activity deliverables must be defined and thoroughly documented. Whatever this work is called—architecting, systems engineering, or something else—it will make the difference between components that mesh properly and integration efforts that fail. When the system decomposition is not done well, the integration activity can consume the time you expected to save, or more. Even worse, it may fail utterly, resulting in components that are completely unusable. Before committing to a plan that uses independent parallel development, explicitly iden-tify when and by whom this analysis will be done, and note the integration risks on your project risk list.

Another approach for schedule compression through revis-ing activity dependencies involves overlap of the work. In the plan, there may be finish-to-start dependencies on the critical path that may be converted to start-to-start dependencies with lags.

In Figure 6-6, the preliminary project plan includes a design activity scheduled for three weeks followed by a coding activity scheduled for four weeks. After thinking about it, the project team may decide that it would be possible to begin coding after only two weeks of design, as there will be enough information to start programming for some of the modules at that point, and staffing will be available to get going. A word of warning, however, is neces-

Figure 6-6. Modifying activity dependencies.

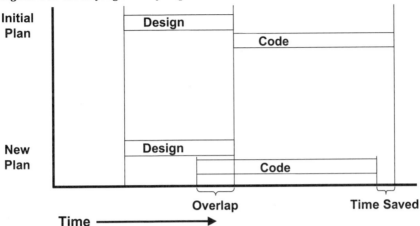

sary. It may seem that converting a finish-to-start dependency to start-to-start dependency with a lag of two weeks would save one week on the schedule. For actual projects this is overly optimistic, as there is an increased likelihood of rework or discovery of something unexpected in the final week of design. When you choose to make this sort of change, increase your duration estimates for all activities that you plan to begin early (in this case, adding about two days to the coding activity estimate), and also explicitly note the new risk.

''CRASHING'' THE SCHEDULE

An additional scheduling technique, common on projects with extreme schedule pressure, is "crashing." In this sense, crashing means applying additional resources to gain speed—as in a "crash program." Not all activities can be crashed. It is not possible to crash activities where one person must do all the work, activities that cannot be partitioned, or activities with time constraints you do not control. A good example of an uncrashable activity is sailing a ship from New York to London. With one ship, it takes five days. With five ships, it *still* takes five days. Four additional ships are not useful in speeding the process of crossing the Atlantic Ocean.

Even when crashing helps, it adds both additional cost and new risks to projects. If an activity is efficiently executed by a team of three people, a team of six will rarely be able to do it in half the time. Involving more people requires extra communication, overhead, and complexity, so resources and time do not vary linearly. This has been observed and documented for all types of projects for a long time, but the best discussion of this for high-tech projects remains *The Mythical Man-Month*, by Fred Brooks. Brooks covers in detail how people get in each other's way and how inefficiencies grow as the number of people working on a project increases. As efficiency drops, project risk increases due to larger staff, potential confusion, work methods, and general complexity.

For all this, when time is critical to your project, these trade-offs may be justified. Crashing a project schedule requires you to locate the activities that can be shortened and to estimate for each what the impact of compression will be, particularly on the project budget. Experienced project leaders usually have a good sense of how to do project work efficiently, so initial plans are generally built using assumptions for staffing and work methods that minimize effort and cost. For any given activity, though, other combinations of staffing and duration may be possible. One person working alone on an activity might take a long time; two working together could take quite a bit less. Adding more people will, for some activities, continue to reduce the activity duration even more. Eventually, though, you reach a point of diminishing returns, where adding more staff makes a negligible difference in the activity duration. A curve describing the relationship between staffing and time has a bend in it at that point, giving it an "L" shape, similar to the curve in Figure 6-7.

For any given activity, there is also a minimum possible duration; no amount of additional staffing, money, or other tactics will allow you to do the work in less time.

Because the initial estimates tend to be near the bend in the curve (where the cost is minimized), shortening projects by crashing can be quite expensive. A common strategy for compressing projects by crashing is to minimize the overall cost by seeking

Figure 6-7. Trade-off between effort and time.

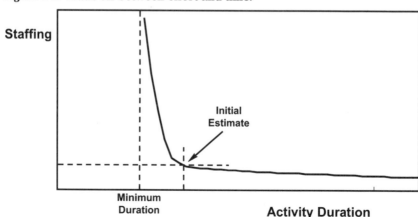

a number of ideas, more than may be needed to meet the project deadline. Examine the schedule for activities that could be crashed, expedited, or otherwise changed in ways that could shorten the project, initially focusing on the critical path(s). Ideas for each activity can then be considered in turn and assessed for both effectiveness and cost.

Normally, you will want to apply the strategies that have the least impact to the project budget, so you need to estimate the cost penalty for each idea. The usual way to do this is to calculate the cost per time (usually per day) associated with the schedule reduction. For example, one idea might be to shorten a development activity, initially estimated to take fifteen work days and consume $4,000 of effort. You believe that this could be reduced to eleven days, saving four, if you bring in an outside contractor to help for a week at a rate of $6,000. Both the initial and compressed approaches to this activity are indicated in Figure 6-8, and the slope of the dotted line connecting them, $1,500 per day, defines the cost penalty for schedule compression.

Ideas for schedule compression can come from a variety of sources. The project team can brainstorm; you can consult peers or experts; or you can research what similar past projects did when they ran into trouble and were forced to work faster. Many effective ideas for crashing originate from actions taken in the past in response to some crisis or project disaster. While not all the actions taken midproject to solve problems are effective, sometimes people come up with great solutions that work. In addition to providing

Figure 6-8. Estimates for "crashed" activity.

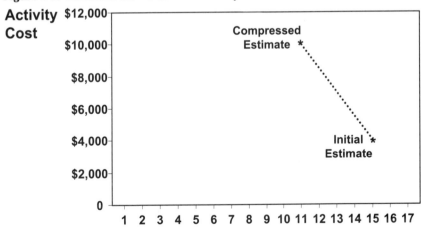

Activity Duration (Days)

a potentially rich source of ideas, historical project information may also offer data on costs and outline the work that will be required.

Typical methods that may prove effective in shortening project activity durations (for a price) include:

- ❏ Adding staff
- ❏ Paying for overtime
- ❏ Hiring outside help to augment staff
- ❏ Outsourcing whole project activities
- ❏ Paying to expedite shipping or services such as printing, testing, fabrication, or installation
- ❏ Upgrading or replacing slower equipment
- ❏ Spreading work over more shifts

For each crashable activity idea you develop, estimate the total cost involved and assess the cost penalty—the expense for each day of schedule improvement—so that you can arrange the ideas from least costly to most expensive, *per day*. Starting with the least costly strategies, make schedule changes that affect critical activities and note the cost of the additional resources. For each modification considered, check that the change does in fact provide a schedule improvement, and monitor for noncritical path activities that become critical. You can continue the process, crashing activities until it is no longer necessary or is not possible. Any schedule compression ideas that you do not use can be held in reserve as possible contingency plans for your project. (Contingency planning is discussed in detail in Chapter 8.) At the conclusion of this process, document any changes you made, and note all the new risks and failure modes, including the new critical and near-critical paths, introduced to your project plan.

Assess Options and Update Plans

After investigating possible scope, resource, and schedule changes, you have the information you need to assess your options and seek the plan that best meets the project objective. Your analysis may result in a credible project plan (including a detailed project schedule, resource plan, and description of major project deliverables) that supports the project objective and any other significant constraints. If so, your next step is risk analysis.

If the "best" plan you can develop is still not very close to the objective, it is evidence that you have a failure-prone project. In this case, you should examine scope, schedule, and resource combinations and develop *at least* two additional plans that achieve slightly different project objectives, such as:

☐ Fewer resources needed, but longer schedule or reduced scope

☐ Increased scope (with higher demonstrable value), but more time or resources required

☐ Shorter schedule, but more resources needed (or scope reduced)

For each option, document relative advantages and risks. These alternative plans can be used to focus the discussions and decision making for the project on facts and possibilities, rather than on politics and emotions. The key to managing projects that will fail because of excessive constraints is fact-based, principled negotiation. (Negotiation of plan-based objectives is a key topic of Chapter 10.)

Incorporate any plan changes that you are empowered to make into your preliminary schedule and other project documents. If you developed alternative plans, document them as well, with any proposed changes they would require that need higher-level approval.

Seek Missing Risks

Your list of project risks grows throughout the defining and planning processes, as noted in the preceding chapters. As your preliminary plans near completion, review them for undetected risks and consider additional risk sources.

REVIEW YOUR PLANS

Although you have collected risk data throughout the planning of project work, it is useful to review your scope definition for any other risks that could arise from:

☐ Required use of new technology and other feasibility issues

☐ External sourcing for a key subcomponent, utility, or tool

☐ Levels of technical complexity significantly higher than those in past projects

❏ Unclear aspects of product definition

❏ Inconsistent specifications

❏ Potential for excessive requirement changes

❏ Unfamiliar or inappropriate development tools or methods

❏ Extreme quality or reliability requirements

❏ Poorly defined acceptance or testing criteria

❏ Loss of proprietary information.

❏ A large number of activities

Also review your preliminary schedule, checking for un-listed risks relating to:

❏ Very large worst-case (or pessimistic "PERT") estimates

❏ Long-duration activities

❏ All activities that lie on or near a critical path

❏ Multiple critical paths

❏ Compressed or "crashed" activities

❏ Merge points in the schedule and major milestones

❏ External dependencies

❏ Estimates with high uncertainty

❏ Projects with deadlines farther out than a reasonable plan-ning horizon

❏ Excessive optimism

❏ Potential project tracking problems

❏ Incorrect schedule logic

❏ Inadvertently omitted project activities

❏ Inexperience with computer project management tools

❏ Learning curve issues with new skills

Review the resource plans as well, to uncover additional risks due to:

❏ Activities that require a large staff

❏ Activities dependent on overcommitted resources

❏ Activities that require skills not currently available

❏ Activities that depend on still unidentified resources

❏ Activities that require a unique or very scarce resource

❏ Geographic or functional separation of staff

❏ Activities that depend on staff also dedicated to other projects

❏ Activities with insufficient resources

❏ Project staff that is new or lacks relevant experience

❏ An overall project team larger than that used in previous successful projects

❏ Productivity impact from the work environment

❏ Potential staff loss through illness, injury, or resignation

❏ Training and staff development requirements

❏ Communications and language difficulties

❏ Potential loss of the project sponsor

ADDITIONAL RISKS

Reviewing the planning documents can uncover many risks, but there are several other methods for detecting potential problems and risks.

Brainstorming

One powerful risk discovery process is brainstorming. With the project team, review the risk list that you have already constructed. Work together to brainstorm other things in the project that could possibly go wrong. Consider risks to the project that may not have come to light during scope definition and project planning. Examine the methods and processes you intend to use, and consider any aspects that are new or that will be particularly difficult. Think about risk that would arise as a consequence of any organizational changes that are rumored or seem likely. Finally, focus on outside factors that might have an impact on your project, such as natural disasters, weather, government or legal changes, and actions of competitors.

Capture every idea without comment, questions, or criticism. Stimulate people to think of new risks triggered by the thoughts of others. List every risk that is mentioned, even those it seems you can do nothing about. Keep the brainstorming going, striving to hear from every member of the project team, until the flow of ideas seems at an end. Conclude the process by restating any risks that are unclear, combining or eliminating risks where there seems to be redundancy, and adding all the new risks to the project risk list.

Retrospective Analysis

A second idea for finding risks in a new project is to look at earlier projects. The old adage "Lightning never strikes twice in the same place" is demonstrably false; lightning strikes the same spot hundreds of times, always the highest place with the best electrical connection to the ground. (If this were not the case, lightning rods would not work.) On projects, the analogous statement—*"That* can never happen again"—is equally untrue. Risks tend to recur in project after project, unless you understand the root cause and do something differently to avoid the problem. Data from earlier work (in the form of project retrospectives, lessons learned, postmortems, postproject analyses, or close-out reports) are a potentially rich source of risk information.

These reports generally contain two types of data useful for risk management: effective practices worth repeating and areas where improvement is possible. In the area of good practices, seek specific ideas from what was done well, practices to repeat or extend, and specific significant accomplishments. Examine your plan to see whether you are taking full advantage of known good practices. In the realm of things that did not go well, review previous project data for problems, assumptions, poor estimates, actual beginnings and ends of major activities compared to plans, complexity of activities undertaken, number of changes proposed and accepted, sources of delay, and other issues. Identify any aspects that impacted progress. Also look for unintended consequences of corrective actions taken, where solving problem "Q" led to new problems "R" and "S." These past problems can point to risks in any of your planned work that is similar, and should be added to your project risk list.

Organizations that take these project processes seriously review project histories regularly and prepare comprehensive checklists and templates that contain common risks for use on new projects. In addition to making common problems more visible, risk templates are an effective tool for stimulating thinking by the project team so that new risks related to past problems can be uncovered. The role of retrospective project analysis in ongoing project risk management is discussed in Chapter 12.

Scenario Analysis

Additional risks may come to light through scenario analysis. Discuss situations expected along the project timeline, step-by-step, asking questions such as, "What might go wrong here?" and "What will be keeping me up at night during this portion of the work?" You can close your eyes and "play a movie in your head" to gain insight into the project's work and the problems it may be exposed to. Techniques familiar to software development organizations, such as inspections and structured walk-throughs, may also be applied to the project plan to reveal weaknesses, omissions, and risks. As you think through project scenarios, test the project assumptions to uncover any that might change.

A similar approach to scenario analysis is the "strengths, weaknesses, opportunities, and threats" (SWOT) analysis. For many projects, particularly those that involve delivering solutions, these aspects are examined early in the project. As the project planning process approaches closure, you should revisit both the identified weaknesses and threats for the project to ensure that any that have not been addressed in your planning are noted as risks.

Risk discovery from outside your project can also be useful. Interviews with peers and experts can be a potentially rich source of information on risks that your project may encounter. Utilizing the experiences and perspectives of others is a potent technique for identifying and managing risks.

Root Cause Analysis

Finally, "cause-and-effect" exercises may be used for risk discovery. Risk management requires knowledge of the root causes that lead to project problems. There are a number of effective techniques for discovering the sources of problems, and, although they are most often applied retrospectively, they can be used to examine future problems. These techniques include failure mode and effect analysis (FMEA), fishbone diagrams, root cause analysis, K-J analysis, or other variations of cause-and-effect investigation. To use these processes to look for potential risks, begin by stating an outcome the project intends to avoid—such as losing a key resource, delay in getting an important input, or significant increases in the cost of some portion of the project. The next step is to challenge the project team to work backward to uncover plausible sources that could cause the problem. In addition to uncovering specific risks that might not otherwise be detected, this exercise often raises the perception of how probable certain problems are likely to be. Before the sources of trouble are articulated, most projects look fairly straightforward and problem-free. After documenting the things that can contribute to project difficulty, you have a much more realistic view of the work, balancing the sometimes excessive optimism that is common early in a new project. Further discussion of root cause analysis as a tool for managing risks is in Chapter 8.

Selected specific risks from the PERIL database are listed in the Appendix to further stimulate your thinking about and discovery of project risks.

Document the Risks

Every time you uncover a risk, write it down. Once all the risks identified have been added to the risk list, review the whole list in preparation for the next steps of analysis and quantification. For each listed risk, check that the description is clear, including a summary of the consequences. Specify the trigger event that signals the occurrence of the risk, and, for risks that are time-specific, also identify when in the project the risk is most likely to occur.

Key Ideas for Constraint Management and Risk Discovery

❏ Minimize differences between project plans and objectives.
❏ Understand and clearly document project priorities.
❏ Use priorities to identify project alternatives.
❏ Explore project opportunities.
❏ Identify and explicitly remove unnecessary project scope.
❏ Determine risks and costs of proposed project changes.
❏ Minimize unknown risk through brainstorming, analysis, and research.

Panama Canal: Improving the Plan (1906)

Many unsuccessful projects, viewed in retrospect, failed because they could not manage the work within mandated constraints. In reviving the Panama Canal project, a great deal of effort went into rethinking the approach to the work, to avoid the most significant issues that plagued the earlier project.

For projects of all types, it is beneficial to invest effort early in investigating whether there are better, faster, more efficient ways to do what is required. New technologies, methodologies, and approaches are born this way. Several key innovations were introduced in the U.S. canal project. Avoiding schedule and cost problems required changes to the equipment used and the methods employed to accomplish the work.

On the equipment side, twentieth-century technology made possible the huge, powerful steam shovels that gave the United States effort a big advantage over the earlier project. New technology also provided equipment suitable for use in the warm, damp, machine-destroying environment of Panama.

As important as the hardware was, however, the *way* the equipment was used made an even bigger difference. John Stevens, as a railroad engineer, saw the canal project as a railroad problem. To him, the canal was "the greatest of all triumphs in American railroad engineering." To keep the huge shovels digging continuously, Stevens developed a system that allowed shovel loads to be dropped onto railroad flatcars that ran along track adjacent to the shovels. The flatcars circulated in large loops out to the dams and other places where these loads could be deposited. When the flatcars arrived at these sites, huge fixed scoops (similar to the fronts of enormous snowplows) cleaned them off for their return to the shovels, with no need for them to stop or pause at any point for this enormous conveyor belt. Using this arrangement and the much larger steam shovels, the U.S. project was soon excavating more in one day than the earlier French project had accomplished in a month.

This system would have been sufficient for the project if the shovels had been simply digging deep holes in one place, but they were not. As the digging proceeded, the shovels had to move, and so did the railroad tracks that carried the flatcars. For this, John Stevens developed an elaborate, elastic method for moving the track, providing a constant, steady stream of empty flatcars flowing by the steam shovels. With this system, twelve men could move almost two kilometers of track in a single day. Using conventional track-laying methods, 600 men would have had difficulty equaling this performance. As the construction continued, excavation in the Culebra Cut widened and deepened, so these methods were used at multiple levels. Each level had its own railroad loop, shovels, and crews. The total track moved in one year approached 2,000 kilometers (more than 1,000 miles). Without these innovations, the canal project would have taken years longer to complete and cost far more, and it might well have been abandoned before completion, like the earlier project.

CHAPTER 7

QUANTIFYING AND ANALYZING ACTIVITY RISKS

"When you know a thing, to hold that you know it, and when you do not know a thing, to allow that you do not know it—this is knowledge."   —CONFUCIUS

Project planning processes serve several purposes, but probably the most important for risk management is to separate the parts of the work that are well understood, and therefore less risky, from the parts that are less well understood. Often, what separates an impossible project from a possible one is isolating the most difficult work early so that it receives the attention and effort it requires. Risk assessment techniques are central to gaining an understanding of what is most uncertain about a project, and they are the foundation for managing risk.

Most of the content of this chapter falls into the "Qualitative Risk Analysis" and "Quantitative Risk Analysis" portions of the Planning Processes in the *PMBOK® Guide.* The focus of this chapter is analysis and prioritization of the identified project risks. Analysis of *overall* project risk is addressed in Chapter 9. The principal ideas in this chapter include:

❐   Risk probability assessment

❐   Risk impact assessment

❐   Risk matrices and tables

❐ PERT

❐ Decision trees

Quantitative and Qualitative Risk Analysis

Risk analysis strives for deeper understanding of potential project problems. Techniques for doing this effectively may provide either quantitative estimates and measures for each risk or qualitative information that places risks into ranges and categories.

Qualitative techniques are easier to apply and generally require less effort. Qualitative risk assessment is often sufficient for rank-ordering risks, allowing you to select the most significant ones for application of the management techniques discussed in Chapter 8.

Quantitative methods strive for greater precision, and they reveal more about each risk. These methods require more work, but, in addition to allowing you to sequence the risks from most to least significant, quantitative analysis also provides data you can use to assess overall project risk and to estimate schedule and/or budget reserves for risky projects.

Although the dichotomy between these approaches is explicit in the *PMBOK® Guide,* analysis methods fall into a continuum of possibilities. They range from qualitative assessment using a small number of categories, through methods that use progressively more and finer distinctions, to the extreme of determining specific quantitative data for each risk. If the primary goal of risk analysis is to prioritize risks to determine which ones are important enough to warrant responses, the easiest qualitative assessment methods may suffice. If you need to assess project-level risk with maximum precision, then you will need to use quantitative assessment methods (though the nature of the available data usually puts a rather modest limit on the accuracy you can attain).

Whatever assessment method you apply, the foundation is always the same simple formula discussed in Chapter 1: "loss" multiplied by "likelihood." The realm of "likelihood" is statistics and probability, domains that many project contributors find confusing and at times counterintuitive. "Loss" in projects is measured in impact: time, money, and related project factors. These two parameters characterize risk, and both must be assessed for each project risk identified.

Risk Probability

The "likelihood," or probability, of a single event is always somewhere between zero (no chance of occurrence) and one (inevitable occurrence). Looking backward from the end of a project, every risk has one of these two values; it either happened or it did not. At the beginning of the project, though, there is uncertainty, and it is logical to assign a value somewhere in between. Qualitative risk assessment methods divide the choices into ranges and require project team members to assign each risk to one of the defined ranges. Quantitative risk assessment assigns each risk a specific fraction between zero and one (or between zero and 100 percent).

By definition, all probabilities fall within this range, but determining what value between zero and one to assign a given risk is often difficult. There are only three ways in practice to set probabilities. For some situations, such as flipping coins and throwing dice, mathematical analysis permits calculation of the expected probabilities. In other situations, a simple model does not exist, but there are many historical events that are sufficiently similar, and empirical data may be used for prediction; this is the basis of the insurance industry. In all other cases, probabilities are basically set by guessing. For complex events that occur seldom, perhaps even never (at least, not yet), you can neither calculate nor measure to determine a probability, so ideas such as referencing analogous situations, scenario analysis, and "gut feel" come into play. For most project risk situations, probabilities fall into the third category and therefore tend to be inexact.

Qualitative methods recognize this lack of precision and do not require specific numerical values. They divide the complete range into two or more nonoverlapping ranges or segments. The simplest qualitative assessment uses two ranges, "more likely than not (.5 to 1)" and "less likely than not (0 to .4999)." Most project teams are able to select one of these choices for each risk with little difficulty, but the coarse granularity of the analysis makes selecting significant risks for further attention fairly arbitrary.

A more common method for qualitative assessment uses three ranges, assigning a value of high, medium, or low to each risk. The definitions for these categories vary, but usually they are:

- ❏ High = 50 percent or higher (Likely)
- ❏ Medium = Between 10 and 50 percent (Unlikely)
- ❏ Low = 10 percent or lower (Very unlikely)

These three levels of probability are quickly and easily determined for risks without undue debate, and the resulting characterization of risk allows you to discriminate adequately between significant and trivial risks.

Other methods use four, five, or more categories. These methods tend to use linear ranges for the probabilities: quartiles for four, quintiles for five, and so forth. (The names assigned to five categories might be: very high, high, moderate, low, and very low.) The more ranges there are, the better the characterization of risk, but the harder it is for the project team to arrive at consensus.

The logical extension of this continues through assessments using integer percentages (one hundred categories) to continuous estimates that allow fractional percentages. While the *apparent* precision improves, the process for determining numerical probabilities may require a lot of overhead, and the data generated are still based primarily on guesses. The illusion of precision can be a source of risk in itself; avoid making subjective information look objective by inappropriate application of quantitative techniques.

Depending on the project, the quality of data available, and the planned uses for risk data, one (or more) of these assessment regimes can generate data on probability. For qualitative assessment methods using five or fewer categories, experience, polling, interviewing, or rough analysis of the risk situation is enough. For quantitative methods, a solid base of historical performance data is the best source, as it provides an empirical foundation for probability assessment. Estimating probabilities using methods such as the Delphi technique (discussed in Chapter 4), computer modeling (discussed later in this chapter), and use of knowledgeable experts (who may have access to much more data than you do) can also potentially improve the quality of quantitative probabilities.

Measurement-based probabilities, when possible, also serve a secondary purpose in project risk management: trend analysis. In hardware projects, statistics for component failure support decisions to retain or replace suppliers for future projects. If custom circuit boards, specialized integrated circuits, or other hardware components are routinely required on projects, quarter-by-quarter or year-by-year data across a number of projects will provide the fraction of components that are not accepted and provide data on whether process changes are warranted to improve the yields and success rates. Managing risk over the long term relies heavily on metrics, which are discussed in more detail in Chapter 9.

Risk Impact

The "loss," or project impact, for an individual risk is not as easily defined as the probability. The minimum is zero, but both the units and the maximum value are specific to the risk. The impact of a given risk may be relatively easy to ascertain and have a single, predictable value, or it may be best expressed as a distribution or histogram of possibilities. Qualitative risk assessment methods for impact again divide the choices into ranges, and the project team assigns each risk to a category on the basis of the magnitude of the risk consequences. For quantitative risk assessment, impact is estimated using units such as days of project slip, money, or some other suitable measure.

Qualitative assessment assigns each risk to one of two or more nonoverlapping categories. A two-range version uses categories such as "low severity" and "high severity," with suitable definitions of these terms related to attaining the project objective. As with probability analysis, the usefulness of only two categories is limited.

Discrimination is improved if you use three ranges, where each risk is assigned a value of high, medium, or low. The definitions for these categories vary, but commonly they relate to the project objective and plan as follows:

- ❐ High = Project objective is at risk (mandatory change to one or more of scope, schedule, and resources).

- ❐ Medium = Project objectives are okay, but significant replanning is required.

- ❐ Low = No major plan changes; the risk is an inconvenience or it will be handled through minor overtime work.

These three levels of project impact are not difficult to assess for most risks and provide fairly good data for sequencing risks according to severity.

Other methods use additional categories, and some partition impact further into specific project factors, such as schedule, cost, and scope. Impact measurement is open-ended; there is no theoretical maximum for any of these parameters (in a literally impossible project, time and cost may be thought of as infinite). Because the scale is not bounded, the categories used for impact are usually geometric, with small ranges at the low end and progressively larger ranges in the upper categories. For an impact assessment that uses five categories, definitions might be:

- ❐ Very low = Less than 1 percent impact on scope, schedule, cost, or quality

- ❐ Low = Less than 5 percent impact on scope, schedule, cost, or quality

❐ Moderate = Less than 10 percent impact on scope, schedule, cost, or quality

❐ High = Less than 20 percent impact on scope, schedule, cost, or quality

❐ Very high = 20 percent or more impact on scope, schedule, cost, or quality

Risks are assigned to a category on the basis of the expected variance of the most significant project parameter, so a risk that represents a 10 percent schedule slip and negligible change to the rest of the project objective would be categorized as "moderate." As with probability assessment, the more ranges there are, the better the characterization of risk, but the harder it is to achieve agreement among the project team.

Similar assessment may also be devised to look at specific kinds of risk separately, such as cost risk or schedule risk, to determine which risks are most likely to affect the highest project priorities.

The most precise assessment of impact defines specific estimates for each risk. Few risks relate only to a single aspect of the project, so this requires a collection of measurement estimates, including at least cost and schedule impact. Cost is conceptually the simplest, because it is unambiguously measured in dollars, yen, euros, or some other easily described unit, and any adverse variance will directly affect the project budget. Schedule impact is not as simple, for two reasons. The impact of a risk is generally in effort, and, as discussed in Chapters 4 and 5, the relation between effort and activity duration is not necessarily straightforward. In addition, not every duration increase for an activity necessarily represents an impact to the schedule. Activities not on a critical path (those with "float" or "slack") generate schedule impact only for adverse variances that are large enough to consume all available schedule flexibility. Estimating cost and schedule variances attributable to risks, as with other project estimating, is neither easy nor necessarily very accurate. Quantitative assessments of risk impact may look precise, but the quality of such estimates is highly variable.

There are other impacts of project risk that are even more difficult to measure. Some risks lead to required overtime or lower the morale of the project team. These represent real impacts on the current project, but they may be relatively small when measured only against the project objective. The longer-term impact, though, is significant if this is a chronic problem encountered frequently on an organization's projects. Mandatory overtime and low motivation are both root causes of turnover, so these impacts may lead to increased probability of other project risks, such as loss of key contributors. Another sort of impact is the effect on relationships with customers, suppliers, and others connected to the project. If a project problem "bruises" such a relationship, consequences in the long term can be quite significant. Increased stress and worry are consequences of risk on troubled projects, as are extra meetings (for global projects, extra meetings in the middle of the night, at least for some people). The impact of these factors on current and future projects may be very difficult to estimate. The correlation among schedule, cost, and other impacts for each risk is often complex. When something in a project is late, there are nearly always both out-of-pocket and other, more subtle costs involved.

Impact assessment on technical projects is not always confined strictly to project parameters. On some projects, concerns about health and safety are significant. Project work may involve poisonous or volatile chemicals, dangerous environments, or unusual modes of travel. While factors such as these are seldom a dominant source of risk impact, you should consider their potential effect on the people involved in your project.

Qualitative impact assessment using three to five categories is usually relatively easy, and it is sufficient for prioritizing risks on the basis of severity. Techniques such as polling, interviewing, team discussion, and reviews of planning data are effective for assigning risks to impact categories. As with probability assessment for each risk, the best foundation for quantitative estimates of impact is history, along with techniques such as Delphi, computer modeling, and consulting peers and experts.

For quantitative assessments of impact in situations that are common, statistics may be available. A good way to provide credible quantitative impact data is to select the mean of the distribution for initial estimates of duration or cost and use the difference between that estimate and the measured "90 percent" point. This principle is the basis for Program Evaluation and Review Technique (PERT) analysis. The PERT estimating technique was discussed in Chapter 4, and other aspects of PERT are covered later in this chapter and in Chapter 9.

Qualitative Risk Analysis

The minimum requirement for risk analysis is a sequenced list of risks, ordered by perceived severity. After assessing "loss" times "likelihood" for each risk, the highest one needs to be at the top of the list and the smallest one at the bottom. If the list of risks is short enough, you can order the list quickly on the basis of a few passes of pair-wise comparisons, switching any adjacent risks where the more severe of the two is lower on the list. The most serious exposures will bubble to the top, and the more trivial ones will sink to the bottom. This technique is best done by a single individual.

A similar technique, related to Delphi, combines data from lists sorted individually by each member of a team. The risks on each list are assigned a score equal to their position on the list, and all the scores for each risk are summed. The risk with the lowest total score heads the composite list, and the rest of the list is sorted by scores in increasing order. If there are significant variances in some of the lists (detected by "clumping" in the aggregated scoring data), further discussion and an additional iteration (as is done in Delphi estimating) may lead to better consensus. The resulting list is more objective than a sequence created by an individual, and it represents the thinking of the whole team.

While these sorting techniques result in an ordered risk list, such a list shows only *relative* risk severity, without indication of the project exposure that each risk represents.

RISK ASSESSMENT TABLES

Qualitative risk assessment based on categorization of both probability and impact provides greater insight into the *absolute* risk severity. A risk assessment table or spreadsheet where risks are listed with category assignments for both probability and impact, as in Figure 7-1, is one approach for this.

Figure 7-1. Risk assessment table.

Risks	Probability	Impact	Overall Risk

After listing each risk, a category is assigned (such as High/ Moderate/Low) for both probability and impact. The last column, "Overall Risk," is filled in by combining the category information in the two columns or by assigning weights to the categories and using the product of the weights. Although any number of categories may be used, the quickest method that results in a meaningful sort uses three categories (defined as in the earlier discussions of probability and impact) and assigns either combinations of the categories or weights such as 1, 3, and 9 for low, moderate, and high, respectively. An example of a sorted qualitative assessment for five risks might look like Figure 7-2.

Figure 7-2. Risk assessment example.

Risks	Probability (H/M/L)	Impact (H/M/L)	Overall Risk
Software Guru Is Not Available	M	H	HM
Consultant Is Incompetent	M	M	M
Purchased Component Comes Late	L	H	M
Software Development Is Too Slow	L	M	ML
Needed Test Gear Is Not Available	L	L	L

For the data in the right column, categories may be combined (as shown), factors multiplied (the numbers would be 27, 9, 9, 3, and 1), or "stop light" icons displayed to indicate risk (with red for high, yellow for moderate, and green for low). From a table such as Figure 7-2, risks above a certain absolute assessment level, such as moderate, can be selected for risk management attention.

RISK ASSESSMENT MATRICES

An alternative method for qualitative risk assessment involves placing risks on a two-dimensional matrix, where the rows and columns represent the categories of probability and impact. The matrices may be two-by-two, three-by-three, or larger. Risk matrices are generally square, but they may be rectangular with different numbers of categories for probability and impact. Figure 7-3 is an example of a five-by-five matrix.

The farther up and to the right a risk is assessed to be, the higher its overall assessment. Risks are selected for management on the basis of whether the cell in the matrix represents a risk above some predetermined level of severity.

ALTERNATIVE ASSUMPTIONS TESTING

Standard project network charts do not permit the use of conditional branching, as system flowcharts and other graphical techniques do. Because it is not uncommon to have places in a

Figure 7-3. Risk assessment matrix.

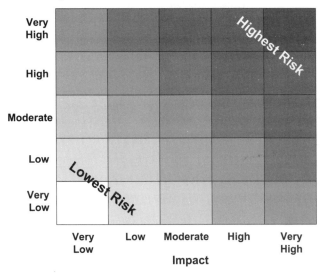

project schedule where one of several possible alternatives, out-comes, or decisions will be chosen, you need some method for ana-lyzing the situation. One qualitative way around this limitation is to construct a baseline plan using the assumption that seems most likely and deal with the other possible outcomes as risks. If it is not possible to determine which outcome may be most likely, it is usual to select the one that represents the longest duration (or highest cost) to use in the baseline plan. Assessing the risk associated with making an incorrect choice involves determining the probability that it may be wrong and any consequences (impact) on the proj-ect. To do this, you also must specifically identify any other poten-tial outcomes, their probabilities, and the consequences to the project if each should occur instead of the outcome you assumed in your plan. Each of these other associated possible outcomes, with probability and impact assessments, then can be listed with project risks and assessed with them.

DATA PRECISION RANKING

Not all risks are equally well understood. Some risks hap-pen regularly, and experience and data concerning them are plenti-ful. Assessment of these risks, and formulation of adequate responses, is not difficult. Other risks in projects arise from the portions of the work that are new, unique, or different compared with work on other projects. Assessment of probability and impact for these risks may be based on imprecise or only partial information, so the assessment of risk may be too low.

Even with qualitative risk assessment, these poorly understood risks can be identified and singled out for special treatment. For each assessment, consider the quality, reliability, and integrity of the data used to categorize probability and impact. If the information seems inadequate, it may be prudent to seek out experts or other sources of better information or to err on the side of caution and adopt higher categories for probability and impact to ensure that the visibility of the risk is elevated and receives sufficient attention.

LIST OF RISKS THAT REQUIRE FURTHER ATTENTION

The main objective of qualitative risk assessment is to identify major risks by prioritizing the known project risks and rank-ordering them, with major risks at the head of the list and minor ones at the bottom. The sequenced list may be assembled using any of the methods described, but the use of three categories (low, moderate, and high) for both probability and impact generally provides a good balance of adequate analysis and minimal effort. However the list is analyzed and sorted, it needs to be partitioned into risks that deserve more consideration and risks that seem too minor to warrant a planned response.

The first several risks on your prioritized list nearly always require attention, but the question of how far down the list to go is not necessarily simple. One idea is to read down the list, focusing on the consequences and the likelihood of each risk until you reach the first one that will not keep you awake at night. The "gut feel" test is not a bad way to select the boundary for a sorted risk list. A similar idea uses consensus; team members individually select the cutoff point and then discuss as a team where the line should be, relying on individual and group experiences. It is also possible to set an absolute limit, such as moderate overall risk, or you can draw a diagonal stair-step boundary from the upper left to the lower right in a matrix. Whatever method you use, it is prudent to check each of the risks that are *not* selected to ensure that there are none that seem to need a response.

Following this examination, you are ready to prepare an abridged list of risks for potential further quantitative analysis and management.

Quantitative Risk Assessment

As stated earlier in the chapter, quantitative risk assessment involves more effort than qualitative techniques, so it is common to do initial sorting and selection of risks qualitatively. This is not absolutely necessary, though, because each of the qualitative methods discussed has a quantitative analogue that can be used to sequence the list. The tables and matrices have their categories for probability and impact replaced by absolute numerical estimates. Quantitative techniques such as sensitivity analysis, more rigorous statistical methods, decision trees, and simulations provide further insight into project risk, and can also be used for overall project risk assessment.

One other distinction between qualitative and quantitative assessment is that in quantitative risk assessment, the estimated impact for each identified risk is explicitly based only on consequences that affect the overall project. Sensitivity analysis, to determine the specific effect of each risk on the project, is an initial requirement for quantitative analysis of each activity risk.

SENSITIVITY ANALYSIS

Not all risks are equally damaging. Schedule impact that arises from activity risks is significant only when the estimated slippage exceeds any available float. For simple projects, a quick inspection of the plan using the risk list will distinguish the risks that are likely to cause the most damage. For more complex networks of activities, using a copy of the project database that has been entered into a scheduling tool is a fast way to detect risks (and combinations of risks) that are most likely to result in project delay. If you make a copy of the project plan and replace the baseline estimates in the copy with longer estimates expected if there are problems, the computer will calculate and display overall project impact. By sequentially entering all the risk data and then backing it out, you can easily detect the quantitative schedule sensitivity for each risk.

In general, all adverse cost variances are summed to estimate budget overrun, but on some projects not all cost impact is accounted for in the same way. If a risk results in an out-of-pocket expense for the project, then it impacts the budget directly. If the cost impact involves a capital purchase, then the project impact may be only a portion of the actual cost, and in some cases the entire expense may be accounted for somewhere else. An increase in cost that is considered part of organizational overhead, such as allocation of a conference room to be used as a "war room" for the duration of a particularly troubled project, is seldom charged back to the project directly. Increased costs for communications, duplication, shipping, and other services considered routine are frequently not borne directly by technical projects. Travel costs in some cases may not be allocated directly to projects. While it is generally true that all cost and other resource impact is proportionate to the magnitude of the variance, it may be worthwhile to segregate potential direct cost variances from any that are indirect.

QUANTITATIVE RISK ASSESSMENT TABLES

For quantitative assessment, the same sort of table or spreadsheet discussed previously can be filled in with numerical probabilities instead of with the categories used for qualitative assessment. As each risk is considered, its estimated impact in cost, effort, time (but only time in excess of any available scheduling flexibility), or other factors is used. Overall risk is then assessed as the product of the impact estimates and the selected probability. One drawback of using this method for sequencing risks is that for some risks it may be very time-consuming to develop consensus for both the impact and the probability. A second, more serious issue is that "impact" may be measured in more than one way (for example, in time and in money), making it difficult to ascertain a single uniform measure of overall risk.

While you could certainly list impacts of various kinds, weighted using the estimated probabilities, you may find that sorting on the basis of these data is not straightforward. This problem can be overcome by selecting one type of impact, such as time, and converting impact of other kinds into an equivalent project duration slip (as was done in the PERIL database). You could also develop several tables, one for cost, another for schedule, and others for scope, quality, safety, or any other type of impact for which you can develop meaningful numerical estimates. You can then sort each table on a consistent basis and select risks from each for further attention. This multiple-table process also requires you to do a final check to detect any risks that are significant only when all factors are considered together.

TWO-DIMENSIONAL QUANTITATIVE ANALYSIS

The qualitative matrix converts to a quantitative tool by replacing the rows and columns with perpendicular axes. Probability may be plotted on the horizontal axis, from zero to 100 percent, and impact may be plotted on the vertical axis. Each risk identified represents a coordinate point in the two-dimensional space, and risks requiring further attention are found in the upper right, beyond a boundary defined as "risky." As with tables, this idea is most useful when all risks can be normalized to some meaningful single measure of impact, such as cost or time.

A variation on this concept plots risks on a pair of axes that represent estimated project cost and project schedule variances, representing each risk using a "bubble" that is sized proportionately with estimated probability instead of a single point. Since impact is higher for bubbles farther from the origin, several boundaries are defined for the graph. A diagonal close to the origin defines significant risk for the large (very likely) bubbles, and other diagonals farther out define significant exposure for the smaller bubbles. In Figure 7-4, there are several risks that are clearly significant. Risk F has the highest impact, and Risk E is, well, risky. Others would be selected on the basis of their positions relative to the boundaries of the graph.

PERT

Program Evaluation and Review Technique (PERT) methodology, discussed briefly in Chapter 4, has assumed a number of

Figure 7-4. Risk assessment graph.

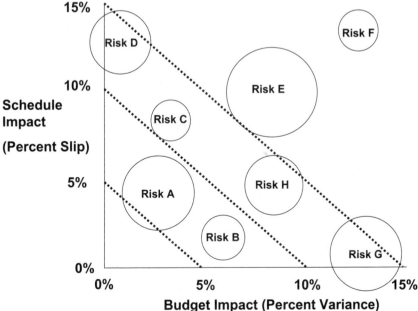

meanings. The most common, which actually has little to do with PERT methodology, is associated with the graphical network of activities used for project planning, often referred to as a "PERT chart." Similar networks are used for traditional PERT analysis, but PERT methodology goes beyond the deterministic point estimates of duration to which so-called PERT charts are generally limited. A second, slightly less common meaning for PERT relates to estimating, which is discussed in the context of schedule risk in Chapter 4. The original purpose of PERT was actually much broader than this.

PERT for Quantitative Activity Risk Analysis

The principal reason PERT was developed in the late 1950s was to help the U.S. military manage risk on large defense projects. PERT was used on the development of the Polaris missile systems, on the NASA manned space projects, including the Apollo moon missions, and on countless other government projects. The motivation behind all of this was the observation that the larger the program became, the more delayed it seemed to be and the higher the cost overruns became. PERT was developed to provide a better basis for setting expectations on these massive, expensive endeavors.

PERT is a specific example of quantitative risk analysis, and it is applied to both schedule (PERT Time) and budget (PERT Cost) exposures. PERT is based on statistical analysis of the project plan, using both estimates of likely outcomes and estimates of the *uncertainty* for these outcomes. PERT techniques may be used to analyze all project activities or only those activities that represent high perceived risk. In either case, PERT also provides data on overall project risk. This application of PERT methodology is covered in Chapter 9.

PERT Time was mentioned in Chapter 4, using three estimates for each activity—an optimistic estimate, a most likely estimate, and a pessimistic estimate—to calculate an "expected estimate." PERT Cost also uses three estimates to derive an expected activity cost, using essentially the same formula:

$$c_e = (c_o + 4c_m + c_p)/6, \text{ where}$$

c_e is the "expected" cost
c_o is the "optimistic" (lowest realistic) cost
c_m is the "most likely" cost
c_p is the "pessimistic" (highest realistic) cost

As with PERT Time, the standard deviation is estimated to be $(c_p - c_o)/6$. A distribution showing this graphically is in Figure 7-5.

Figure 7-5. Cost estimates for PERT analysis.

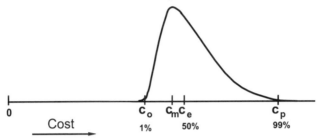

PERT Cost estimates are generally done in monetary units (e.g., pesos, rupees, euros), but they may also be evaluated in effort (person-hours, engineer-days) instead of, or in addition to, the financial estimates.

The earlier discussion of estimating focused on developing credible duration estimates, using pessimistic (or worst-case) estimates to adjust the baseline estimates used for planning. Whether or not the estimates in a preliminary project plan are derived this way, PERT analysis of activity-associated risks is an effective way to assess both cost and schedule impact.

Probability Density Functions

Risk impact discussed so far in this chapter has been based on single-point, deterministic estimates. PERT assumes a continuum of possibilities, defined by a statistical distribution (or, less commonly, by discrete data values that define a histogram). The commonly used formulas assume a Beta distribution, a bell-shaped probability density function that may be symmetric (equivalent to the Normal distribution) or one skewed to the right or left, depending on its parameters. Figure 7-5 is an example of a Beta distribution for activity cost. The formulas also assume that the optimistic and pessimistic estimates bound nearly all the possibilities, with about 98 percent (or in other variants 90 or 80 percent) of the distribution inside the range bounded by the optimistic and pessimistic estimates.

Other distributions may also be used for modeling potential outcomes. These include:

❏ Triangular (a linear rise from optimistic estimate to the most likely, followed by a linear decline to the pessimistic estimate, Figure 7-7)

❏ Normal (the Gaussian bell-shaped curve, with the most likely and expected values halfway between the extremes, Figure 7-8)

❐   Uniform (all values in the range are assumed equally likely, also with the most likely and expected values both at the midpoint, Figure 7-9)

There are also more exotic distributions.

Although dozens of statistical distributions and limitless histograms are possible, the precise *shape* of the distribution turns out to be relatively unimportant, because the shape of the distribution has only a minor effect on the two parameters that matter the most in risk analysis: the mean and the standard deviation of the distribution. Assessment of risk in PERT relies only on these two parameters, which tend to be roughly equivalent regardless of the distribution you chose. In addition, although it is theoretically possible to carry out a PERT analysis mathematically, it is impractical. PERT analysis is nearly always done by computer simulation (based on pseudorandom number generation and algorithms that approximate the chosen distributions) or by rough manual methods that estimate the results. The choice of a distribution type for each activity has little effect on quantitative assessment of risk for most projects.

For those who may be interested, some examples follow that show why the choice of a probability density function for the estimates is not terribly crucial. If you do not need convincing of this, just note that any approach that you find easy to work with can produce useful quantitative risk data, and skip ahead to the discussion of setting the estimate ranges for PERT.

PERT has generally assumed that the three estimates used are all located along a continuum. The shape of the distribution that these estimates define does not have a substantial effect on the resulting analysis, even if only two estimates are used, one "most likely" and a second "worst-case." These set the range and are sufficient to provide useful estimates of risk. Between the two limits, on the basis of the expected time (or cost) variance, PERT formulas generate results for risk assessment.

For Figure 7-6, the optimistic estimate is assumed identical to the most likely. If the plan estimates the activity duration as t_e, the calculated expected duration, schedule risk impact (assuming this activity is schedule-critical) is most of the difference between t_e and t_p.

When values are plugged into the formula to calculate the expected duration—for example, using fifteen days for t_o and t_m and twenty-one days for t_p—the PERT formula results in a t_e of sixteen days.

A similar result, mathematically much simpler, could be estimated using a triangular distribution, as in Figure 7-7.

Figure 7-6. Two-estimate PERT Beta distribution.

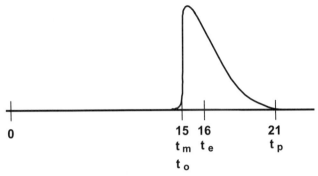

Figure 7-7. Triangular distribution.

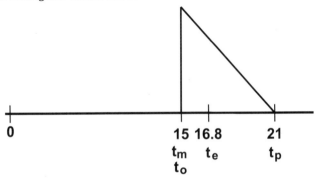

For a triangular distribution, the point at which the areas to the right and left are equal occurs slightly less than 30 percent of the way along the triangle's base. (It is 1 minus the square root of .5, or .292893, which is many more digits of accuracy than this analysis warrants. Even .3 is greater precision than necessary.) Using the same estimates as before for t_o, t_m, and t_p, the estimate for t_e is just under 16.8 days.

Symmetric distributions increase the expected estimate a little more. Using a Normal distribution (Figure 7-8) or a simple Uniform distribution (Figure 7-9) for the probability distribution that lies between the range limits results in an expected value for this example of eighteen days.

The PERT formula for the Beta distribution in Figure 7-5 estimates sixteen days, and all the other examples are a bit higher. For a quantitative risk assessment, some value above the mean is selected to represent impact (the "90 percent" point is common). Although these points are also not identical for the various distributions, they all are quite close together, near the upper (t_p) estimate. Risk assessment is related to the *variance* for the chosen

Figure 7-8. Normal distribution.

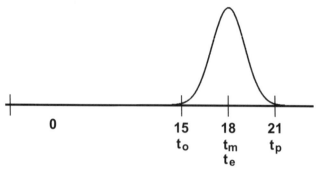

Figure 7-9. Uniform distribution.

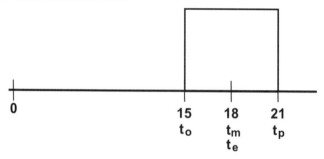

distribution, which for these examples will all be similar because, in each case, the range is the same.

If t_p is twenty-one days, the "90 percent" point for all of these distributions is about twenty days (rounded off to the nearest whole day). Whichever distribution might be selected, there is only a "moderate" risk (roughly 10 percent of the time) that the sixteen-day expected duration will be four or more days late. There are many PERT tools and techniques capable of calculating all of this with very high precision, displaying many (seemingly) significant digits in the results. Considering the precision and expected accuracy of the input data, though, the results are at best accurate only to the nearest whole day. Arguing over the "best" distribution to use and endlessly fretting over how to proceed are not a good investment of your time. Almost any reasonable choice of distribution will result in comparable and useful results for risk analysis, so use the choice that is easiest for you to implement.

At the project level, where PERT data for all the activities is combined, the distributions chosen for each activity become even more irrelevant. The larger the project, the more the overall analysis for project cost and duration tends to approximate a Normal bell-shaped curve (more on this in Chapter 9).

Setting Ranges for PERT

What *does* matter a great deal for risk assessment is the range specified for the estimates. Setting the range to be too narrow (which is a common bias) materially diminishes the quantitative perception of risk. Risk, assessed using PERT analysis, is based on the total expected variation in possible outcomes, and this varies directly with the size of the estimate range.

Arriving at credible upper and lower limits for cost and duration estimates is usually the most difficult aspect of PERT. One way to develop these data is through further analysis of potential root causes for each activity that has substantial perceived risk. As is discussed in Chapter 4, the most powerful tool for estimating the upper limit of an activity duration is to seek worst-case scenarios and be as realistic as possible concerning the consequences of potential problems. It is easy to minimize or overlook the potential impact of risk scenarios, particularly when planning is not thorough.

When there is sufficient historical information available, the limits (and possibly even the shape) of the distribution may be inferred from the data population. Discussions and interviews with experts, project stakeholders, and contributors may also provide information that will be useful in setting credible range boundaries.

In any event, one quantitative assessment of risk impact for each activity is determined using the difference between the expected and the pessimistic (or worst-case) PERT estimates. There is more about using PERT methodology for project-level risk assessment in Chapter 9.

DECISION TREES

Decision trees may also be used to assess risks when only a small number of options or potential outcomes are possible. Decision analysis for risks is a quantitative version of the project assumption testing (discussed earlier with other qualitative assessment techniques). Decision trees are generally used to evaluate several options prior to selecting one of them to execute. The concept is applied to risk analysis in a project by using the weights and estimates to ascertain potential impact for specific alternatives.

Whenever there are points in the project where several options are possible, each can be planned and assigned a probability (the sum for all options totaling 100 percent). As with PERT, an "expected" estimate for either duration or cost may be derived by weighting the estimates for each option and summing these figures to get a "blended" result. Using the data in Figure 7-10, a project

Figure 7-10. Decision tree for duration.

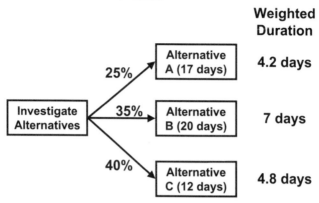

Weighted Duration

25% → Alternative A (17 days) — **4.2 days**

35% → Alternative B (20 days) — **7 days**

40% → Alternative C (12 days) — **4.8 days**

"Expected" Duration = 16 days

plan containing a generic activity (that could be any of the three options) with an estimate of sixteen days would result in a more realistic plan than simply using the twelve-day estimate in the "most likely" option. The schedule exposure of the risk situation here may be estimated by noting the maximum adverse variance (an additional four days, if the activity is schedule-critical) and associating this with an expected probability of 35 percent.

Decision analysis may also be used to guide project choices based on costs. It provides information on the options that offer the lowest expected cost, as well as the lowest expected cost variance. Whenever there are several ways to proceed in a project—for example, by either upgrading existing equipment or purchasing new hardware—decision analysis can be effective in determining the choice that minimizes project risks. The analysis of costs in Figure 7-11 argues for replacement to minimize cost variance (none, instead of the $20,000 to $120,000 associated with upgrade) and for upgrade to minimize the *expected* cost. As is usual on projects, there is a trade-off between minimizing project parameters and minimizing risk—you must decide which is more important and balance the decisions with your eyes open.

SIMULATION AND MODELING

Decision trees are useful for situations where you have discrete estimates. In more complex cases, options may be modeled or simulated using Monte Carlo or other computer techniques. If the range of possibilities for an activity's duration or cost is assumed to be a statistical distribution, the standard deviation (or

Figure 7-11. Decision tree for cost.

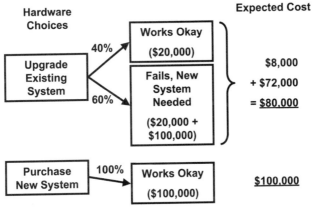

variance) of the distribution is a measure of risk. The larger the range selected for the distribution, the higher the risk for that activity. For single activities, modeling with a computer is rarely necessary, but when several activities (or the project as a whole) are considered together, computer-based simulations are useful and effective. Both software tools and manual approximations for this are key topics in Chapter 9.

Key Ideas for Activity Risk Analysis

❏ Assess probability and impact for each project risk.
❏ Use qualitative risk analysis to prioritize risks.
❏ Apply quantitative risk analysis techniques to significant risks.
❏ If you use PERT, keep it simple.

Panama Canal: Risks (1906–1914)

As with any project of the canal's size and duration, risks were everywhere. On the basis of assessment of cost and probability, the most severe were diseases, mud slides, the constant use of explosives, and the technical challenges of constructing the locks.

Diseases were less of a problem on the U.S. project, but health remained a concern. Both of the first two managers cited tropical disease among their reasons for resigning from the project. Life in the tropics in the early 1900s was neither comfortable nor safe. The enormous death toll from the earlier project made this exposure a top priority.

Mud slides were common during both the French and the U.S. projects, as the soil of Panama is not stable, and earthquakes made things worse. Whenever the sloping sides of the cut collapsed, there was danger to the working crews and potential serious damage to the digging and railroad equipment. In addition to this, it was demoralizing to face the repair and rework following each slide, and the predicted additional effort required to excavate repeatedly in the same location multiplied the cost of construction. This risk had very high impact to both schedule and budget; despite precautions, major setbacks were frequent.

Explosives were in use everywhere. In the Culebra Cut, massive boulders were common, and workers set off dynamite charges to reduce them to movable pieces. The planned transit for ships through the manmade lakes was a rain forest filled with large, old trees, and these, too, had to be removed with explosives. In the tropics especially, the dynamite of that era was not very stable. It exploded in storage, in transit to the work sites, while being set in place for use, and in many other unintended situations. The probability of premature detonation was high, and the risk to human life was extreme.

Beyond these daunting risks, the largest technical challenge on the project was the locks. They were gigantic mechanisms, among the largest and most complex construction ever attempted. Although locks had been used on canals for a very long time, virtually all of them had been built for smaller boats navigating freshwater rivers and lakes. Locks had never before been constructed for large ocean-going ships. (The canal at Suez has no locks; as with the original plan for Panama, it is entirely at sea level.) The doors for the locks were to be huge and, therefore, very heavy. The volume of water held by the locks when filled was so great that the pressure on the doors would be immense, and the precision required for the seams where the doors closed to hold in the water was also unprecedented for manmade objects so large. The locks would be enormous boxes with sides and bottoms formed of concrete, which also was a challenge, particularly in an earthquake zone. For all this, the biggest technological hurdle was the requirement that all operations be *electric*. Because earlier canals were much smaller, usually the lock doors were cranked open and shut and the boats were pulled in and out by animals. (To this day, the trains used to guide ships into and out of the locks at Panama are called "electric mules.") The design, implementation, and control of a canal using the new technology of electric power—and the hydroelectric installations required to supply enough electricity—all involved emerging, poorly understood technology. Without the locks, the canal would be useless, and the risks associated with resolving all of these technical problems were large.

These severe risks were but a few of the many challenges planners faced on the canal project, but each was singled out for substantial continuing attention. Their responses are summarized at the end of the next chapter, in which tactics for dealing with risk are covered.

CHAPTER 8

MANAGING ACTIVITY RISKS

"Statistics are no substitute for judgment."

—HENRY CLAY, U.S. Senator

Risk assessment provides a prioritized list of risks. Using the list, it becomes clear just how much trouble your project is in. An accumulation of significant scope risks may indicate that your project is *literally* impossible. Too many schedule or resource risks may indicate that your project is unlikely to complete within its constraints. Project risk management is a potent tool for transforming a seemingly impossible project into a merely challenging one.

Managing risk begins with your prioritized list of significant risks, but these details and statistics are just the starting point; you must then add your judgment and decide how to proceed. For each of the significant risks, you need to seek root causes to determine your best management strategy. For risks where the project team has influence over the root cause, you can develop and analyze ideas to reduce or eliminate the risk and then modify the project plans to incorporate these ideas wherever it is feasible. For risks that cannot be avoided or that remain significant, you can then develop contingency plans for recovery should the risk occur.

Most of the content of this chapter falls into the "Risk Response Planning" portion of the Planning Processes in the *PMBOK® Guide,* but it also draws from other Planning Processes. The principal concepts this chapter covers include:

❐ Root cause analysis
❐ Risk categorization

❒ Avoidance

❒ Mitigation

❒ Transfer

❒ Contingency planning

❒ Passive acceptance

Root Cause Analysis

What, if anything, can be done about a risk depends a great deal on its causes. For each identified risk that is assessed as significant, you must determine the source and type of risk that it represents.

The process for cause-and-effect analysis is not a difficult one. For risk analysis, it begins with the listed risks and their descriptions. Effective root cause analysis depends on a consistent and thorough understanding of the project's risks, so it helps to start by reviewing the list with the project contributors so that they can describe each risk in their own words.

The next step is to brainstorm possible sources for the risk. Any brainstorming process will be effective so long as it is successful in determining conditions or events that may lead to the risk. You can begin with major cause categories (such as scope, schedule, or resource) or simply think about specific factors that may lead to the risk. However you begin the analysis, complete it by organizing the information into categories of root cause. As in any brainstorming, it is best to focus on the quantity of ideas, not the quality. Even an idea that seems very unlikely may trigger an important thought for someone participating in the analysis. Some redundancy between the categories is common, and removing it is a matter of personal choice.

Cause-and-effect analysis using fishbone diagrams, so called because of their appearance, was popularized by the Japanese quality movement guru Dr. Kaoru Ishikawa (they are also sometimes called Ishikawa diagrams). These diagrams may be used to display root causes of risk visually, allowing deeper understanding of the source and likelihood of potential problems. Once you have organized the ideas into a branching diagram similar to the one in Figure 8-1, review it to see whether that perspective on the risk stimulates any additional thinking. Note that the causes may themselves have multiple potential sources. Continue the root cause analysis process for each significant risk in the project.

Figure 8-1. Fishbone diagram example.

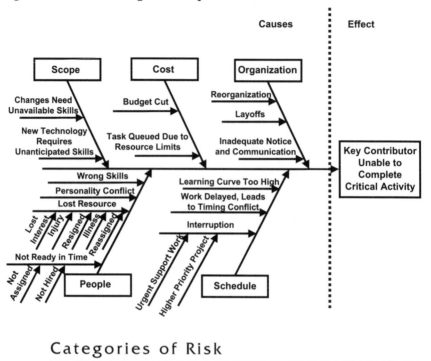

Categories of Risk

In dealing with risk, there are really only two rather simple options. In an advertisement some years ago, the options were demonstrated pictorially using an egg. On the left side of the picture was a falling egg, headed for a pillow held in a person's hand. On the right side was a fallen egg, broken and oozing over the flat, hard surface it had smashed into, with a second hand swooping in holding a paper towel. The left side was titled "Prevention" and the right side "Recovery." Management of risk in projects always involves these tactics—prevention to deal with causes, and recovery to deal with effects.

The three categories of project risk are *controllable known* risks, *uncontrollable known* risks, and *unknown* risks. All the significant listed project risks are known risks and are either under your control or not. For each of these risks it is possible to plan for response, at least in theory, and that is the topic of this chapter. The third category, unknown risks, is hidden, so specific planning is not generally of much use. The best method for managing unknown risk involves setting project reserves, in schedule or budget (or both), on the basis of the measured consequences of unanticipated problems on similar past projects. Keeping track of specific past problems also converts your past unknown risks into known risks. Managing unknown project risk is addressed in more detail in Chapter 10.

Root cause analysis not only makes known project risks more understandable but also shows you how to manage each risk. Depending on the root cause or causes, you can determine whether the risk arises from factors you can control and may therefore be preventable or whether it is due to uncontrollable causes. When the causes are out of your control, risk can only be managed through recovery. These strategies are summarized in Figure 8-2.

Known controllable risks are at least partially under the control of the project team. Risks such as the use of a new technology, small increases in complexity or performance of a deliverable, or pressure to establish aggressive deadlines are examples of this. Working from an understanding of the root causes for these problems, you may be able to modify project plans to avoid or minimize the risk.

For known uncontrollable risks, the project team has essentially no influence on the source of the risk. Loss of key project staff members, business reorganizations, and external project factors such as weather are examples. For these problems, the best tactic is to deal with effects after the risk occurs, recovering with a contingency plan you prepared in advance.

It is common for a root cause analysis to uncover both some causes that you can control and some that you cannot, for the same risk. Responding to risks with several possible sources may require both replanning and preparation for recovery.

While the dichotomy between *controllable* and *uncontrollable* may seem simple, it often is not. The perceived root causes of a risk vary depending on the description of the risk. To take the example of the fishbone diagram in Figure 8-1, many of the root causes seem out of the control of the project team, as the risk is described as the loss of a particular person. If the exposure were redefined to be the loss of a particular skill set, which is probably more accurate, then the root causes would shift to ones that the project might influence through cross-training, negotiating for additional staff, or other actions.

Figure 8-2. Risk management strategies.

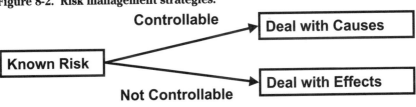

Even when a risk seems to be uncontrollable, the venerable idea from quality analysis of "Ask why five times" may open up the perspective on the risk and reveal additional options for response. If weather, earthquakes, or other natural disasters are listed as risks to particular activities, probe deeper into the situation to ask why and how that particular problem has an impact on the project. The risk may be a consequence of a project assumption or a choice made in planning that could be changed, resulting in a better, less problematic project. Shifting the time, venue, infrastructure, or other parameters of risky activities may remove uncontrollable risks from your project, or at least diminish their impact.

Risk Response Planning

Two basic options are available for risk management: dealing with *causes* and dealing with *effects*. There are, however, a number of variations on both of these themes. Dealing with causes involves risk prevention—either eliminating the risk (avoidance) or lowering its probability or potential impact (mitigation). Avoidance of risks means changing the project plan or approach to remove the root cause of the risk from your project. One way to avoid falling off a cliff is to stay away from cliffs. Mitigating actions rarely remove a risk completely, but they do serve to reduce it. Some mitigating actions reduce the probability of a risk event, such as checking the air pressure in your automobile tires before a long trip. Other mitigations reduce the risk impact, such as wearing a seat belt to minimize injury. Neither of these actions prevents the problem, but they do serve to reduce the overall risk by lowering the "loss" or the "likelihood."

Similarly, some risks are transferred to others. Many kinds of financial risks are transferred to insurance companies; you may purchase coverage that will compensate your losses in the event of a casualty that is covered by the policy. Again, this does not remove the risk, but it does reduce the financial impact should the risk occur. Transfer of risk deals with causes if the impact of the risk is primarily financial, but in most cases it is used to deal with risk effects—aiding in the recovery.

Dealing with the effect of a risk may be done either in advance (contingency planning) or after the fact (passive acceptance). Some risks are too minor or too expensive to consider preventing. For minor risks, acceptance may be appropriate; simply decide to deal with the consequences of the problem if and when it occurs. For more serious problems where avoidance, mitigation, and transfer are ineffective, impractical, or impossible, contingency planning is the best option.

For some risks, one of these ideas will be sufficient; for others, it may be necessary to use several.

TIME LINE FOR KNOWN RISKS

As was discussed briefly in Chapter 6, each activity risk has a signal, perhaps more than one, indicating that the risk has crossed over from a possibility to a certainty. This signal, or trigger event, may be in advance of the risk or coincident with it. It may be visible to everyone involved in the project, or it may be subtle and hidden. For each risk, strive to define a trigger event that provides as much advance notification of the problem as possible. Consider this risk: "A key project team member quits." One possible trigger event might be the submission of a resignation letter. This is an obvious trigger, but it is a late one. There are earlier triggers to watch for, such as a drop in motivation, erratic attendance, frequent "personal" telephone calls, or even an uncharacteristic improvement in grooming and dress. These triggers are not foolproof, and they require more attention and effort to monitor, but they may also foreshadow other problems even if the staff member does not intend to leave.

In addition to one or more trigger events, identify the portions of the project plan where the risk is most probable, being as precise as possible. For some risks there may be a single exposure related to one specific activity; more general risks (such as loss of key staff members) may occur throughout the project.

Risk management decisions and plans are made in advance of the trigger event, and they include all actions related to avoidance, mitigation, or transfer, as well as preparation for any contingent actions.

Risk management responses that relate to recovery fall on the project timeline after the risk trigger but are only used if necessary. For each significant risk that you cannot remove from the project, assign an owner to monitor for the trigger event and to be responsible for implementing the contingency plan or otherwise working toward recovery. The risk management time line is summarized in Figure 8-3.

DEALING WITH RISK CAUSES

After each risk is categorized and you have identified those risks for which the project team can influence some or all of the causes, you are ready to begin developing response possibilities

Figure 8-3. Risk management timeline.

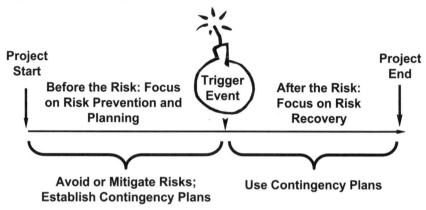

for prevention, including avoidance, mitigation, and transfer. Analyze all the options you and your team develop, examining both the cost of the idea and its potential benefits. If good, cost-effective ideas are proposed, the best of them are candidates for inclusion in your draft project plan. Prevention ideas must earn their way into the project plan. Even excellent ideas that completely remove a risk should be bypassed if their overall cost exceeds the expected "loss times likelihood" of the risk.

The final process step is to integrate all accepted risk prevention ideas into your preliminary project plan and review the plan for new risks or unintended consequences as a result of the changes.

Generating Ideas for Each Risk

There are many ways to develop risk responses. A common method is brainstorming with the project team. This is widely used in planning where it is advantageous to start with a number of possible choices. It is also useful to discuss risks with peers and others who may have relevant experiences, and it may be worthwhile to consult experts and specialists for types of risks that you are not familiar with.

Few known risks are completely novel, so it is quite possible that many of the risks you face have been addressed on earlier projects. A quick review of project retrospective analyses, final reports, "lessons learned," and other archived materials may provide information on what others did in response to similar risk situations they encountered. In addition to finding things that did not work and that are worth avoiding, you may find useful ideas that effectively deal with the risks you need to manage.

There are also many ideas available in the public domain, in papers, books, articles, and on the Web. References on project management, particularly those that are tailored to projects similar to yours, are filled with advice, and some of it may be very valuable. Life cycles and project management methodologies also provide direction and useful ideas for risk prevention and avoidance.

A number of possible preventive actions follow in the next several pages, including tactics for risk avoidance, mitigation, and transfer. These may be useful in seeding a brainstorming exercise or in planning for a specific response. The ideas listed here include some that may be appropriate only for particular kinds of technical projects, but many are useful for any sort of work.

Strategies for Avoiding Risks

Risk avoidance is the most effective way to deal with the causes of risks, because it obliterates them. Unfortunately, avoidance is not possible for all project risks, because many risks are tightly coupled with the requirements of technical projects. Avoiding risks in your project requires you to reconsider choices and decisions you made in defining and planning your project. Most of Chapters 3, 4, and 5 concerned use of project planning processes to identify risks. While some of the risks you discovered may be unavoidable consequences of your project, a review of the current state of your plan may turn up opportunities to replan the work in ways that remove specific serious risks. Tactics for avoiding scope risks suggested by the material in Chapter 3 include:

- ❑ Identify the minimum acceptable deliverable; avoid overdesign.

- ❑ Negotiate and clearly document all interface deliverables expected from other projects.

- ❑ Avoid untried, unfamiliar, or "bleeding edge" technology whenever practical.

- ❑ Plan to design using standard, modular, or better-understood methods. Look for ways to achieve project specifications using older, well-established technologies.

- ❑ Buy instead of make.

- ❑ Avoid "not invented here" thinking; be willing to leverage work done by others.

Many of your schedule risks are consequences of decisions you made in preparing your preliminary schedule. You may be able to remove sources of schedule risk using ideas covered in Chapter 4:

- ❒ Reduce the number of critical paths.
- ❒ Modify the work to have fewer activity dependencies.
- ❒ Schedule the highest uncertainty activities as early as possible.
- ❒ Avoid having the same staff members work on two successive or concurrent critical (or near-critical) activities.
- ❒ Decompose lengthy activities further.
- ❒ Reschedule work to provide greater flexibility.

Resource risks may also be a consequence of choices you made in resource planning. Explore opportunities to avoid these risks using the concepts of Chapter 5:

- ❒ Obtain names for all required project roles.
- ❒ Get explicit availability commitments from all project staff (and from their managers).
- ❒ Work to limit commitments by project staff to other projects, maintenance and support work, and other time conflicts. Explicitly document all that remain.
- ❒ Modify plans to reduce the load on fully loaded or overcommitted resources.
- ❒ Use the best people available for the most critical activities.
- ❒ Educate team members to use more efficient or faster methods, and do it early in the project.
- ❒ Use mentoring to build teamwork and establish redundancy for critical skills
- ❒ Upgrade or replace older equipment to make work more efficient, and do it in the beginning of the project.
- ❒ Automate manual work when possible.
- ❒ Locate and gain access to experts to cover all skill areas not available on the project team.
- ❒ Minimize dependence on a single individual or other resource for project work.
- ❒ When you use outside services, use the same suppliers that you (or others that you trust) have used successfully in the past.

❏ Establish contract terms with all suppliers that are consistent with project objectives.

Avoidance tactics are not limited to these ideas by any means. Anything that you can realistically do to eliminate the root cause of a risk has potential for risk avoidance.

General Risk Mitigation Strategies

While avoidance is very effective in managing risk, it can never deal with all your significant project risks; at least some of them are intrinsic to your project. Mitigation strategies that reduce the probability or impact of a potential problem are the next choice for risk management. Some generic ideas for risk mitigation include:

❏ Good communication

❏ Use of specialists *and* generalists

❏ Strong sponsorship

❏ Continuing user involvement

❏ Clear decision priorities

One of the least expensive and strongest preventive actions a project leader can take is to communicate more—and more effectively. Risks and risk consequences that are visible always affect the way that people work. If all the team members are aware how painful the project will become following a risk, they are likely to proceed, to the best of their ability, to work in ways that minimize the risk. You should discuss risks regularly. Post risk lists on walls, on Web sites, and in other places people will see them. Include risk status information in status reporting. In addition to specific risk data, also establish unambiguous project documentation that is easily accessible by the whole team. Communication can significantly reduce risk probabilities. Communicate. Communicate. Communicate.

Another broad strategy for managing risk relates to project staffing. Difficult projects benefit from having a mix of specialists and generalists. Specialists are essential on technical projects because no one can know everything, and the specialist can generally complete assigned work in his or her specialty much faster than a generalist. However, a project team composed *only* of specialists is not very robust and tends to run into frequent trouble. The reason is that project planning on specialist-heavy projects is often intense and detailed for work in the specialists' areas and remarkably sketchy for other work. Also, such teams often lack broad problem-solving skills. Generalists on a project (nearly always including the project leader) are needed to fill in the gaps and ensure that as much of the project work as possible is initially made visible. Generalists are also best at finding and solving cross-disciplinary problems. As the head generalist, the project manager should always reserve at least a small percentage of his or her time for problem solving, helping out on troubled activities, and general fire-fighting. Even if the project leader has a solid grasp of all the technical project issues, it is useful to have other generalists on the team in case several things on the project go wrong at the same time. Generalists can reduce the time to solution for problems of all kinds and reduce schedule impact.

Managing project risk is always easier with friends in high places. Establish and work to sustain strong sponsorship for your project. While strong sponsorship does not ensure a risk-free project, weak (or no) upper-level sponsorship is a significant source of risk. Form a good working relationship with the project sponsor(s), and work to understand their expectations for project information. Reinforce the importance and value of the project regularly, and don't let sponsors forget about you. Plan to update your management frequently on project progress and challenges, and involve management early in problems and escalations that require more authority than the project team has. Validate project objectives with sponsors and customers, and work to set realistic expectations. Using your budget and staffing plans, get commitments for adequate funding and project talent. Strong sponsorship reduces timing impact of risks and reduces the probability of many kinds of resource risk.

Project risk also increases, particularly on lengthy projects, whenever the project team is disconnected from the ultimate customers for the deliverable. Establish and maintain contact with the end users or with people who can represent them. Seek strong user buy-in, and work with the customer to define the project scope and to validate all acceptance and testing criteria. Establish *measurable* criteria, and determine what will be required for the users to deem the project a success. Identify the individual or individuals who will have the final word on this and keep in contact with them. The probability of scope risk and the likelihood of late project schedule difficulties are both reduced by meaningful user involvement.

A final general strategy for lowering project risk is to set clear decision priorities for the project. Validate the priorities with both the sponsors and the end users, and ensure that the project priorities are well known to the project team. Base project decisions on the priorities, and know the impact of failing to meet each priority established for the project. This not only helps manage scope risks but also permits quick decisions within the project that minimize schedule impacts.

Mitigation Strategies for Scope and Technical Risks

Mitigation of scope risks involve shifts in approach and potential changes to the project objective. Ideas for mitigating scope risks include:

- ❏ Explicitly specify project scope and all intermediate deliverables, in measurable, unambiguous terms, including what *is not* in the deliverable. Eliminate "wants" early—make them part of scope or drop them.

- ❏ Gain acceptance for and use a clear and consistent specification change management process.

- ❏ Build models, prototypes, and simulations.

- ❏ Test with users, early and often.

- ❏ Deal with scope risks promptly.

- ❏ Obtain funding for any required outside services.

- ❏ Translate, competently, all project documents into relevant languages.

- ❏ Minimize external dependency risks.

- ❏ Consider the impact of external and environmental problems.

- ❏ Keep all plans and documents current.

More on each of these ideas follows.

The most significant scope risks in the PERIL database are due to changes. Minimizing change risk involves the first two tactics—scope definition and change management. Scope definition, discussed in detail in Chapter 3, increases risk both when it is incomplete and when it is too inclusive.

Scope risk is high for projects with inadequate specifications. While it is true that thorough, clear definition of the deliverable is often difficult on technical projects, failure to define the results adequately leads to even greater difficulty. For any project to be ultimately successful, every specification must eventually be uncovered and met. If the project is allowed to meander toward this end, dragging along lists of options and working with unstable assumptions, changes will be frequent, expensive, and painful. Excessive change is an inevitable price of inadequate scope definition. Since project scope determines the work breakdown, inadequate scope definition results in unidentified activities, causing unpredictable impact to project timing, effort, and cost.

Closely inspect the list of features to be included to verify that all the requested requirements are in fact necessary. The Pareto principle can be applied effectively to most technical projects, defining an alternate scope that provides much, if not nearly all, of the project's value by implementing only the most essential capabilities. Such a project will be smaller, shorter, and less costly and represents lower risk. It is often possible to deliver base functionality and then extend it in a follow-on project at a lower total cost than that for a single project with more comprehensive scope. Viewing project scope as a continuum that may be expanded over time using a succession of less risky projects is a very effective tool for minimizing scope risk on technical projects. Evolutionary software development methodologies employ this principle to both manage scope risk and deliver useful functionality to users as quickly as possible.

Setting project scope more aggressively than is necessary is also a common source of scope risk. The "blot out the sun" technical project, which includes every possible feature, bell, whistle, and capability that seems possible (plus some that will be added later when they occur to the project team), is not only excessively long and expensive but also extremely difficult to manage. One common method used for the all-inclusive project is the concept of "musts" and "wants." The project team lists the absolute requirements as "musts" and also creates a list of desirable other inclusions as "wants." While this is appropriate during initial planning, maintaining the list of options throughout the project guarantees many project scope changes. As preliminary planning concludes and the time to commit to your project draws near, you need to be brutal. The list of features that it would be nice to have must shrink. Each listed "want" must either be added to project scope as a firm requirement or dropped. Any optional features carried into development will require effort, even early in the project, that would be better spent doing more essential project work. Work to freeze project scope using lists of what "is" and what "is not" in the project, instead of musts and wants. Scope definition adds all the "musts" to the "is" list and commits to their delivery. All "wants" are either accepted as requirements and added to the "is" list or are demoted to the "is not" list and are excluded from the project scope. A process that defines scope by freezing what "is" and what "is not" in the project deliverable at the conclusion of initial planning is a key tactic for mitigating this sort of change risk.

The second necessary tactic for reducing change risk is to uniformly apply an effective process for managing *all* changes to project scope. To manage risks on large, complex projects, the process is generally very formal, using forms, committees, and extensive written reporting. For technical projects done under contract, risk management also requires that the process be described in detail in the contract signed by the two parties. On smaller projects, even if it is less formal, there still must be uniform treatment of all proposed changes, considering both their benefits and their expected costs. For your project, adopt a process that rejects all changes that fail the cost-justification test. Also, ensure that the process provisionally rejects any change that impacts the project's overall objective, even when the change is proposed by the project's sponsor or customer. Such changes represent a new project and are acceptable only if all stakeholders agree to the shifts in the project, including any increases in cost and timing. A significant increase in scope with no adjustment in the resources or deadline nearly always represents unacceptably high risk. It is not enough to *have* a change management process; mitigating scope risks requires its disciplined *use*.

Scope risks are often hard to evaluate at the beginning of technical projects. One way to gain better insight is to schedule work during planning to examine feasibility and functionality questions as early as possible. Use prototypes, simulations, and models to evaluate concepts with users. Schedule early tests and investigations to verify whether untried technologies are likely to work. Plan for walkthroughs and scenario discussions in order to spread awareness and to identify potential problems and defects early enough to correct them. Also consider scale risks. Even if there are no problems during small-scale, limited tests, scope risks may still remain that will be visible only during full-scale production. Plan for at least some rudimentary tests of functionality in full-scale operation as early in the project as is practical. Schedule work to uncover issues and problems near the beginning of the project, and be prepared to make changes or to abandon the project based on what you learn.

While it is risky to defer difficult or unknown activities until late in the project, it may be impractical to begin with them. In order to get started, you may need to complete some simpler activities first and then move on to more complicated activities as you build expertise. In any case, however, develop your plans to schedule the more risk-prone activities as early in your project as you can.

Lack of skills on the project team also increases scope risk, so define exactly how you intend to acquire all needed expertise. If you intend to use outside consultants, plan to spend both time and effort in their selection, and ensure that the necessary funding to pay for them is in the project budget. If you need to develop new skills on the project team, identify the individuals involved and plan so that each contributor is trained, in advance, in all the needed competencies. If the project will use new tools or equipment, schedule installation and complete any needed training as early in the project as possible.

Scope problems also arise from faulty communications. If the project depends on a distributed team that speaks several languages, identify all the languages needed for project definition and planning documents, and plan for their translation and distribution. Confusion arising from project requirements that are misinterpreted or poorly translated can be expensive and very damaging, so verify that the project information has been clearly understood in discussions, using interpreters if necessary. It is also critical to provide written follow-up after meetings and telephone discussions.

Scope often depends on the quality and timely delivery of things the project receives from others. Mitigating these risks requires clear, carefully constructed specifications to minimize the possibility that the things that you get are consistent with the request but are inappropriate for the project's intended use. If you have little experience with a provider, it may be prudent to find and use a second source in addition to the first, even though this can increase the cost. A second source can lower the probability of the project getting stuck due to delivery of a failed component, a deliverable that has performance or quality problems, or dependence on "vaporware." The cost of a redundant source may be very small compared to the cost of a delayed project.

External factors also lead to scope risks. Natural disasters such as floods, earthquakes, and storms, as well as not-so-natural disasters like computer viruses, may cause loss of critical information, software, or necessary components. While there is no way to prevent the risks, provision for some redundancy, adequate frequent backups of computer systems, and reduced dependency on one particular location can minimize the impact of this sort of risk.

Finally, managing scope risk also requires tracking the initial definition with any and all changes approved during the project. You can significantly lower scope risk by adopting a process that tightly couples all accepted changes to the planning process, as well as making the consequences of scope decisions visible throughout the project.

Mitigation Strategies for Schedule Risks

Tactics for mitigating schedule risks include making additional investments in planning and revising your project approach. Some ideas to consider include:

- Use "expected" estimates when worst cases are significant.
- Schedule highest-priority work early.
- Schedule proactive notifications.
- If you must use new technology, explore how you *could* use older methods.
- Use parallel, redundant development.
- Send shipments early.
- Be conservative in estimates for training and new hardware.
- Break projects with large staffs into parallel efforts.
- Partition long projects into a sequence of shorter ones.
- Schedule project reviews.
- Reschedule work coincident with known holidays and other time conflicts.
- Track progress with rigor and discipline.

More detail on each of these ideas follows.

The riskiest activities in the project tend to be the ones that have very significant worst-case estimates. For any activity where the most-likely estimate is a lot lower than what could plausibly occur, calculate an "expected" duration using the PERT formula. Use these estimates in project planning to provide some reserve for particularly risky work and to reduce the schedule impact.

Project risk is lower when you schedule activities related to the highest priorities for the project as early as possible, moving activities of lower priority later in the project. For each scheduled activity, review the deliverables, and specify how and when each will be used. Wherever possible, schedule the work so that there is a time buffer between when each deliverable is complete and the start of the activities that require them. If there are any activities that produce deliverables that seem to be unnecessary, either validate their requirement with project stakeholders or remove the work from the project plan.

Many schedule risks are caused by delays that may be avoided through more proactive communication. Whenever decisions are needed, plan to remind the decision makers at least a week in advance and get commitment for a swift turnaround. If specialized equipment or access to limited services will be required, put an activity in the plan to review your needs with the people involved somewhat before the scheduled work. If scarce equipment for some kinds of project work is a chronic problem, propose adding capacity to lower the risk on your project, as well as for all other parallel work. The preventive maintenance schedules for production systems are generally determined well in advance. Inquiring during project planning about availability of needed services and then synchronizing plans with the maintenance schedules can reduce conflicts and delays.

New things—technology, hardware, systems, or software—are very common sources of delay. Manage risk by seeking alternatives using older, known capabilities unless using the new technology is an absolute project requirement. A "lower-tech" alternative may in some cases be a better choice for the project anyway, or it could serve as a standby option to be used if necessary in case an emerging technology proves not to be quite ready. Identify what you would need to do or change in the project to complete your work without the newer technology; this information can provide both pressure and motivation to the project team to do what is necessary to get the new technology to work.

One cause of significant delay is developing a specific design and then sending it out to be built or created before it can be tested. It may take weeks to get the tangible result of the design back, and if it has problems the entire cycle must be repeated, doubling the duration (or worse—it may not work the second time, either). In areas such as chip design, more than one chip will be made on each wafer, anyway, and it might be useful to design a number of slightly different versions that can all be fabricated at the same time. Most of the chips will be of the primary design, but other variations created at the same time can also be tested, thus increasing the chances of having a component that can be used to continue with project work. There are other cases where slightly different versions may be created in parallel, such as printed circuit boards, mechanical assemblies, and other newly designed hardware. While this could increase the project cost, protecting the project schedule is often a much higher priority. Varying the parameters of a design and evaluating the results is also useful for quickly understanding the principles involved. The deliverables created in current and future projects will benefit from this deeper understanding.

Delays due to shipping problems are significant on many projects and in many cases can be avoided simply by ordering or shipping items earlier in the project. Just because it is generally thought to take a week to ship a piece of equipment from San Jose, California, to Bangalore, India, does not mean you should wait until a week before it is needed in India to ship it. There are only two ways to get something done sooner—work faster or start earlier. With shipping, expediting may not always be effective, so it is prudent planning to request and send things that require physical transport well ahead of the need, particularly when it involves complex paperwork and international customs regulations.

Similarly, delay may result from the need to have new equipment or new skills for the project. The time necessary to get new equipment installed and running or to master new skills may prove longer than you think. If you underestimate how long it will take, project work that depends on the new hardware or skills could have to wait. Planning proactively for these project requirements removes many risks of this sort from your project (and, as mentioned earlier, it also lowers the chances that you might lose, or never get, the required funding). Estimate these activities conservatively, and schedule installations, upgrades, and training as early in your project as practical—well before they are needed.

Large projects are intrinsically risky. If a project requires more than twenty full-time staff members, explore the possibility of partitioning it into smaller projects responsible for subsystems, modules, or components that can be developed in parallel. However, when you decompose a large program into autonomous smaller projects, be sure to clearly define all interfaces between them both in terms of specifications required and timing. While the independent projects will be easier to manage and *less* risky, the overall program could be prone to late integration problems without adequate systems-level planning and strong interface controls.

Long projects are also risky. Work to break projects longer than a year into phases that produce measurable outputs. A series of evolutionary projects of short duration create value sooner than a more ambitious longer project, and the shorter projects are more likely to fall within a reasonable planning horizon of six months or less. This is one of the most important aspects of evolutionary software development, such as extreme programming or other agile methodologies. Mandating delivery of intermediate results sooner is an effective way to lower both schedule and scope risk.

If a lengthy project must be undertaken as a whole, you can adopt a "rolling-wave" planning philosophy, planning the current and next phase in detail whenever you transition from one phase to the next and making adjustments to the project as you proceed to reflect what has been learned in the previous phase. Adjustments at phase transition include changes to plans for future phases, changes to the project deliverable, shifts in project staffing, and changes to other parameters of the project objective. Rolling-wave planning does mean that at the end of each phase, the project team needs to conduct a thorough project review and to be prepared to continue as planned, continue with changes, or abort the project.

Schedule risk also arises from time conflicts outside the project. Check the plan for critical project work that coincides with paid holidays, the end of financial reporting periods, times when people are likely to take vacations or otherwise be distracted, and so forth. Verify that intermediate project objectives and milestones are consistent with the personal plans of the staff members responsible for the work. On global projects, collect data for each region to minimize problems that may arise when part of the project team will be unavailable. When there are known project time conflicts with any of these nonproject factors, modify the plan to avoid them, either by accelerating the work to complete earlier or scheduling it to fall later.

Finally, commit to rigorous activity tracking throughout the project, and periodically schedule time to review your entire plan: the estimates, risks, work flow, project assumptions, and other data.

Mitigation Strategies for Resource Risks

As with schedule risks, there are many tactics for resource risk mitigation. Some ideas for minimizing resource risk include:

- ❑ Avoid planned overtime.
- ❑ Build teamwork and trust on the project team.
- ❑ Use "expected" cost estimates where worst-case activity costs are high.
- ❑ Obtain firm commitment for funding and staff.
- ❑ Keep customers involved.
- ❑ Anticipate staffing gaps.
- ❑ Minimize safety and health issues.
- ❑ Encourage team members to plan for their own risks.
- ❑ Staff risky work with successful problem solvers.
- ❑ Rigorously manage outsourcing.
- ❑ Detect and address flaws in the project objective promptly.
- ❑ Rigorously track project resource use.

More on each of these tactics follows.

One of the most common avoidable resource risks on technical projects is required overtime. Starting a project with full knowledge that the deadline is not possible unless the team works overtime for much of the project's duration is a prescription for failure. Whenever the plan shows requirements for effort in excess of what is realistically available, rework the plan to eliminate the condition. Even on well-planned projects, there are always plenty of opportunities for people to stay late, work weekends and holidays, lose sleep, and otherwise devote time to the project from their side of the "work/life" balance. Technical projects get done because people want them to be successful and are willing to put in the extra effort that it requires. Projects that are planned to require overtime (or, even worse, are not planned at all and result in massive overtime) are in trouble from the beginning for two reasons: productivity is low and turnover is high. Projects that involve significant overtime are rarely motivating, especially in the long run. People strive to avoid these projects, not to participate in them. The people who are stuck on them do not work at full efficiency. Tom DeMarco and others have written about the phenomenon of the "mental undertime" that accompanies required overtime, so productivity suffers. In addition, at least some of the project team will be looking for somewhere else to work. If they are successful, the project will lose team members; if not, they are still expending time off the project, and the available effort for the project is further depleted.

Realistically, managing resource risk on technical projects nearly always requires at least some unplanned overtime. Unanticipated activities (no WBS can ever be absolutely comprehensive), coverage for staff members who have emergencies, execution of contingency plans, and recovery from all the risks either not identified or below the "cut line" for management—all of these may require overtime. What you want to avoid are project plans that contain significant *planned* overtime. If you use up all the reasonably available overtime to do scheduled work, any difficulties that arise may leave the project little choice but to crash and burn.

Resource risk is lower on projects whenever motivation is high. Motivation is a key factor in how people respond to overtime, and low motivation is frequently a root cause of many resource-related risks. Technical projects are nearly always difficult. When they are successful, it is not because they are simple; it is because people working on them want to be successful—they care about the project. Project leaders who are good at building teamwork and getting people working on the project to trust and care about each other are much more successful than project leaders who work at a distance, using just electronic mail and printed Gantt charts. Successful projects require effective teamwork, so plan to get the staff members together physically for at least a short start-up workshop. Particularly if they will spend most of the project separated as a "virtual" or a global team, having them meet face-to-face is a tried-and-true tactic for beginning a project with a cohesive, motivated team. Another method for connecting and motivating people uses mentoring to establish additional capabilities on the team where critical skills are scarce. The development of junior people is prudent risk management, and when project contributors want to develop new skills, being mentored can be very motivating for them. The senior people who serve as mentors may resist, but two benefits to them are a reduction in their work (and stress) when it can be assigned to others and the explicit recognition of their past accomplishments and experience. (Flattery will often get you to places that straightforward requests cannot.)

Teamwork across cross-functional project boundaries is also important. The more involvement in project planning, start-up or launch activities, and other meaningful work with others you plan early in the project, the more team cohesion there will be. People who know and trust one another will back one another up and help to solve one another's problems. People who do not know one another well tend to mistrust one another and create conflict, arguments, and unnecessary project problems. Working together to plan and initiate project work transforms it from the "project leader's project" to "our project."

Financial risk is also significant for many projects. For activities in the project that have a worst-case cost that is significantly higher than the most likely cost, use the PERT formula to estimate an "expected cost," and use this estimate to reflect the potential financial exposure. Use "expected costs" in determining the proposed project budget.

As with schedule risk, adequate sponsorship is essential to resource risk management. Get early commitment from the project's sponsor for staffing and for funding, on the basis of planning data (a detailed discussion of negotiating for this follows in Chapter 10). The priority of the project is also under the control of the project sponsor, so work to understand the relative priority of the project in his or her mind. Strive to obtain the highest priority that is realistic for your project (and document this in writing). If the project has more than one sponsor, determine who has the highest influence on the project. In particular, it is good to know who would be able to make a decision to cancel your project so that you can take good care of that person and keep him or her aware of your progress. It is also useful to know who in the organization above you would suffer the most serious consequences if your project does not go well, because these managers have a personal stake in your project, and they will likely be useful when risk recovery requires escalation.

Too little involvement of customers and end users in definition, design, and testing is also a potential resource risk, so obtain commitments early on for all activities that require it. Also, plan to provide reminders to them in advance of the project work that needs their participation.

Risks resulting from staffing gaps can be reduced or detected earlier through more effective communication. Assess the likelihood that project staff (including yourself) might join the project late because of ongoing responsibilities in prior projects that are delayed. Get credible status reports from these projects, and determine how likely it is that the people working on them will be available to work on your project. If the earlier projects are ending with a lot of stress and overtime, reflect the need for some recovery time and less aggressive estimates in your project plans for the affected team members. Also, plan to notify any contributors with part-time responsibilities on your project in advance of their scheduled work.

Loss of project staff due to safety problems is not common on technical projects, but a review of activities looking for known dangerous work is still a good idea. Modify plans for any activities that you suspect may have health or safety risks to minimize the exposure. You may be able to make changes to the environment, time, and place for the work or to the practices used that may mitigate the risk. Also consider the experience and skills of the staff that may be exposed to risks, and work to replace any contributors with too little relevant background.

For each activity where the people who will do the work are a potential risk source, involve them in developing the response. In addition to potentially helping you to find more, and better, ideas for prevention, this will tend to sensitize them to the impact of the problem and can greatly reduce the likelihood of the risk.

For new, challenging, or otherwise risky activities, strive to find experienced contributors who have a reputation for effective problem solving. While you cannot plan and schedule innovation, you can identify people who seem to be good at it.

Outsourcing is a large and growing source of resource risk on projects. The discussion in Chapter 5 includes a number of exposures, and mitigating these risks requires discipline and effort. For each contract with a service provider that your project depends upon, designate a liaison on the project team to manage the relationship. Do this also for other project teams in your own organization that you need to work with. If you plan to be the liaison, ensure that there is sufficient time allocated for you to do this in the resource plan (in addition to meeting all your other responsibilities). Involve the owner of each relationship in selection, negotiation, and finalization of the agreement. Ensure that the agreement is sufficiently formal (a contract with an external supplier, a "memo of understanding" or similar document for an internal supplier) and that it is specific as to both time and technical requirements for the work consistent with your project plan. Provide incentives and penalties in the agreement when appropriate, and, whenever possible, schedule the work to complete earlier than your absolute need.

With any project work performed outside the view of the project team, schedule reviews of early drafts of required documents. Also, participate in inspections and interim tests, and examine prototypes. Identify and take full advantage of any early opportunities to verify tangible evidence of progress. Plan to collect status information regularly, and work to establish a relationship that will make it more likely that you will get credible status, including bad news, throughout your project.

A significant risk situation on fee-for-service projects is a lack of involvement of the technical staff during the proposal and selling phases. When a project is scoped and a contract commitment is made before the project team has any awareness of the project, resource risks (not to mention schedule and scope risks) can be enormous. This "price to win the business" technique is far too common in selling fee-for-solution projects, and it often leads to seemingly large and attractive fixed-price revenue contracts that are later discovered to involve even larger and extremely unattractive costs. Some projects sold this way may even be impossible to deliver at all. Prevention of this risk would be reasonably easy using time-travel technology, by turning back the clock and involving the project team in setting the terms and conditions for any agreement. Since that is impossible, and since this risk may already be a certainty when the project team gets into project and risk planning, the only recourse is to mitigate the situation insofar as possible.

Minimizing the risks associated with committed projects based on little or no analysis requires the project team to initiate the processes of basic project and risk planning as quickly as it can, doing bottom-up planning based on the committed scope. Using best-effort planning information, uncover any expectations for timing and cost that must be shifted into line with reality. Timing expectations are visible to all, so any shifts there must be dealt with internally, as well as with the customer, which could require contract modifications. Resource and cost problems may be hidden from the customer, but they still require internal adjustment

and commitment to a realistic budget for the project, even if it significantly exceeds the amount that can be recovered under the contract. If this is all done quickly enough, before everyone has
mentally settled into expectations based on the "price to win" contract, it may even be possible to adjust the fees in the contract.
While it may be tempting to adopt a "safe so far" attitude and hope
for the miracle that would allow project delivery consistent with
the flawed contract, delay nearly always makes things worse. The
last, best chance to set realistic expectations for such a project
is within a few days of its start. After this, the situation becomes
progressively uglier and more expensive to resolve.

It is also important to document and make these "price to
win" situations visible, in order to minimize the chances of future
recurrence. Organizations that chronically pursue business like
this rarely last long.

Finally, establish resource metrics for the project, and track
them against realistic planning data. Track progress, effort, and
funding throughout the project, and plan to act quickly when the
information shows that the trends show adverse variances against
the plan.

Risk Transference

Risk transference is most effective when you are dealing
with risks whose impact is primarily financial. The best-known form
of transfer is insurance: for a fee, someone else bears the financial
consequences of a risk. Transfer works to benefit both parties, because the purchaser of the insurance avoids the risk of a potentially catastrophic monetary loss in exchange for paying a small (in
comparison) premium, and the seller of the insurance benefits by
aggregating the fees collected to manage the risk in a large population of insurance buyers, who may be expected to have a stable
and predictable "average" risk. In technical projects, this sort of
transfer is not extremely common, but it is used. Unlike other strategies for mitigation, transfer does not actually do anything to lower
the probability or diminish the nonfinancial impact of the risk. With
transfer, the risk is accepted, and it either happens or it does not.
However, any budgetary impact will fall outside the project, limiting the resource risk impact.

Transfer of scope and technical risk is often the justification
for outsourcing, and this sometimes works very well. If the project
team lacks a needed skill, hiring an expert or consultant to do the
work transfers the activities to people who may be in a better position to get it done. Unfortunately, the risk does not actually transfer
to the third party; the project still belongs to the team, so it still

bears the risk of nonperformance. Should things not go well, the fact that the bill for services will not need to be paid will be of small consolation. Even the possibility of legal action is unlikely to help the project. This sort of transfer as a risk prevention strategy is very much a judgment call. In some cases, the risks accepted may significantly exceed the risks managed, no matter how well you write the contract.

IMPLEMENTING PREVENTIVE IDEAS

Avoidance, mitigation, and transfer nearly always have costs, sometimes very significant ones. Before you adopt any ideas to avoid or reduce risks, some analysis is necessary. For each risk to be managed, estimate the expected consequences in quantitative terms. For each proposed option to deal with the risk, assess the marginal costs and timing impact involved. After comparing this data, cost-effective preventive actions dealing with risk causes can be integrated into the project plan.

Comparing Costs and Benefits

The first step in this analysis is to determine the expected cost of the risk, the "loss times likelihood." For this, you need the probability in numerical terms, as well as estimates of the risk impact in terms of financial, schedule, and possibly other factors.

For a risk that is assessed as "moderate" probability, the historical records may provide an estimated probability of 15 percent, about one chance in six. The impact of risks is also difficult to estimate in many cases, as was discussed in Chapter 7, but some assessment is required. Whether the impact is in money, time, or both, it is weighted using the probability to derive an expected amount. For a risk that represents three weeks of schedule slip and $2 million in cost, the expected risk impact will be about one-half week (which is probably not that significant) and $300,000 (which would be, for most projects, very significant). In each case, this is 15 percent of the total impact, shown graphically in Figure 8-4.

The consequences of each idea for avoiding or mitigating the risk in time and money may be compared with the expected impact estimates to see whether they are cost-justified. If an idea only mitigates the risk—lowering the impact or probability of the problem—then the comparison is between the cost for mitigation and difference between the "before and after" estimates for the risk.

Determining whether a preventive is justified is always a judgment call, and it may be a difficult one. It is made more so

Figure 8-4. Expected impact.

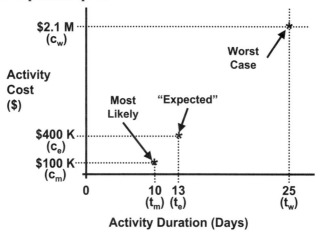

because the data are often not very precise or dependable and the fact that it is human nature to prevent problems if possible. Just because you *can* prevent a risk, though, does not mean that you should. Seeking a risk-free project is illogical for two reasons. First, it isn't possible. All projects have some residual risk, no matter how much you do to avoid it. Second, a project with every possible risk prevention idea built into the plan will be far too expensive and time-consuming to ever get off the ground. For each potential idea that reduces project risk, compare the expected costs of the risk with the cost of prevention before building it into the project plan. In the case given, with the expected half-week of delay and $300,000 in expense, an idea that requires a week of effort and costs $1.5 million would most likely not be adopted, as this "cure" is nearly as bad as the relatively unlikely risk. This situation would be similar to paying more for insurance than the cost of the expected loss. A preventive that costs less and requires little effort, though, may very well represent a prudent plan modification. Even if some of the ideas you generate for risk prevention are not cost-justified, the same (or similar) approaches may still have application as contingency plans.

You will usually generate a number of cost-effective ideas, so the next step is to select ideas for implementation that can lower project risk impact or probability at justifiable cost, and integrate them into the preliminary project plan.

Updating the Plan

For each cost-justified risk avoidance, mitigation, or transfer idea, shifts in the project planning documents are necessary.

Most ideas require additional or different work, so there are changes to the project WBS or revisions to effort and duration estimates for existing activities. Any added work requires staffing, so the profiles in the resource plan also require updating. If the resulting plan has problems meeting existing project constraints, additional replanning is required, which may create new risks. Before adoption, each idea for risk prevention must earn its way into the project by lowering, not increasing, project risk. Before any modifications, review the plan for unintended consequences, and document the justification for all additional project work.

DEALING WITH RISK EFFECTS

Avoidance, mitigation, and transfer, when justified and added to the project, all serve to make a project less risky, but risks inevitably remain. You may have no influence on the root causes of some risks or may find no preventive action for them that is cost-effective. You may have mitigation strategies that help with other risks but still leave substantial residual risk. For most of the significant risks that remain, you should develop contingency plans, although for some cases you may decide to passively accept the risk.

Contingency planning deals with risk effects by generating plans for recovery or "fallback." The process for contingency planning is entirely the same as for any other project planning, and it should be conducted at the same level of detail and using the same methodologies and tools as other project planning.

For each risk managed with a contingency plan, you begin with the trigger event that signals the occurrence of the risk. The most effective risk trigger precedes the risk consequences by as much as possible. Early triggers increase the number of potential recovery options, and in some cases they may permit you to reduce the impact of the risk, so verify that the trigger you have is the best available.

Each risk also must be assigned to an owner, who will develop the initial contingency plan, monitor the project for the trigger event, and be responsible for maintaining the contingency plans. He or she must be particularly vigilant whenever the risk trigger is less obvious. If the risk should occur, the risk owner is responsible for beginning to execute the contingency plan, working toward project recovery. The owner of a project risk is most often the same person who owns the project activity related to the risk, but for risks with particularly severe, project-threatening consequences, the project leader may be a better choice.

General Contingency Planning Strategies

Contingency planning for risks often starts with leftover ideas. Some ideas may have been considered for schedule compression (discussed in Chapter 6) but were not needed. Others might be risk prevention strategies that were not adopted in the preliminary baseline plan for cost or other reasons. While some of these ideas may be simply adopted as contingency plans without modification, in other cases they may need to be modified for "after the fact" use. Prevention strategies such as using an alternate source for components or schedule compression strategies such as expediting late project printing activities can be documented as contingency plans with no modification. Some risk avoidance ideas can serve as contingencies after minor changes. Dropping back to an older technology, for example, might require additional work to back out any dependencies on the failed newer technology, and other project change is likely to be required.

Contingency planning in itself is a powerful risk prevention tool, as the process of planning for recovery shows clearly how difficult and time-consuming it will be to recover from problems. This provides additional incentive for the project team to work in ways that make risks less likely to occur. You should strive to make risks and risk planning as visible as possible in project communication. Your project team can work to avoid only the potential problems that they are aware of.

Contingency Planning Strategies for Schedule Risks

Whenever a risk results in a significant delay, the contingency plan must seek an alternate version of the work flow that provides either a way to expedite work so that you can resume the project plan at some later point or an alternate way to complete the project that minimizes impact to the project deadline.

Recovery involves the same concepts and ideas used for schedule compression, discussed in Chapter 6. The baseline plan will require revision to make effort available for recovery immediately following the risk, so other work must be shifted, changed, or eliminated. You may be able to delay the start of less crucial planned activities, postponing them to later in the project. Any noncritical activity work that is simultaneous to or scheduled to follow the risk event may be interrupted or postponed to allow more focus on recovery. Some activity dependencies may be revised so that project activities are done out of the planned sequence, freeing contributors to work on the problem. In all of these cases, necessary activities shift later in the schedule, increasing the impact of future risks and creating new failure modes and exposures as more and more project work becomes schedule-critical.

It may even be possible to eliminate planned work if it is nonessential or to devise quicker approaches to project activities that could obtain similar, but possibly less satisfactory, results. Eliminating work and adopting "shortcuts" are generally best done as part of the main baseline plan, but for some projects it may be possible to defer these decisions until later in the work, using them on an as-needed basis.

"Crashing" project activities scheduled for later in the project to decrease their duration may also permit later starts that can free up project effort for recovery, if the project has sufficient budget reserve or access to the additional staffing to make this possible. Adding staff to the project to work on recovery may also be an option, but you should get specific commitment for any resources required. Also, include all training and project familiarization required as part of your baseline plan to minimize the disruption inevitable with new staff. Without adequate preparation, this tactic might delay your project even more.

It may not be possible to replan the project to protect the deadline, especially when the risk involves work near the scheduled end of the project. In this case, the goal of contingency planning is to minimize the unavoidable slippage and to provide the data necessary to document a new, later completion date.

A generic schedule contingency strategy involves establishing some schedule reserve for the project. Establishing schedule reserve is explored in more detail in Chapter 10.

CONTINGENCY PLANNING STRATEGIES FOR RESOURCE RISKS

For risks that create significant resource increases, contingency planning involves revising the resource plans to protect the project budget, or at least to limit the damage. Again, the process for this parallels the discussion for dealing with resource constraints in Chapter 6.

The most common strategy is also one of the least attractive—working overtime and on weekends and holidays. This tried-and-true recovery method works adequately on most projects, provided the resource impact is minimal and project staffing is not already expected to work significantly beyond the normal workday and workweek. If the amount of additional effort required is very high, or if the project team is stretched too thin when the risk occurs, this contingency strategy may backfire and actually make things worse by lowering motivation and leading to higher staff turnover.

For some projects, there may be contributors who are assigned to the project but are underused during part of it. If this is the case, shifting work around in the schedule may allow them to assist with risk recovery and still effectively meet other commitments. This tactic, like dealing with schedule risks using float, tends to increase overall project risk later in the project.

Eliminating later work or substituting approaches other than those planned may also reduce the resources needed for work later in the project, but this is generally more appropriately handled as part of the initial plan. If the work is not essential, or if there is a quicker way to obtain an acceptable result, these choices ought to be reflected in the baseline plan, not viewed as potential jetsam to fling overboard if necessary.

Particularly for resource risks, it may be impossible to avoid damage to the overall resource plan and budget. All adverse variances increase the total project cost, so there may be few or no easy ways left to cut back other expenses to compensate. Minimizing the impact of risk recovery involves contingency planning that revises resource use in ways that protect the budget as much as possible. Tactics such as assigning additional staff to later critical path activities or "borrowing" people from other, lower-priority projects may have very little budget impact. Expediting external activities using incentive payments and outsourcing work planned for the project team may also be possible, but seek approval in advance for the additional cost as part of your contingency planning. If a contingency plan requires any training or other preliminary work to be effective, make these activities part of your baseline project plan.

A generic resource contingency strategy involves establishing a budget reserve for the project, similar to the schedule reserve discussed earlier. Budget reserve is discussed further in Chapter 10.

Contingency Planning Strategies for Scope Risks

Contingency planning for scope risks is not too complicated. The plans involve either protecting the specifications for the deliverable or reducing the scope requirements. Attempting to preserve the requirements is done by adding more work to the schedule (using tactics summarized previously), using more resource, or both. In most cases, it is very difficult to assess in advance the magnitude of change that this may require, as the level of difficulty in fulfilling requirements for technical projects is highly variable—

from relatively trivial in some cases to impossible in others. Contingency plans for scope risks usually provide for some level of recovery effort, followed by a review to determine whether to continue, modify the scope, or abandon the project.

For many technical projects, scope risks are managed by modifying the project objective to provide most of the value of the project deliverable in a way that is consistent with schedule and resource objectives. The process for this, similar to that discussed in Chapter 6, starts with a prioritized list of specifications. It may be possible to drop some of the requirements entirely or to defer them to a later phase or project. There may also be potential for relaxing some of the requirements, making them easier to achieve. While this can be done effectively for some projects in advance, contingency planning for scope risks generally includes a review of project accomplishments and any shifts in assumptions, so your decisions on what to drop will be based on current data.

Passive Acceptance

For some risks, it may not be possible, or worthwhile, to plan specifically for recovery. Acceptance, as a general risk management technique, includes both transfer and contingency planning, because in both of these situations the risk causes are not influenced and the risk either happens or does not. For transfer and for contingency planning, specific responses are provided in advance to assist in recovery. For some risks, though, neither of these options may be practical. When the consequences of a risk are sufficiently unclear, as may be the case for scope and some other risks in technical projects, planning for recovery in advance may be impossible. An example of this might be a stated requirement to use new technology or hardware for the project. In such a case, many potential problems, ranging from the trivial to a complete disaster, are possible.

When a specific risk response is not an option, there are a number of choices. If the risk is sufficiently serious, it may be the best course to abandon the project altogether as too risky or to consider a major change in the objective. For situations that are less damaging, you may choose to proceed with the project having no specific risk response, passively accepting the risk (and hoping for the best). If you adopt this alternative, it is prudent to document the risk as thoroughly as possible and to provide for some project-level schedule and budget reserves to be used in managing the passively accepted known risks, as well as your unknown project risks.

Document All Risk Plans

For risks with multiple potential consequences or particularly severe effects, you may want to generate more than one contingency plan. Before finalizing a contingency plan (or plans), review for overall cost and probable effectiveness. If you do develop more than one response for a risk, prioritize the plans, putting first the plan you think will be most effective.

Document all contingency plans, and include the same level of detail as in the project plans: WBS, estimates, dependencies, schedule, resources required, the expected project impact, and any relevant assumptions. For each risk response plan, clearly specify the trigger event to detect that the risk has happened. Also, include the name of the owner who will monitor the risk trigger, maintain the contingency plan, and be responsible for its execution if the risk occurs.

As part of the overall project documentation, document your risk response plan, and work to make the risks visible. One method for increasing risk awareness is to post a "top ten" risk list (revised periodically) either on the project Web site or with posters on the walls of project work areas. Ensure adequate distribution and storage of all risk plans, and plan to review risk management information at least quarterly.

Some projects define and maintain a risk register as part of their risk response plan. For each managed risk, the register includes:

- ❐ A detailed description of the risk
- ❐ The risk owner, plus any others with assigned roles and responsibilities
- ❐ The activities affected by the risk (including WBS codes)
- ❐ Any qualitative or quantitative risk analysis results
- ❐ A summary of risk response actions in the project plan
- ❐ The risk trigger event
- ❐ Expected residual risk exposure
- ❐ A summary of contingency and fallback plans

Add risk plans to the other project documentation, and choose an appropriate location for storage that is available to all project contributors and stakeholders.

Managing a Specific Risk

Some years ago, a large multinational company initiated a yearlong effort to establish a new European headquarters. Growth over the years had spread people, computers, and other hardware all over Geneva, Switzerland, and the inconvenience and expense for all of this had grown unacceptable. The goal was to consolidate all the people and infrastructure into a modern, new headquarters building. This effort involved a number of high-profile, risky projects, and I was asked to manage one of them.

One particularly risky aspect of the project involved moving two large, water-cooled mainframe computers out of the older data center where the systems had operated for some years and into a more modern center in the new headquarters building. In the new location, the systems would be co-located with all the other headquarters computers and the telecommunications equipment that tied them to other sites in Europe and around the world. Both systems were critical to the business, so each was scheduled to be moved over a three-day holiday weekend. It was essential that each system be fully functional in the old data center at the end of the week before the move and fully functional in the new data center before the start of business following the holiday, three days later.

Most of the risks were fairly mundane, and they were managed through thorough planning, adequate staffing, and extensive training, all committed months in advance. Other precautions, such as additional data backups, were also taken. The move itself was far from mundane, though, because the old data center, for some reason, had been established on the fifth floor of a fairly old building. The elevator in the building was very small, about one meter square, and could carry no more than the weight of three or four people (who had to be on very friendly terms). When the systems were originally moved into the building, a system-size door had been cut into the marble façade of the building, and a crane with a suspended box was used to move the systems into the data center. Over the years, upgrades and replacements had been moved in and out the same way.

Up to the time of this project, only older hardware being replaced had ever been moved out of the data center this way. In these cases, if there had been a mishap it would have not affected operations, since the older systems were moved out only once the replacement systems were successfully moved in. For the relocation project, this was not the case. Both systems had to be moved out, transported, and reinstalled successfully, and any problem that started twenty meters in the air would result in a significant and expensive service interruption far longer than the allocated three days.

The new data center was, sensibly, at ground level; eliminating the need to suspend multimillion-dollar mainframes high in the air was one of the reasons the project was undertaken. Successful completion of the project would mean ground-level systems in the new data center and far easier maintenance for all future operations.

In addition to the obvious risk of a CPU plummeting to the ground, the short timing of the project also involved other exposures such as weather, wind, traffic, injuries to workers, problems with the crane, and many other potential difficulties. The assessment of risk for most of these situations resulted either in adjustments in staffing, shifts in the plan, or passive acceptance, because there was sufficient experience and people were confident that most of the potential problems could be managed during the move.

The one remaining risk that concerned all of us was that one of the mainframe computers might smash into the sidewalk. The consequences of this could not be managed during the three-day weekend, so a lot of analysis went into exploring ways to manage this risk.

Risk assessment was the subject of significant debate, particularly with regard to probability. Some thought it "low," saying, "This is Switzerland; we move skiers up the mountains this way all the time." Others, particularly people from the United States, were less optimistic. In the end, the consensus was "moderate." There was less debate on risk impact, which in this case had a very literal meaning. In addition to issues of cost and delay, there were significant other concerns such as safety, the large crater in the pavement, noise, and computer parts bouncing for blocks around.

The primary impact was in time and cost and was deemed "high," so considerable planning went into mitigating the risk. A number of ideas were explored, including disassembly of the system for movement in pieces using the elevator, building a lift along the side of the building (the two systems were to be moved a month apart, so this cost would have covered both), using padding or some sort of cushion for the ground, and a number of other even less practical ideas. The disassembly idea was considered seriously but was deemed inappropriate due to timing and the discouraging report from the vendor that "those systems do not always work right initially when we assemble them in the factory." The external lift idea was a good one, but hardware that could reach to the fifth floor was unavailable. A large net or cushion would have minimized the spread of debris but seemed unlikely to ensure system operation. It was not until the problem was reframed that the best idea emerged. The risk was not really the loss of that particular system; it was the loss of a *usable* system.

A plan to purchase a new system and install it in advance in the new data center would make the swift and successful move of the existing hardware unnecessary. Once operations were trans-

Suspending computing in Geneva.

ferred to the new hardware, the old system could be lowered to the street, and successful, if sold as used equipment. This was a very effective plan for avoiding the risk, but it had one problem—cost. The difference between the salvage value of the current machine and the purchase price of a new one was roughly $2 million. This investment was far higher than the expected consequences of the risk, so it was rejected as part of the plan. We decided to take as many precautions as possible and accept the risk.

All this investigation made the contingency planning easy, as the research we had done into acquiring a new system was really all that was necessary. We ordered a new system and got a commitment from the vendor to fill the order with the next machine built if there were any problems moving the existing system. (The vendor was happy to agree to this, as it was heavily involved in many aspects of the relocation.) Once the move had been competed successfully, the order could be canceled with no penalty.

The consequences documented for the contingency plan were that the system would be unavailable for about three weeks, and the cost of the replacement system would be roughly $3 million.

As it happened, the same staff and basic plan was employed for both mainframe moves, and both went without any incident. Although the contingency plan was not used, everyone felt that the risk planning had been a good investment. The process revealed clearly what we were facing, and it heightened our awareness of the overall risk. It uncovered many related smaller problems that were eliminated, which saved time and made the time-critical work required much easier. It also made all of us confident that the projects had been very carefully and thoroughly planned and that we would be successful. Even when risk management cannot eliminate all the risks, it is worthwhile to the project.

Key Ideas for Managing Activity Risks

❏ Determine root causes.
❏ Avoid, mitigate, or transfer risks when feasible.
❏ Develop contingency plans for remaining significant risks.
❏ Document risk plans and keep risk data visible.
❏ Thirty grams of prevention is worth half a kilogram of cure (approximately).

Panama Canal: Risk Plans (1906–1914)

Risk management represented one of the largest investments for the Panama Canal project. Of the risks mentioned in Chapter 7, most were dealt with in effective and, in several cases, innovative ways.

The risk of disease, so devastating on the earlier project, was managed through diligence, science, and sanitation. The scale and cost of this effort was significant, but so were the results. Widespread use of methods for mosquito control under the guidance of Dr. William Gorgas was effective on a scale never seen before. Specific tactics used, such as frequently applying thin films of oil on bodies of water and the disciplined dumping of standing water wherever it gathered (which in a rain forest was nearly everywhere), were so effective that their use worldwide in the tropics continues to this day. Once the program for insect control was in full effect, Panama was by far the healthiest place anywhere in the tropics. Yellow fever was eliminated. Malaria was rare, as were tuberculosis, dysentery, pneumonia, and a wide range of other diseases common at the time. Not only were the diseases spread by mosquitoes virtually eliminated, but also work went much faster without the annoyance of the omnipresent insects. Although some estimates put the cost at ten dollars for every mosquito killed, the success of the canal project depended heavily on Dr. Gorgas to ensure that the workers stayed healthy. This risk was managed thoroughly and well.

For the risk of frequent and sudden mud slides, there were no elegant solutions. As the work commenced, it seemed to many that "the more we dug, the more remained to be dug." Unfortunately, this was true; it proved impossible to use the original French plan for the trench in the Culebra Cut to have sides at forty-five degrees (a 1:1 slope). This angle created several problems, the largest of which was the frequent mud slides. In addition, the sides of the cut pressed down on the semisolid clay the excavators were attempting to remove, which squeezed it up in the center of the trench. The deeper the digging, the more the sides would sink and the center would rise; like a fluid, it would seek its level. The contingency plan was inelegant but ultimately effective—more digging. The completed canal had an average 4:1 slope, which minimized the mud slides and partially stabilized the flowing clay. This brute-force contingency plan not only resulted in the need to dispose of much more soil but also represented about triple the work. Erosion, flowing clay, and occasional mud slides continue to this day, and the canal requires frequent dredging to remain operational.

Dealing with the risks involved with building the enormous locks required a number of tactics. As with the mud slides, the massive concrete sides for the locks were handled by brute force and overengineering. Cement was poured at Panama on a scale never done before. The sides of the locks are so thick and so heavily reinforced that, even after nearly ninety years of continuous operation, with thousands of ship passages and countless earthquakes, there are very few cracks or defects. The locks still look much as they did when they were new.

The mechanical and electrical challenges were quite another matter. The locks were colossal machines with thousands of moving parts, many huge. Years of advance planning and experimentation led to ultimate success. The canal was a triumph of precision engineering and use of new steels. Vanadium alloy steels used were developed initially for automotive use, and they proved light and strong enough to serve in the construction of doors for the locks. Holding the doors tightly closed against the weight of the water in a filled lock required a lot of mass, mass that the engineers wanted to avoid moving each time the doors were opened or closed. To achieve this, the doors were made *hollow*. Whenever they are closed, they are filled with water before the lock is filled, providing the necessary mass. The doors are then drained before they are opened to allow the ships raised (or lowered) to pass through.

Even with this strategy, moving doors of this size and weight required the power of modern engines. The choice of electrical operation proved very difficult and required much innovation (the first all-electric factory in the United States was barely a year old at the time of this decision), but electricity did provide a number of advantages. With electric controls, the entire canal system can be controlled centrally. Scale models were built to show the positions of each lock in detail. The lock systems are all controlled using valves and switches on the model, and mechanical interlocks beneath the model prevent errors in operation, such as opening the doors on the wrong end of a lock or opening them before the filling or draining of water is complete. Complete status can be monitored for all twelve locks.

When George Goethals began to set all of this up, he realized that neither he nor anyone else had ever done anything like it. For most of the controls and the more than 1,000 electric motors the canal required, Goethals managed risk by bringing in outside help. He awarded a sizable contract to a rapidly growing U.S. company known for its expertise in electrical systems. Although it was still fairly small and not known internationally, the General Electric Company had started to attract worldwide attention by the time the Panama Canal opened. This was a huge contract for GE, and it was its first large government contract. Such a large-scale collaboration of private and public organizations was unknown prior to this project. The relationship between Goethals and GE served as the model for the Manhattan Project during World War II and for countless other modern projects in the United States and elsewhere. For good or ill, the modern military-industrial complex began in Panama.

Despite the project's success in dealing with most risks, explosives remained a significant problem throughout construction. As in many contemporary projects, loss of life and limbs while handling explosives was common. Although stringent safety precautions helped, the single largest cause of death on the second Panama Canal project was TNT, not disease. For this risk, the builders found no solutions or viable alternatives, so throughout the project they were quite literally "playing with dynamite."

CHAPTER 9

QUANTIFYING AND ANALYZING PROJECT RISK

"Knowledge is power."   —FRANCIS BACON

Information is central to managing projects successfully.
Knowledge of the work and of the potential risk serves as the first
and best defense against problems and project delay. The overall
assessment of project risk provides concrete justification for necessary changes in the project objective, so it is one of the most powerful tools you have for failure-proofing difficult projects. Project-
level risk rises steeply for projects with insufficient resources or
excessively aggressive schedules, and risk assessments offer compelling evidence of the exposure this represents. Knowledge of
project risk also sets expectations for the project appropriately,
both for the deliverables and for the work that lies ahead.

Most of the content of this chapter falls into the "Qualitative Risk Analysis" and "Quantitative Risk Analysis" portions of the
Planning Processes in the *PMBOK® Guide*. The focus of this chapter
is the analysis of overall project risk, building on the foundation of
analysis and response planning for known *activity* risks discussed
in the two preceding chapters. The principal ideas covered in this
chapter include:

❏ Project-level risk

❏ Aggregated risk responses

❏ Questionnaires and surveys

❏ Project simulation and modeling

- ❏ Analysis of scale
- ❏ Project appraisals
- ❏ Project metrics
- ❏ Financial metrics

Project-Level Risk

Considered one by one, the known risks on a project may seem relatively easy to deal with, or overwhelming, or somewhere in between. Managing risk at the activity level is necessary, but it is not sufficient; you also need to develop a sense of overall project risk. Overall project risk arises, in part, from all the activity-level data combined, but it also has a component that is more pervasive, coming from the project as a whole. High-level project risk assessment was discussed in Chapter 3, using methods that required only information available during initial project definition. Those high-level techniques—the risk framework, the risk complexity index, and the risk assessment grid—may also be reviewed and revised according to your project plans.

As the preliminary project planning process approaches completion, you have much more information available, so you can assess project risk more precisely and thoroughly. There are a number of useful tools for assessing project risk, including statistics, metrics, and modeling tools such as the Program Evaluation and Review Technique (PERT). Risk assessment using planning data may be used to support decisions and make recommendations for project changes, project control, and project execution.

COMMON PROJECT RISKS

Generic sources of project risk are many. In *Assessment and Control of Software Risks*, Capers Jones lists as the top five:

1. *Inadequate measures.* If cost and effort measures are inaccurate or missing, there is little precision in project planning and high, uncontrolled costs.

2. *Excessive schedule pressure.* Setting project deadlines too aggressively leads to poor quality, low morale, high attrition, and project cancellation.

3. *Management malpractice.* Project leaders good at technical work but not skilled in definition, planning, estimating, track-

ing, communication, and project control produce poor results and very high levels of inefficiency.

4. *Creeping user requirements.* Inadequate specification change control wastes money and effort and causes rework.

5. *Very large projects.* Sheer size is a project risk; the larger the project, the more likely it is to end in cancellation. Jones reports that the largest projects are generally canceled a year or more after the original deadline, having spent at least double the intended budget, in most cases without providing any salvageable output.

USES OF PROJECT RISK DATA

As discussed in Chapter 1, risk information has many uses, including helping sponsors to select and compare potential projects. Project risk data can build support for less risky projects, and it may lead to cancellation of higher-risk projects. It can also be used in setting relative project priorities. High-risk projects may warrant lower priority. Raising project priority may significantly reduce project risk by opening doors, reducing obstacles, making resources available, and reducing queues. Risk assessment is also important in managing a portfolio of projects. The mix of ongoing projects should represent an appropriate risk profile, including both lower- and higher-risk projects in proportions consistent with business strategies. Without adequate project risk information, all these decisions will be made using guesswork.

Project risk assessment may also be used to reduce the risk of individual projects. Project-level risk assessments may reveal sources of project risk that are part of the project infrastructure. Fine-tuning the overall project by making structural and other changes can drop risk significantly. The overall assessment of risk also provides a data-driven justification for establishing management reserve for the project. Taking into account overall risk, managers may set the project objectives with aggressive targets, along with commitments and expectations that are less aggressive. The window between the aggressive target and the project's commitment can be sized to reflect project risk and uncertainty. For example, a target project schedule might call for completion of the project in twelve months, but taking risk analysis into consideration, it would not be late unless it requires more than fourteen months. Both schedule and resource reserves are common for risky projects.

Finally, project risk data are useful in communication. Documentation of project risk can be vital in discussions with sponsors and managers—it is harder for them to argue with facts and data than it is to argue with you. Risk information also builds awareness of project uncertainties on the project team.

The techniques, tools, ideas and metrics described in this chapter will assist you in all of this.

Aggregating Risk Responses

One way to measure project risk is to add up all the expected consequences for all of the contingency plans established for the project. This is not just a simple sum; the total is based on the estimated cost (or time) involved multiplied by the risk probability—the "loss times likelihood" for the whole project.

One way to calculate project-level risk is by accumulating the consequences of the contingency plans. To do this, you sum the expected costs for all the plans—their estimated costs weighted by the risk probabilities. Similarly, you can calculate the total expected project duration increase required by the contingency plans using the same probability estimates. For example, if a contingency plan associated with a risk having a 10 percent probability will cost $10,000 and slip the project by ten days, the contribution to the project totals will be $1,000 and one day, respectively.

Another way to generate similar data is by using the differences between PERT–based "expected" estimates and the "most likely" activity estimates. Summing these estimates of both cost and time impact for the project generates an assessment roughly equivalent to the contingency plan data.

While these sums of expected consequences provide a baseline for overall project risk, they tend to underestimate total risk, for a number of reasons. First, this analysis assumes that all project risks are independent, with no expected correlation. On real projects, this assumption is generally incorrect; some project risks are much more likely after other risks have occurred. Project activities are linked through common methodologies, staffing, and other factors. Second, a project has a limited staff, so whenever there is a problem, nearly all of the project leader's attention (and much of the project team's) will be on recovery. While distracted by problem solving, the project leader will focus much less on all the other project activities, making additional trouble elsewhere that much more likely.

Another big reason that overall project risk is underestimated using this method is that the sums do not yet account for project-level risk factors. Overall project-level risk factors include:

- ❐ Experience of project manager
- ❐ Weak sponsorship
- ❐ Reorganization, business changes
- ❐ Regulatory issues
- ❐ Lack of common practices (e.g., life cycle, planning)
- ❐ Market window or other timing assumptions
- ❐ Insufficient risk management
- ❐ Ineffective project decomposition, resulting in inefficient work flow
- ❐ Unfamiliar levels of project effort
- ❐ Low project priority
- ❐ Poor motivation and team morale
- ❐ Weak change management control
- ❐ Lack of customer interaction
- ❐ Communications issues
- ❐ Poorly defined infrastructure
- ❐ Inaccurate (or no) metrics

The first two factors on the list are particularly significant. If the project leader has little experience running similar projects successfully, or the project has low priority, or both, you can increment the overall project risk assessment from summing expected impacts by at least 10 percent for each. Similarly, make adjustments for any of the other factors that may be significant for the project. Even after these adjustments, the risk assessment will still be somewhat conservative, because the effect of any "unknown" risk in your project has not been included.

Compare the total expected project duration and cost impacts related to project risks with your preliminary baseline plan. Whenever the expected risk impact for either time or cost exceeds 20 percent of your plan, the project is very risky. You can use these data on cost and schedule risk to adjust your project plan, justify management reserve, or both.

Questionnaires and Surveys

Questionnaires and surveys are a well-established technique for assessing project risk. These can range from simple, multiple-response survey forms to assessments using computer spreadsheets or any other suitable format or computer tool. However a risk assessment tool is implemented, it will be most useful if you customize it for your project.

Many organizations have and use risk surveys. If there is a survey or questionnaire commonly used for projects similar to yours, it may require very little customizing, but it is always a good idea to review the questions and fine-tune the instrument before using it. If you do not have a standard survey format, the following example is a generic three-option risk survey that can be adapted for use on a wide range of technical projects.

This survey approach to risk assessment also works best when the number of total questions is kept to a minimum, so review the format you intend to use and select only the questions that are most relevant to your project risks. You may need to modify existing questions or to create new risk evaluation questions to maximize the usefulness of the survey for your project. It also helps to keep the responses simple. If you develop your own survey, limit the number of responses for each question to no more than four clearly worded responses.

Once you have finalized the risk assessment questionnaire, the next step is to get input from each member of the core project team. Ask each person who participated in project planning to respond to each question, and then collect their data.

Risk survey data are useful in two ways. First, you can analyze all the data to produce an overall assessment of risk. This can be used to compare projects, to set expectations, and to establish risk reserves. Second, you can scan the responses question by question to find particular risks—questions where the responses are consistently in the high-risk category. Risk surveys can be very compelling evidence for needed changes in project infrastructure or other project factors that increase risk. For high-risk factors, ask, "Do we need to settle for this? Is there any reason we should not consider changes that will reduce project risk?" Also, investigate any questions with widely divergent responses, and conduct additional discussions to establish common understanding within the project team.

Instructions for the Project Risk Questionnaire

The following document is a generic risk questionnaire, typical of surveys commonly used on technical projects. The results of using this sort of tool are qualitative and not intended to provide high-precision analysis of comparative risk between different projects.

Before using the following survey, read each one of the questions and make changes as needed to reflect your project environment. Strike out any questions that are irrelevant, and add new questions if necessary to reflect risky aspects of your project. Effective surveys are *short*, so delete any questions that seem less applicable. Section 2, "Technical Risks," normally requires the most intensive editing. The three sections focus on:

- ❐ Project external factors (such as users, budgets, and schedule constraints)

- ❐ Development issues (such as tools, software, and hardware)

- ❐ Project internal factors (such as infrastructure, team cohesion, and communications)

Add or delete questions in these categories to make this tool more useful to you.

To use the survey, distribute copies to key project contributors and stakeholders (at least one other person in addition to yourself), and ask each person to select one of the three choices offered for each question.

To interpret the information, assign values of 1 to selections in the first column, 3 to selections in the middle column, and 9 to selections in the third column. Within each section, sum up the responses, then divide each sum by the number of responses tallied. For example, if three people answered all seventeen questions in Section 1—for a total of fifty-one questions—and the weighted responses sum to 195, the result is 3.82, or medium risk. Within each section, use the following evaluation criteria:

Low risk: 1.00–2.50

Medium risk: 2.51–6.00

High risk: 6.01–9.00

Average the three section results to determine overall project risk, using the same criteria. Although the results of this kind of survey are qualitative, they can help you to identify sources of high risk in your project. For any section with medium or high risk, consider changes to the project that might lower the risk. Within each section, look for responses in the third column. Brainstorm ideas, tactics, or project changes that could shift the response, reducing overall project risk.

Risk Questionnaire

For each question below, choose the response that best describes your project. If the best response seems to lie between two choices, check the one of the pair further to the right.

Section 1. Project Parameter and Target User Risks

1-1. Scope (project deliverable specification) stability.

❐ Change is unlikely   ❐ Small change is possible   ❐ Changes are likely or definition is incomplete

1-2. Project Budget/Resources.

❐ Committed and realistic   ❐ Probably sufficient, with margin/reserve defined   ❐ Insufficient or unknown

1-3. Project Deadline.

❐ Realistic   ❐ Possible; margin/ reserve defined   ❐ Overly aggressive or unrealistic

1-4. Total project length.

❐ Less than 3 months   ❐ 3–12 months   ❐ More than 12 months

1-5. Total effort-months estimated for the project.

❐ Less than 30   ❐ 30–150   ❐ More than 150

1-6. Peak size of core project team (key contributors critical to the project).

❐ 5 or fewer   ❐ 6–12   ❐ More than 12

1-7. Project manager experience.

❐ Finished more than one comparable project successfully   ❐ Finished a project about the same size successfully   ❐ None, or has done only smaller or shorter projects

1-8. User support for the project objective (scope, schedule, and resources).

❐ Enthusiastic   ❐ General agreement   ❐ Small or unknown

1-9. Prioritization of scope, schedule and resources (constrained, optimized, accepted).

❐ Known and agreed upon; only one parameter constrained   ❐ Two parameters are constrained, but one is flexible   ❐ No priorities set or all parameters are constrained

1-10. Number of different types of users (market segments).

❐ 1   ❐ 2   ❐ 3 or more

1-11. Project team interaction with users during project.

☐ Frequent and easy   ☐ At project start and end only   ☐ Little or none

1-12. User need for the project deliverable.

☐ Verified as critical to user's business   ☐ Solves a problem; increases user efficiency   ☐ Not validated or unknown

1-13. User enthusiasm generated by the project deliverable at project start.

☐ High   ☐ Some   ☐ Little or none

1-14. User acceptance criteria for the project deliverable.

☐ Well defined   ☐ Nearly complete   ☐ Definition incomplete

1-15. User environment and process changes required to use the project deliverable.

☐ None   ☐ Minor   ☐ Significant

1-16. User interface to operate or use the project deliverable.

☐ Identical to one now in use   ☐ Similar to one now in use   ☐ New or represents major changes

1-17. Testing planned with actual users of the project deliverable.

☐ Early, using models or prototypes   ☐ Midproject, at least for key subdeliverables   ☐ Late in project; Beta test

Section 2. Technical Risks

General

2-1. Complexity of development.

☐ Less than recent successful projects   ☐ Similar to recent successful projects   ☐ Unknown or beyond recent similar projects

2-2. Development methodology.

☐ Standardized   ☐ Similar to other recent projects   ☐ Ad hoc, little, or none

2-3. Minimum team experience with critical development technologies.

☐ More than 1 year   ☐ 6 months to 1 year   ☐ Little or none

2-4. Tools, workstations, and other technical resources.

☐ Established, stable, and well understood   ☐ All have been used before   ☐ Some new facilities or tools required

2-5. Planned reuse from earlier projects.

☐ More than 75 percent   ☐ 40 percent to 75 percent   ☐ Little or none

2-6. Early simulation or modeling of deliverable.

☐ Will be done with existing processes   ☐ Planned, but will need new processes   ☐ Not planned or not possible

2-7. Technical interfaces required (connections of this project's deliverable into a larger system or to deliverables from independent projects).

❐ None (stand-alone) and well understood	❐ Fewer than 5, and all are to existing systems	❐ More than 5 or more than 1 that is new (parallel development)

Hardware

2-8. Hardware technology incorporated into deliverable.

❐ All established, existing technology	❐ Existing technology in a new application	❐ New, nonexistent, or unknown technology

2-9. Testing.

❐ Will use only existing facilities and processes	❐ Will use existing facilities with new processes	❐ Unknown, or new facilities needed

2-10. Component count.

❐ Number and type similar to recent successful projects	❐ Similar number, but some new parts required	❐ Unknown, larger number, or mostly unfamiliar components

2-11. Component sources.

❐ Multiple reliable, managed sources for all key components	❐ More than one identified source for all key components	❐ A single (or unknown) source for at least one key component

2-12. Component availability (lead times, relative to project duration).

❐ Short lead time for all key components	❐ One or more key components with long, but known, lead times	❐ One or more key components with unknown lead time

2-13. Mechanical requirements.

❐ All significant processes used before	❐ Some modification to existing processes required	❐ New, special, or long lead processes needed

Software

2-14. Software required for deliverable.

❐ None or off-the-shelf	❐ Mostly leveraged or reused	❐ Mostly new development

2-15. Software technology.

❐ Very high-level language only (4GL)	❐ Standard language (C++, Java, PERL, COBOL)	❐ New or low-level language (assembler)

2-16. Data structures required.

❐ Not applicable or relational database	❐ Other database or well-defined files	❐ New data files

2-17. Data conversion required.

❏ None required ❏ Minor ❏ Major or unknown

2-18. System complexity.

❏ No new control or algorithm development ❏ Little new control or algorithm development ❏ Significant new or unknown development

2-19. Processing environment of deliverable.

❏ Single system ❏ Multisystem, but single site ❏ Distributed, multisite system

Section 3. Structure Risks

3-1. Project sponsorship and management commitment to project objective (scope, schedule, and resources).

❏ Enthusiastic ❏ Supportive ❏ Neutral or none

3-2. Project priority.

❏ High ❏ Moderate ❏ Low

3-3. Project manager experience.

❏ Success on recent similar project ❏ Managed part of a recent similar project ❏ Low or none on this sort of project

3-4. Project manager authority.

❏ Most project decisions made by PM ❏ Limited decision making and budget control ❏ None; all decisions escalated to others

3-5. Project manager focus.

❏ Full-time on this project ❏ More than half time spent managing this project ❏ Less than half time spent managing this project

3-6. Project plan.

❏ Plan is realistic and bottom-up ❏ Plan seems possible and has defined reserve for schedule/ budget ❏ Plan is unrealistic or no plan exists

3-7. Project version control and change management.

❏ Well-defined and rigorously used process ❏ Informal but effective process ❏ Little or no change control

3-8. Project life cycle.

❏ Well defined, with clear milestones and phase deliverables ❏ Defined, but not rigorously used ❏ No formal life cycle

3-9. Project staffing.

❏ Available and committed ❏ All key people identified ❏ Significant staffing unknowns remain

3-10. Subprojects.

| ❐ This project is independent of other work | ❐ All related subprojects are well defined and coordinated | ❐ Related subprojects are loosely coupled or not clearly defined |

3-11. Project work environment.

| ❐ Your site; workplace known and conducive to project progress | ❐ Some work must be done in an unknown or poor work environment | ❐ Mostly off-site or in a poor work environment |

3-12. Staffing commitment.

| ❐ All key people are full-time | ❐ Mix of full-time and part-time staffing | ❐ All part-time or external staffing |

3-13. Team separation.

| ❐ Co-located | ❐ Single site | ❐ Multisite |

3-14. Team enthusiasm for the project.

| ❐ High | ❐ Adequate | ❐ Reluctant or unknown |

3-15. Team compatibility.

| ❐ Most of team has worked together successfully | ❐ Some of team has worked together before | ❐ New team |

3-16. Lowest common manager for members of the core project team.

| ❐ Project leader | ❐ Up to two levels in same organization | ❐ More than two levels up, or none |

3-17. Number of outside organizations or independent projects that this project depends on for inputs, decisions, or approvals.

| ❐ None | ❐ One other | ❐ More than one |

3-18. Project dependence on external subcontractors or suppliers.

| ❐ Little or none (<10 percent) | ❐ Minor (10–25 percent) | ❐ Significant (>25 percent) |

3-19. Quality of subcontractors.

| ❐ High—with relevant experience (or no subcontractors used) | ❐ Good—solid references from trusted sources | ❐ Doubtful or unknown |

3-20. Project communication.

| ❐ Frequent (weekly) face-to-face status gathering and written reporting | ❐ Sporadic, informal, or long-distance status and reporting | ❐ Ad hoc or none |

3-21. Project tracking.

| ❐ Frequent (weekly) reporting of actual progress vs. plan | ❐ Project leader tracks and deals with plan exceptions reactively | ❐ Informal or none |

3-22. Project documentation.

☐ Accurate, current documents are on-line for project team ☐ Current status and schedule are available to project team ☐ Documents known only to project leader, or none

3-23. Project issue resolution.

☐ Well-defined process; issues tracked and closed promptly ☐ Informal but effective process ☐ Issues are not easily resolved in a timely fashion

Project Simulation and Modeling

The best-known project modeling methodology is the Program Evaluation and Review Technique (PERT), discussed in Chapter 4 with regard to estimating and in Chapter 7 for analysis of activity risk. These uses are beneficial, but the original purpose of PERT was quantitative *project* risk analysis, the topic of this chapter. There are several approaches to using PERT, as well as other useful simulation and decision analysis tools available for project risk analysis.

PERT FOR PROJECT RISK ANALYSIS

PERT was not developed by project managers. It was developed in the late 1950s at the direction of the U.S. military to deal with the increasingly common cost and schedule overruns on very large U.S. government projects. The larger the programs became, the bigger the overruns. Generals and admirals are not patient people, and they hate to be kept waiting. Even worse, the U.S. Congress got involved whenever costs exceeded the original estimates, and the generals and admirals liked that even less.

The principal objective of PERT is to use detailed risk data to predict possible project outcomes. For schedule analysis, project teams are requested to provide three estimates: a "most likely" estimate that they believe would be the most common duration for work similar to the activity in question, and two additional estimates that define a range around the "most likely" estimate that includes nearly every other realistic possibility for the work.

Shown in Figure 9-1, the three PERT Time estimates are: at the low end, an "optimistic" estimate, t_o; in the middle somewhere, a "most likely" estimate, t_m; and at the high end, a "pessimistic" estimate, t_p.

Originally, PERT analysis assumed a continuous Beta distribution of outcomes defined by these three parameters, similar to the graph in Figure 9-1. This distribution was chosen because it is

Figure 9-1. PERT estimates.

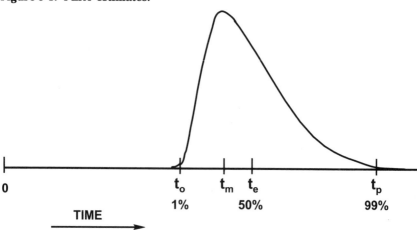

relatively easy to work with in computer simulations and it can skew to the left (as in Figure 9-1) or to the right when the three estimating parameters are asymmetric. When it is symmetric, the Beta distribution is the Normal distribution (the Gaussian, bell-shaped curve).

PERT Time

PERT Time analysis using computer simulation takes these data and generates a random sample from the distribution associated with each project activity. These samples are then used as duration estimates to calculate the critical (longest) path through the network using standard critical path methodology (CPM) analysis. If PERT Time analysis were only done once, it would not be any more useful for risk analysis than CPM, but the PERT methodology repeats the process over and over, each time using new randomly generated activity duration estimates consistent with the chosen ranges. For each new schedule, CPM is used to calculate the project's critical path, and over many repetitions PERT builds a histogram of the results.

Current PERT and other computer modeling tools offer many alternatives to the Beta distribution. You may use Triangular, Normal, Poisson, and many other distributions, and with most software you can even enter histograms defining discrete estimates with associated probabilities. (For example, you may expect a 50 percent probability that the activity will complete in fifteen days, a 40 percent chance that it will complete in twenty days, and a 10 percent chance that it will complete in thirty days. These scenarios are generally based on probabilities associated with known risks for which incremental estimates are made—the five-day slip associated with a contributor who may need to take a week of leave to deal with a family situation, the fifteen-day slip associated with a problem that requires completely redoing of all the work).

As discussed in Chapter 7, the precise choice of the distribution shape is not terribly important, even for activity-level risk analysis. At the project level, it becomes even less relevant. The reason for this is that the probability density function for the summation of randomly generated samples of most types of statistical distributions (including all the realistic ones) always resembles a Normal, bell-shaped, Gaussian distribution. This is a consequence of the central limit theorem, well established by statisticians, and it is why the output of PERT analysis nearly always looks like a symmetric, bell-shaped curve. The Normal distribution has only two defining parameters, the mean and the variance (the square of the standard deviation). Early on with PERT, it was recognized that you could calculate these two parameters for the Beta distribution the activity estimates, using the formulas referenced earlier:

$$t_e = (t_o + 4t_m + t_p)/6, \text{ where}$$

t_e is the "expected" duration—the mean
t_o is the "optimistic" duration
t_m is the "most likely" duration
t_p is the "pessimistic" duration

and

$$\sigma = (t_p - t_o)/6, \text{ where}$$

σ is the standard deviation

For many projects, the expected duration and standard deviation can be calculated for the project as a whole fairly easily. First, build a network of project activities using the calculated "expected" PERT durations for all estimates. Then, do a critical-path analysis to identify all critical activities. When there is a single, dominant critical path for the "expected" project, the expected duration for the project is the result you just generated—the sum of all the expected durations along the critical path. The standard deviation for the project, one measure of overall project risk, can be calculated from the estimated standard deviations for the same activities. PERT uses the following formulas:

$$t_{proj} = \sum_{i=CP_{first}}^{CP_{last}} t_{ei} \qquad \sigma_{proj} = \sqrt{\sum_{i=CP_{first}}^{CP_{last}} \sigma_i^2}$$

Where

$$t_{proj} = \text{Expected project duration}$$
$$CP_i = \text{Critical path activity } i$$
$$t_{e_i} = \text{``Expected'' } CP \text{ estimate for activity } i$$
$$\sigma_{proj} = \text{Project standard deviation}$$
$$\sigma_i^2 = \text{Variance for } CP \text{ activity } i$$

These formulas work well whenever there is essentially only one critical path, or schedule failure mode, for the project. PERT gets more complicated when there are additional paths in the project that are roughly equivalent in length to the longest one. When this occurs, these formulas *underestimate* the expected project duration (it is actually slightly higher), and they *overestimate* the standard deviation. For project networks that have several "longest" paths, a full PERT analysis using computer simulation provides better results than the formulas. The reason these formulas are inaccurate was introduced in Chapter 4, in the discussion of multiple critical paths. There, the distinction between "Early/on time" and "Late" was a sharp one, with no allowance for degree. PERT analysis uses distributions for each activity and creates a spectrum of possible outcomes for the project, but the same logic—more failure modes lead to lowered success rates—is unavoidable. Since *any* of the parallel critical paths may end up being the longest for each simulated case, each of them contributes to the result for the project as a whole. The simple project considered in Chapter 4 had the network diagram in Figure 9-2, with one critical path across the top ("A-D-J") and a second critical path along the bottom ("C-H-L").

PERT analysis, as should be expected, shows that there is about one chance in four that the project will complete on time or earlier than the expected durations associated with each of the critical paths. The distribution of possible outcomes has about one-

Figure 9-2. Project with two critical paths.

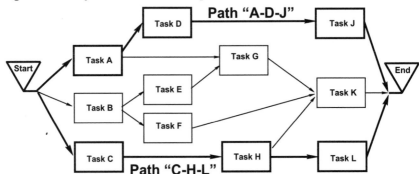

quarter of the left tail below the expected dates, and the peak and right tail are above it, similar to Figure 9-3. The resulting distribution is still basically bell-shaped, but, compared with the distributions expected for each critical path, it has a larger mean and is narrower (a smaller standard deviation).

To consider this quantitatively, imagine a project plan using "50 percent" expected estimates that has a single dominant critical path of one hundred days (five months) and a standard deviation of five days. (If the distribution of expected outcomes is assumed symmetric, the PERT optimistic and pessimistic durations—plus or minus three standard deviations—would be roughly 85 days and 115 days, respectively). PERT analysis for the project says you should expect the project to complete in five months (or sooner) five times out of ten, and in five months plus one week over eight times out of ten (about five-sixths of the time)—pretty good odds.

If a second critical path of one hundred days is added to the project with similar estimated risk (a standard deviation of five days), the project expectation shifts to one chance in four of finishing in five months or sooner. (Actually, the results of the simulation based on one thousand runs shows 25.5 percent. The results of simulation should never be expected to match the theoretical an-

Figure 9-3. PERT results.

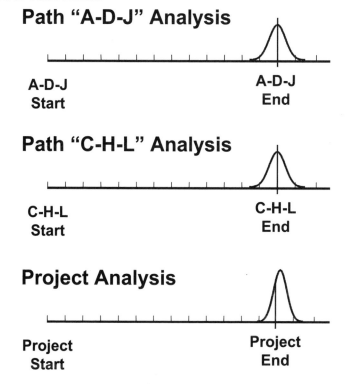

Path "A-D-J" Analysis

A-D-J
Start

A-D-J
End

Path "C-H-L" Analysis

C-H-L
Start

C-H-L
End

Project Analysis

Project
Start

Project
End

swer exactly.) In the simulation, the average expected project duration is a little less than 103 days, and the similar "five-sixths" point is roughly 107 days. This is a small shift (about one-half week) for the expected project, but it is a very large shift in the probability of meeting the date that is printed on the project Gantt chart—from one chance in two to one chance in four.

Similar simulations for three and four parallel critical paths of equivalent expected duration and risk produce the results you would expect. For three paths of one hundred days, the project expectation falls to one chance in eight of completing on or before one hundred days (the simulation showed 13 percent) and an expected duration of roughly 104 days. The project with four failure modes has one chance in *sixteen* (6.3 percent in the model), and the mean for the project is a little bit more than 105 days. The resulting histogram for this case, based on 1,000 samples from each of four independent, Normally distributed parallel paths with a mean of one hundred days and a standard deviation of five days, is in Figure 9-4. (The jagged distribution is typical of simulation output.)

For these multiple critical path cases, the distribution mean increases, and the range compresses somewhat, reducing the expected standard deviation. The reason for this is that the upper data boundary for the analysis is unchanged, while each additional critical path tends to further limit the effective lower boundary. For the case in Figure 9-4, the project duration is always the *longest* of the four, and it becomes less and less likely that this maximum will be near the optimistic possibilities with each added path. Starting with a standard deviation for each path of five days, the resulting distribution for a project with two similar critical paths has a standard deviation of about 4.3 days. For three paths it is just under four days, and with four it falls to roughly 3.5 days, the statistic for the example in Figure 9-4. The resulting distributions also skew slightly to the left, for the same reasons; the data populating the histograms is being compressed, but only from the *lower* side.

Figure 9-4. PERT histogram.

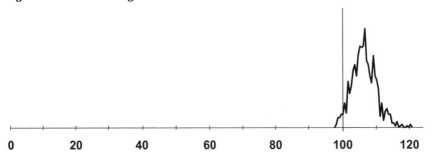

| 0 | 20 | 40 | 60 | 80 | 100 | 120 |

PERT Cost

PERT analysis is most commonly performed for duration estimates, but it can also be used for effort and cost estimates. As with PERT Time, PERT Cost generates expected estimates for activities, as well as for the entire project. Unlike the PERT Time analysis, where only data from the calculated critical path are needed, PERT Cost sums the expected cost data and variance information from *all* project activities. Because of this, the formulas analogous to PERT Time for deriving project-level cost results are equivalent to simulation.

Using PERT

True PERT analysis software uses computer simulation, and for this reason the whole idea of PERT was impractical before the late 1950s. Starting then, simulations using Monte Carlo techniques began to be widely used to analyze many kinds of complex systems, including projects. Initially, PERT was very expensive (and slow), so it was undertaken only for the largest, most costly projects. This is no longer an issue with today's inexpensive desktop systems.

The issue of data quality for PERT analysis was also significant in early implementations, and this drawback persists. Generating range estimates remains difficult, especially when defined in terms of "percent tails," as is generally done in PERT literature. Considering that the initial single-point "most likely" estimate may not be very precise or reliable, the upper and lower boundary estimates are likely to be even worse. Since at least some of the input data are inexact, the "garbage in/garbage out" problem is a standard concern with PERT analysis.

This, added to the temptation to misuse the "optimistic" estimates by overeager managers and project sponsors, has made sustained use of PERT for technical projects difficult. This is unfortunate, because even if PERT analysis is applied only to suspected critical activities using manual approximations, it can still provide valuable insight into the level of project risk, and some methods require only modest additional effort. There are a number of approaches to PERT and PERT–like analysis, from manual approximations to full computer simulation. A summary of choices follows.

Manual PERT Approximation

One way to use PERT concepts is based on a technique discussed earlier. If you have a project scheduling tool, and project schedule information has been entered into the database, most of the necessary work is already done. The duration estimates in the database are a reasonable first approximation for the optimistic estimates, or the most likely estimates (or both). To get a sense of project risk, make a copy of the database (*before* you save it as a baseline), and enter new estimates for each activity where you have developed a worst-case or a pessimistic estimate. The Gantt chart based on these estimates will display end points for the project that are further out than the original schedule. By associating a Normal distribution with these points, a rough approximation of the output for a PERT analysis may be inferred.

The method used for scaling and positioning the bell-shaped curve can vary, but at least half of the distribution ought to fall between the lower "likely" boundary and the upper "pessimistic" limits defined by the end points of the two Gantt charts. Since it is very unlikely that all the things that could go wrong in the project will actually happen, the upper boundary should line up with a point several standard deviations from the mean, far out on the distribution tail. (Keep in mind, however, that none of your unknown project risk is yet accounted for.) The initial values in the scheduling database are probably somewhere below the mean of the distribution, though the exact placement should be a function of perceived accuracy for your estimates and how conservative or aggressive the estimates are. A histogram similar to Figure 9-5, using the initial plan as about the 20 percent point (roughly one standard deviation below the mean) and the worst-case plan to define the 99 percent point (roughly three standard deviations above the mean) is not a bad first approximation.

If the result represented by Figure 9-5 looks unrealistic, it may improve things if you calculate "expected" estimates, at least for the riskiest activities on or near a critical path. If you choose to do the arithmetic, a third copy of the database can be populated with "expected" estimates, defining the mean (the "50 percent" point) for the Normal distribution. The cumulative graph of project completion probabilities equivalent to Figure 9-5 looks like Figure 9-6.

Figure 9-5. PERT approximation.

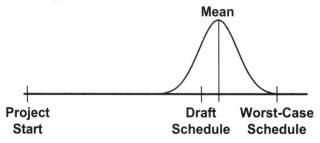

Figure 9-6. PERT estimates.

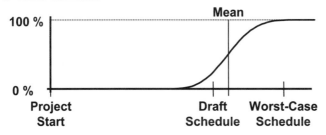

Although this sort of analysis is still subjective, the additional effort it requires is small once you generate a preliminary schedule for the project, and it provides valuable insight regarding project risk.

One of the most valuable things about analytical tools such as PERT is that they provide a very concrete, specific result. Either the results of a PERT analysis will look reasonable to you or they will seem "wrong." If the results seem realistic, they will probably be useful. If they look unrealistic, it usually indicates that additional work and planning are warranted. Odd PERT results are a good indication that your activity list is incomplete, your estimates are inaccurate, you missed some dependencies, you underestimated some risks, or your preliminary plan has some other defect.

Even this "quick and dirty" PERT approximation provides insight into the thoroughness of your project plan.

Using Computer Spreadsheets

Particularly for resource analysis, a computer spreadsheet such as Lotus 1-2-3 or Microsoft Excel is a very easy way to quickly assess three cost (or effort) estimates to derive an overall project-level budget analysis. A list of all the activities in one column with the "most likely" and range estimates in adjacent columns can be readily used to calculate expected estimates and variances for each activity and for the project as a whole. Using the PERT formulas for cost, it is simple to accumulate and evaluate data from all the project activities (not just from the critical path). The sum of all the expected costs and the calculated variance can be used as an approximation for PERT analysis of the project budget. Assuming a Normal distribution centered on the sum of the expected cost estimates with a spread defined by the calculated standard deviation shows the range that may be expected for project cost.

You could also generate "expected" duration estimates for the project by entering three duration estimates into the same spreadsheet. You can then use these "expected" duration estimates to locate your project critical path, either by manual inspection (for small projects) or by importing the data into a computer scheduling tool. If the "expected" project has a single, dominant critical path, the overall project PERT Time analysis may be derived with good accuracy, using the spreadsheet and the PERT formulas, but you must include only the activities associated with the longest path in your project network. The project PERT analysis generated this way is essentially similar to the manual approximation method discussed previously, with a Normal distribution centered on the sum of the expected duration estimates for the critical path and a spread defined by the calculated standard deviation.

For projects that have several paths roughly equal to the critical path, this method still may be used, but it will underestimate the expected project duration and overestimate the standard deviation.

Computer Scheduling Tools

True PERT analysis capability is not common in computer-based scheduling tools, and what is available tends to be implemented in quirky and mysterious ways. (This is not to be confused with the generating of "PERT" charts to display the network of project activities. All scheduling tools generate at least some rudimentary version of "PERT" charts. As discussed before, these charts are unrelated to PERT analysis and project risk.) This section mentions a number of scheduling tools, but it is far from exhaustive. Mention of a tool is not meant to imply that it is good, and nothing negative is implied about any tools that are omitted.

There are dozens of applications available for project scheduling, ranging from minimalist products that implement rudimentary activity analysis to high-end, Web-enabled enterprise applications. Often, families of software offering a range of capabilities are sold by the same company. Almost any of these tools may be used for determining the project critical path, but risk and PERT analysis using most of these tools, even some fairly expensive ones, often requires the manual processes discussed already or purchase of additional, specialized software (more on this specialized software follows).

Some rudimentary PERT analysis capability in scheduling software begins to show up in the midlevel products, which includes Microsoft Project, CA SuperProject, Scitor Project Scheduler, and other single-user products with prices comparable to home-office software. However, PERT capability in these products, if it is done at all, is based on calculations, not simulation.

For example, a very basic PERT capability was introduced

into Microsoft Project 98 and continues in more current versions. It is possible to enter the three estimates into a "PERT Entry Sheet" and have the software use these data to calculate the duration estimates that are used in the database for the primary project Gantt chart. Except for the mislabeling of "most likely" as "expected" and then calling the calculated weighted average "estimated" instead of "expected," MS Project works much as it should for basic PERT schedule analysis. It even will generate optimistic, "most likely" (mislabeled "expected"), and pessimistic Gantt views for you to look at that are based on the three entered estimates, but it does not calculate an expected variance.

If you carefully read the descriptions of what the software does, and what data should be entered where, using MS Project and other similar software can be a convenient way to assemble project PERT data. Generating PERT results similar to the manual approximation and spreadsheet methods is not difficult, but only for schedule analysis. (Even *basic* project resource analysis is not a strong feature of midrange computer scheduling tools.)

High-end project management tools, which are both more capable and more costly than the ubiquitous midrange tools, frequently provide at least some built-in "what if?" capability for risk analysis. These products have more complex user interfaces, multi-user capability, and, consequently, steeper learning curves. Open-Plan Professional, from Welcom Software Technology, provides full integrated PERT analysis, and other high-end products, such as Primavera Enterprise and Project Workbench, from Niku, provide optional capabilities. Even with the high-end tools, though, PERT analysis requires an experienced project planner with a solid understanding of the process.

PERT Simulation Tools

Tools that provide true simulation-based PERT functionality are of two types. If you plan to implement full PERT capability, you will need either to locate PERT analysis software compatible with your project scheduling tool or to select a stand-alone PERT analysis application. Again, there are many, many options available in both of these categories; the examples mentioned are not endorsements, nor are omissions intended as criticism.

There are quite a few applications designed to provide simulation-based risk analysis that either integrate into high-end tools or "bolt on" to midrange scheduling packages. If such an add-on capability is available for the software you are using (or plan to use), you can do a PERT analysis without having to reenter or convert any of your project data. With the stand-alone software, project information must be input a second time or exported. Unless you also need to do some nonproject simulation analysis, add-on PERT analysis software is also generally a less expensive option.

Two tools that implement PERT directly for Microsoft Project are Risk+, from C/S Solutions, and @Risk, from Palisade Corporation. Each of these products offers similar capability at roughly the cost of a midrange scheduling tool. The exact functions offered and the user interface differ somewhat, but each product, even in its basic version, offers the necessary functions, operates with data entered into the MS Project database, and supports a number of reporting options.

Similar risk analysis software is available for the products in the Primavera suite, including its Monte Carlo add-on software. Other available project management tools also support partner-supplied PERT modules. The marketplace for these tools evolves rapidly, and versions (and even product names) change often, so it is a good idea to do some research before committing to specific risk management software to use with your scheduling tool.

Even if you are using scheduling software that can't perform PERT analysis, there are still ways to do it. The easiest solutions to implement are simulation applications specifically designed to do project schedule analysis. Data exported from MS Project and quite a few other scheduling tools can be used by tools such as Pertmaster Professional +Risk, from Pertmaster, Ltd., and Predict! Risk Analyser, from Risk Decisions, Ltd. These tools and others, including both Risk+ and @Risk, can also operate on data stored in computer spreadsheets. Exporting the data from a scheduling tool can be difficult the first time, but, once established, the process is fairly painless.

In addition to products specifically designed for PERT analysis, there are also general-purpose simulation applications that could be used, including decision-oriented software packages such as Crystal Ball, from Decisioneering Corporation, and Analytica, from Lumina Decision Systems, both of which are designed to interface with data in spreadsheets and other data formats. You can even perform PERT analysis using general-purpose statistical analysis software such as the SAS products from the SAS Institute, Minitab, from Minitab, Inc., and the SPSS products from SPSS, Inc. For the truly masochistic, it is even possible to do PERT analysis using only a spreadsheet—Microsoft Excel includes functions for generating random samples from various distribution types, as well as statistical analysis functions for interpreting the data.

Implementing PERT

As you can see, there are many methods for evaluating projects using PERT concepts. Some are quick and relatively easy to do and provide subjective but still useful insight into project risk. Other, more robust PERT methods offer very real risk management benefits, but they also carry costs, including investment in software, generation of more data, and increased effort. Before deciding to embark on a full-scale PERT analysis on a project, especially the first time, you must carefully consider the costs and added complexity.

A primary benefit of PERT analysis (shared to some degree with the approximate techniques discussed earlier) is the graphic and visible contrast between the deterministic-looking schedule generated by point-estimate critical path methods and the range of possible end points (and associated probabilities) that emerge from PERT analysis. The illusion of certainty fostered by single-estimate Gantt charts is inconsistent with the actual risk present in technical projects. The easy-to-see output from PERT analysis is a good antidote for excessive project optimism.

In addition, PERT tools that use Monte Carlo simulation techniques are able to display project schedules more realistically in cases where the project has more than one critical (or very near-critical) path, and some PERT analysis tools even provide for project branching and "decision-tree" type analysis. Project scheduling tools assume that all choices and decisions can be made during planning and cemented into an unchanging project plan, which is not very realistic for most technical projects.

All this benefit from using PERT is far from free. (In projects there are always trade-offs.) For one thing, it can be a lot of work, and generating realistic input data forces project staff members to do even more of the sort of analysis that they already dislike doing. PERT analysis, like most analytical methodologies, can generate extremely precise-looking output, creating an illusion of precision. The actual precision of the output generated can never be any better than that of the *least* accurate inputs. Rounding the results off to whole days is about the best you can expect, yet results with many decimal places are reported by some software. This illusion of precision is particularly ironic considering the quality of typical project input data. Generating useful estimates and the effort of collecting, entering, and interpreting PERT information represent quite a bit of work.

In project environments that currently lack systematic project-level risk analysis, it may be prudent to begin with a modest PERT effort on a few projects and expand as necessary for future projects.

OTHER PROJECT MODELING AND DECISION SUPPORT

Project risk analysis also includes decision making. There are many techniques for decision making, varying from informal examination of small decisions to elaborate processes used in complex, difficult situations. One frequently used technique employs decision trees, discussed in Chapter 7. When they are simple, these branching diagrams are not difficult to evaluate through inspection. As decisions get more complicated, there are software applications and more analytical techniques available. Some decisions also benefit from more elaborate analysis, using the same simulation and statistical methods used for full-scale PERT-type project analysis. There are many computer tools available for decision modeling and analysis.

Decision-Making Process

Good decisions result from systematic group dialogue to reach agreement on one choice among a set of alternatives. More consistent decisions result from an organized process with sufficient formality to ensure thoroughness and broad participation. The overall process includes:

❒ Defining the issue or question requiring a decision

❒ Determining how, and when, and by whom the decision will be made

❒ Forming options and selecting decision criteria

❒ Analyzing options and making the decision

The first step in the decision process is to clearly define the issue requiring a decision. To avoid jumping into problem-solving mode too quickly, you should initially focus on the question "What problem are we solving?" Use root cause analysis to understand the underlying source of the issue, not just the obvious symptoms. If clarification of the overall problem proves impossible, decompose it into smaller, more tractable subproblems. Frame the issue by identifying how the decision will be used, and summarize the issue in a concise statement.

Effective decision making requires participation by the right people. Involve people who will be affected by the decision, as well as those who will need to approve the choice that you make. Also, identify the experience, knowledge, and skills required for a good decision, and get commitment from qualified people to participate in the decision-making process.

While some decisions must be made quickly, with very little discussion or group input involved, other decisions require consensus, or even unanimity. Determine how you will arrive at a decision, and gain support for your process. Set a deadline for the decision that will allow adequate time for discussion and analysis.

Once you have determined the issue and how to proceed, develop a set of options or alternative solutions for the problem statement, using methods such as brainstorming, cause-and-effect diagrams, root cause analysis, and creative problem solving. Also, identify any criteria that are important for the decision. Define measurable criteria and prioritize them by relative importance. Evaluation criteria could include factors such as speed, cost, total required effort, and the number of people involved. Discussing the criteria and their relative weights improves understanding of the issue and leads to group buy-in for the decision.

You can evaluate simple decisions using a "pros and cons" list or a simple matrix with weighted decision criteria. For more complex situations, spreadsheets or software tools may help with your evaluation. However you evaluate your potential options, use the information to prioritize the alternatives. Discuss the top several items; if there are people who believe that the top item is not the best choice, explore why. Whenever an analytical process results in the "wrong" answer, it may indicate that your assumptions or data are faulty. Your criteria, weights, or evaluations may need adjustment, or you may need further discussion to develop consensus. Before adopting any of the alternatives, check for any unintended consequences or risks.

When you reach agreement, stop the discussion. Verify support for the decision among all those involved, communicate your decision, and put it into action.

Decision Support Software

As with project analysis tools, there is no dearth of computer applications to help with decision making. Some software available is related to the PERT tools already discussed, such as Precision Trees, from Palisade Corporation, the same company that offers the @Risk application. Other tools for decision-tree analysis include DPL, from Applied Decision Analysis, and DATA, from Treeage Software. There are also a number of packages that support implementation of the matrix-oriented analytical hierarchy process, including Expert Choice, from Expert Choice, Inc., but evaluating decisions using a matrix of evaluations of weighted criteria is not that complicated for many decisions, whether done manually or using a computer spreadsheet.

Several of the simulation-support tools discussed for PERT analysis are also useful for analyzing decisions, such as Crystal Ball, from Decisioneering Corporation, and Analytica, from Lumina

Decision Systems. Simulation capability allows deeper exploration of the range of possible outcomes from decisions, which can be valuable in evaluating very complex decisions.

Analysis of Scale

Quantitative project analysis using all the preceding techniques, either with computer tools or using manual methods, is based on details of the project work—activities, decisions, worst cases, resource issues, and other planning data. It is also possible to assess risk on the basis of the overall size of the project, because the overall level of effort is another important risk factor. Projects only 20 percent larger than previous work represent significant risk.

Scale analysis is based on the overall effort that the project plan calls for. Projects fall into three categories—low risk, normal risk, and high risk—determined by the anticipated effort as compared with earlier, successful projects. Scale assessment begins by accumulating the data from the bottom-up project plan to determine total project effort, measured in a suitable unit such as "effort-months." The calculated project scale can then be compared with the effort actually used on several recent, similar projects. In selecting comparison projects, look for work that had similar deliverables, timing, and staffing so that the comparison will be as valid as possible. If the data for the other projects are not in the form you need, do a rough estimate using staffing levels and project duration. If there were periods in the comparison projects where significant overtime was used, especially at the end, account for that effort, as well. The numbers generated do not need to be exact, but they do need to fairly represent the amount of overall effort actually required to complete the comparison projects.

Using the total of planned effort-months for your project and an average from the comparison projects, determine the risk:

Low risk   Less than 60 percent of the average

Normal risk   Between 60 percent and 120 percent of the average

High risk   Greater than 120 percent of the average

These ranges center on 90 percent rather than 100 percent because the comparison is between actual past project data, which include all changes and risks that occurred, and the current project plans, which do not. Risk arises from other factors in addition to size, so consider raising the risk assessment one category if:

- ❐ The schedule is significantly compressed
- ❐ The project requires new technology
- ❐ 40 percent of the project resources are either external or unknown

Project Appraisal

Scale analysis can be taken a further step, both to validate the project plan and to get a more precise estimate of risk. The technique requires an "appraisal," similar to the process used whenever you need to know the value of something, such as a piece of property or jewelry, but you do not want to sell it to find out. Value appraisals are based on the recent sale of several similar items, with appropriate additions and deductions to account for small differences. If you want to know the value of your home, an appraiser examines it and finds descriptions of several comparable homes recently sold nearby. If the comparison home has an extra bathroom, a small deduction is made to its purchase price; if your house has a larger, more modern kitchen, the appraiser makes a small positive adjustment. The process continues, using at least two other homes, until all factors normally included are assessed. The average adjusted price that results is taken to be the value of your home—the current price for which you could probably sell it.

The same process can be applied to projects, since you face an analogous situation. You would like to know how much effort a project will require, but you are not in a position to execute all the work to find out. The comparisons in this case are two or three recently completed similar projects, for which you can ascertain the number of effort-months that were required for each. (This starts with the same data the scale analysis technique uses.)

From your bottom-up plan, calculate the number of effort-months your project is expected to take. The current project can be compared to the comparison projects, using a list of factors germane to your work. Factors relevant to the scope, schedule, and resources for the projects can be compared, as in Figure 9-7 (which was quickly assembled using a computer spreadsheet).

One goal of this technique is to find comparison projects that are as similar as possible so that the adjustments will be small and the appraisal can be as accurate as possible. If a factor seems

Figure 9-7. Project appraisal.

Project : ____Zinfandel____   Effort-Months (Planned)   [100]

	Project A		Project B		Project C	
	Comparison	Change in Effort	Comparison	Change in Effort	Comparison	Change in Effort
Effort-Months (actual)	110		80		107	
Scope: Functionality	Similar	0	3%	2.4	Similar	0.0
Usability	-3%	-3.3	Similar	0	Similar	0.0
Reliability	Similar	0	3%	2.4	Similar	0.0
Performance	5%	5.5	Similar	0	-3%	-3.2
Supportability	Similar	0	Similar	0	Similar	0.0
Technology	-5%	-5.5	5%	4	-3%	-3.2
Resources: Maximum Staff	-3%	-3.3	3%	2.4	-5%	-5.4
Control	Similar	0	Similar	0	Similar	0.0
Staff Experience	3%	3.3	Similar	0	Similar	0.0
Geographical Separation	Similar	0	5%	4	Similar	0.0
Schedule: Total Length	-5%	-5.5	Similar	0	3%	3.2
Net Adjustments	-8%	-8.8	19%	15.2	-8%	-8.6
Indicated Effort-Months		101.2		95.2		98.4

Mean Effort-Months   [98.3]

"similar," no adjustment is made. When there are differences, adjust conservatively, such as:

Small differences   Plus or minus 2–5 percent

Larger differences   Plus or minus 7–10 percent

The adjustments are *positive* if the current project has the higher risk and *negative* if the comparison project seems more challenging.

The first thing you can use a project appraisal for is to test whether your preliminary plan is realistic. Whenever the adjusted comparison projects average to a higher number of effort-months than your current planning shows, your plan is almost certainly missing something. Whenever the appraisal indicates a difference greater than about 10 percent compared with the bottom-up planning, work to understand why. What have you overlooked? Where are your estimates too optimistic? What activities have you not captured? Also, compare project appraisal effort-month estimates with the resource goal in the original project objective. A project appraisal also provides early warning of potential budget problems.

One reason project appraisals are generally larger than the corresponding plan is risk. The finished projects include the consequences of all risks, including those that were invisible early in the work. The current project planning includes only data on the known risks for which you have incorporated risk prevention strategies. At least part of the difference between your plan and an appraisal results from the comparison projects' "unknown" risks, contingency plans, and other risk response efforts.

In addition to plan reviews, project appraisals are also useful in project-level risk management. Whenever there is a major difference between the parameters of the planned project and the goals stated in the project objective, the appraisal shows why this is so, convincingly and in a very concise format. A project appraisal is a very effective way to begin discussion of options and trade-offs with the project sponsor, which is addressed in Chapter 10.

Project Metrics

Project measurement is essential to risk management. It also provides the historical basis for other project planning and management processes, such as estimation, scheduling, controlling, and resource planning. Metrics drive behavior, so selecting appropriate factors to measure can have a significant effect on motivation and project progress. Bill Hewlett, a founder of HP, was fond of saying, "What gets measured gets done." Metrics provide the information needed to improve processes and to detect when it is time to modify or replace an existing process. Established metrics also are the foundation of project tracking, establishing the baseline for measuring progress. Defining, implementing, and interpreting a system of ongoing measures is not difficult, so it is unfortunate that on many projects these steps either are not done at all or are done poorly.

Establishing Metrics

Before deciding what to measure, carefully define the behavior you want and determine what measurements will be most likely encourage that behavior. Next, establish a baseline by collecting enough data to determine current performance for what you plan to measure. Going forward, you can use metrics to detect changes, trigger process improvements, evaluate process modifications, and make performance and progress visible.

The process begins with defining the results or behavior you desire. For metrics in support of better project risk management, a typical goal might be "Reduce unanticipated project effort" or "Improve the accuracy of project estimates." Consider what you might be able to measure that relates to the desired outcome. For unanticipated project effort, you might measure "total effort actually consumed by the project versus effort planned." For estimation accuracy, a possible metric might be "cumulative difference between project estimates and project results, as measured at the project conclusion."

Metrics are of three basic types: predictive, diagnostic, and retrospective. An effective system of metrics generally includes measures of more than one type, providing for good balance.

❑ *Predictive metrics* use current information to provide insight into future conditions. Because predictive metrics are based on speculative rather than empirical data, they are typically the least reliable of the three types. Predictive metrics include the initial assessment of project "return on investment," the output from the quantitative risk management tools, and most other measurements based on planning data.

❑ *Diagnostic metrics* are designed to provide current information about a system. On the basis of the latest data, they assess the state of a running process and may detect anomalies or forecast future problems. The unanticipated effort metric suggested before is based on earned value, a useful diagnostic project metric.

❑ *Retrospective metrics* report after the fact on how the process worked. Backward-looking metrics report on the overall health of the process and are useful in tracking trends. The estimating accuracy example already mentioned is based on the estimating quality factor metric as defined by Tom DeMarco, a retrospective metric discussed in more detail later in this chapter.

MEASURING PROJECTS

The following section includes a number of useful project metrics. No project needs to collect all of them, but one or more measurements of each type of metric, collected and evaluated for all projects in an organization, can significantly improve the planning and risk management on future projects. These metrics relate directly to projects and project management. A discussion of additional metrics, related to financial measures, follows this section.

When implementing any set of metrics, you need to spend some time collecting data to validate a baseline for the measurements before you make any decisions or changes. Until you have a validated baseline, measurements will be hard to interpret, and you will not be able to determine the effects of process modifications that you make. There is more discussion on selecting and using metrics in Chapter 10.

Predictive Project Metrics

Most predictive project metrics relate to factors that can be calculated using data from your project plan. These metrics are fairly easy to define and calculate, and they can be validated against corresponding actual data at the project close. Over time, the goal for each of these should be to drive the predictive measures and the retrospective results into closer and closer agreement. Measurement baselines are set using project goals and planning data.

Predictive metrics are also useful in helping you anticipate potential project problems. One method of doing this is to identify any of these predictive metrics that is significantly larger than typically measured for past, successful projects—a variance of 15 to 20 percent represents significant project risk. (The first metric, "total effort," is the basis for the "project scale" risk assessment discussed earlier in the chapter.) A second use for these metrics is to correlate them with other project properties. After measuring factors such as unanticipated effort, unforeseen risks, and project delays for ten or more projects, some of these factors may reveal sufficient correlation to predict problems with fair accuracy.

Some predictive project metrics include:

☐ *Total project effort*: effort-month total for all project activities.

☐ *Budget at completion* (BAC): the monetary equivalent of total project effort. This metric is associated with project earned value analysis.

☐ *Project appraisal*: the expected total project effort based on comparisons with completed similar projects, adjusting for significant differences.

☐ *Project complexity index*: the sum of several deliverable-related factors, multiplied by a scale factor (described in Chapter 3).

☐ *Aggregated schedule risk*: the sum of all project slippage expected, based on using contingency plans and weighted by probability of use.

☐ *Aggregated budget risk*: the sum of all additional project costs expected, based on using contingency plans and weighted by probability of use.

❐ *Survey-based risk assessment score*: collaborative accumulation of risk data from project staff using a customized set of assessment questions.

❐ *Logical project length*: the maximum number of distinct activities on any network path.

❐ *Logical project width*: the maximum number of parallel activities found in the project network.

❐ *Logical project complexity*: the ratio of activity dependencies to activities.

❐ *Project independence*: the ratio of internal activity dependencies to all dependencies.

❐ *Project staffing*: maximum number of project staff.

❐ *Sum of activity durations*: total duration of all activities if executed sequentially.

❐ *Sum of total activity float*: total float (or slack) accumulated from all planned activities.

❐ *Project density*: the ratio of the sum of activity durations to the sum of activity durations plus the sum of total activity float.

Diagnostic Project Metrics

Diagnostic metrics are based on measurements taken throughout the project, and they are used to detect adverse project variances and project problems, either in advance or as soon as is practical. Measurement baselines are generally set using a combination of stated goals and historical data from earlier projects. Diagnostic metrics are comparative measures, either trend-oriented (comparing the current measure with earlier measures) or prediction-oriented (comparing measurements with corresponding predictions, generally based on planning).

A large family of diagnostic project metrics relates to the concept of earned value analysis (EVA). This technique for project measurement and control begins with allocating the portion of the project budget associated with project activities (the costs associated with effort) to each of the planned project activities. The sum of all these allocated bits must exactly equal 100 percent of the project staffing budget. As the project executes, EVA collects data on actual costs and actual timing for all completed activities so that ratios and differences may be calculated. The definitions for these diagnostic metrics follow, stated in financial terms. The mathematics of EVA are identical for equivalent metrics that are based on effort data (person-hours planned versus person-hours actually consumed), and a parallel set of metrics defined this way are sometimes used. The terminology for earned value analysis was changed in the *PMBOK® Guide*, 2000 edition, but both the new and the still commonly used older terminology are included here.

Like PERT analysis, the value of EVA for technical projects is the subject of much discussion. It can represent quite a bit of overhead, and, for many types of technical projects, tracking data at the level required by EVA is thought to be overkill. If the metrics for EVA seem impractical, the related alternative of activity closure index, which provides similar diagnostic information on the basis of the higher granularity of whole activities, provides similar information with a lot less effort. EVA typically can accurately predict project overrun at the point where 15 percent of the project staffing budget is consumed. Activity closure rate is less precise, but even it will accurately spot an overrun trend well before the project halfway point.

Some diagnostic project metrics include:

❑ *Earned value (EV), or budgeted cost of work performed (BCWP)*: a running accumulation of the costs that were planned for every project activity that is currently complete. The terms are synonymous, but EV is currently preferred in the *PMBOK® Guide*.

❑ *Actual cost (AC), or actual cost of work performed (ACWP)*: a running accumulation of the actual costs for every project activity that is currently complete. The terms are synonymous, but AC is currently preferred in the *PMBOK® Guide*.

❑ *Planned value (PV), or budgeted cost of work scheduled (BCWS)*: a running accumulation of the planned costs for every project activity that was expected to be complete up to the current time. The terms are synonymous, but PV is currently preferred in the *PMBOK® Guide*. (PV is really a predictive project metric, because all the values for the whole project may be calculated from the baseline plan as an ever increasing amount of money. PV starts at zero, and at the project end it is equal to the budget at completion. PV may be treated as a diagnostic metric for earned value analysis, calculated periodically along with EV and AC.)

❑ *Cost performance index (CPI)*: the ratio of earned value to actual cost. This ratio is the primary diagnostic metric used for EVA. When it is one or higher, the project is spending money (or equivalently, effort) at a rate that is equal to or less than the planned rate. When it is less than one, the "burn rate" for the project is too high, and it indicates a possible project budget overrun.

☐ *Schedule performance index (SPI)*: the ratio of earned value to planned value. This ratio may be used to predict schedule problems, providing that resource use throughout the project is relatively constant. If resource use varies with project timing, SPI has limited usefulness.

☐ *Cost variance (CV)*: the difference between earned value and actual cost, a measurement of how much the project is over or under budget. A cost variance percentage may be calculated as a ratio of CV to earned value. The CV percentage reports the current budget variance as a fraction. CV, like CPI, may be used to predict project overrun.

☐ *Schedule variance (SV)*: the difference between earned value and planned value. Like the SPI metric, this absolute monetary difference is of value only if resource use is flat over time. Schedule variance percentage, the ratio of SV to earned value, presents the same information as a fraction.

☐ *Activity closure index*: the ratio of activities closed in the project so far to the number expected based on a linear extrapolation—in other words, for an N-week project, 1/N of the total number of activities per week. For example, by week six of a thirty-six-week project with 200 planned activities, roughly thirty-three activities should be complete. If only thirty are closed, the ratio is .9, indicating a potential schedule problem. This is a less complex, and less precise, variation on earned value analysis.

☐ *Cumulative slip*: the running sum for all activities of early schedule finish date minus actual activity completion date.

☐ *Risk closure index*: the ratio of risks closed (avoided, encountered, or otherwise no longer a risk) in the project divided by the number expected on the basis of a linear extrapolation.

Retrospective Project Metrics

Retrospective metrics are backward-looking and may be assessed only at the close of a project. Measurement baselines are based on prior history, and these metrics are most useful for longer-term process improvement.

Some retrospective project metrics include:

❐ *Estimation quality factor (EQF)*: the ratio of project cost multiplied by duration, divided by an accumulated estimating error factor

❐ *Performance to planned schedule*: a variance measured in workdays or as a percentage of the planned schedule

❐ *Performance to planned budget*: a variance measured in financial terms or as a percentage of the planned budget

❐ *Life-cycle phase effort percentages* (for *your* life cycle)

❐ *Testing effort* as a percent of total project effort

❐ *Performance to standard estimates* for required or standardized project activities

The first metric listed, EQF, requires some explanation. Introduced in *Controlling Software Projects* by Tom DeMarco, EQF is a measure of how quickly erroneous estimates are detected and corrected. It is a unitless ratio based on the actual project duration multiplied by the actual project cost, divided by an accumulated estimating error factor. The estimating error factor is accumulated for the project by summing over the whole project the absolute value of the difference between the project cost estimate and the final project cost, multiplied by the amount of time the estimate was believed accurate. If the estimate was changed several times, the estimating error factor will be a number of these products, added together.

EQF sounds harder to calculate than it is, and it is evaluated only once per project. A graph with the project duration on the X axis and project budget on the Y axis defines a rectangle (as shown in Figure 9-8), the area of which is the numerator for EQF. The plot of cost estimates by date throughout the project defines a series of rectangles that share either a top or a bottom border with the larger rectangle that defines the numerator. The areas of all the smaller rectangles (shaded in the figure) added together are the denominator for EQF.

If the initial project cost estimate is exactly right and never changed, EQF is infinite, because you are dividing by an estimating error factor of zero. If the cost estimate starts at zero and stays there through the entire project, EQF is one, which is the effective minimum. (EQF lower than one is possible, but only for projects that begin with enormously padded budgets.) A project that increases the estimate linearly once a week until the project is done has an EQF of two, equal to a project that estimates the cost at one half the final figure and never changes it.

Figure 9-8 shows an EQF of roughly four (the grey area is

Figure 9-8. EQF example.

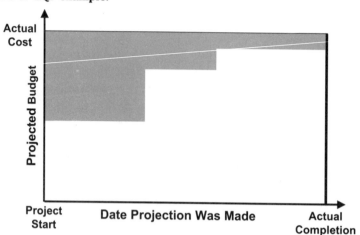

about one quarter of the larger rectangle). This is about where one R&D lab at Hewlett-Packard started when it calculated EQF for several completed projects. Over a period of about a year, the average project in the lab improved to an EQF of almost 20, representing a typical overall estimating error of about 5 percent—very respectable. What gets measured *gets done.*

FINANCIAL METRICS

Project risk extends beyond the normal limits of project management, and project teams must consider and do what they can to manage risks that are not strictly "project management." There are a number of methods and principles used to develop predictive metrics that relate to the broad concept of return on investment (ROI), and an understanding of these is essential to many types of technical projects. As discussed in Chapter 3 with market risks, ROI analysis falls only partially within project management's traditional boundaries. Each of the several ways to measure ROI comes with benefits, drawbacks, and challenges.

The Time Value of Money

The foundation of most ROI metrics is the concept of the time value of money. This is the idea that a quantity of money today is worth more than the same quantity of money at some time in the future. How much more depends on a rate of interest (or discount rate) and the amount of time. The formula for this is:

$$PV = FV/(1 + i)^n, \text{ where}$$

PV is present value
FV is future value
i is the periodic interest rate
n is the number of periods

If the interest rate is 5 percent per year (.05) and the time is one year, $1 today is equivalent to $1.05 in the future.

Payback Analysis

Even armed with the time-value-of-money formula, it is rarely easy to determine the worth of any complex investment with precision, and this is especially true for investments in projects. Project analysis involves many (perhaps hundreds) of parameters and values, multiple periods, and possibly several interest rates. Estimating all of these data, particularly the value of the project deliverable after the completion of the project, can be very difficult.

The most basic ROI model for projects is simple payback analysis, which assumes no time value for money (equivalent to an interest rate of zero). This type of ROI metric has many names, including break-even time, payback period, or the "return map." Payback analysis adds up all expected project expenses and then proceeds to add expected revenues, profits, or accrued benefits, period by period, until the value of the benefits balances the costs. As projects rarely generate benefits before completion, the cumulative financials swing heavily negative, and it takes many periods after the revenues and benefits begin to reach "break even."

The project in the graph in Figure 9-9 runs for about five months, with a budget of almost $500,000. It takes another six

Figure 9-9. Simple payback analysis.

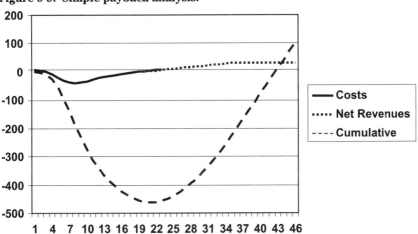

months, roughly, to generate returns equal to the project's expenses. Simple payback analysis works fairly well for comparing similar-length projects to find the one (or ones) that recover their costs most rapidly. It has the advantage of simplicity, using predictive project cost metrics for the expense data and sales or other revenue forecasts for the rest.

Refining simple payback analysis to incorporate interest (or discount) rates is not difficult. The first step is to determine an appropriate interest rate. Some analyses use the prevailing cost of borrowing money, others use a rate of interest available from external investments, and still others use rates based on business targets. The rate of interest selected can make a significant difference when evaluating ROI metrics.

Once an appropriate interest rate is selected, each of the expense and revenue estimates can be discounted back to an equivalent present value before it is summed. The discounted payback or break-even point again occurs when the sum, in this case the cumulative present value, reaches zero. For a nonzero interest rate, the amount of time required for payback will be significantly longer than with the simple analysis, since the farther in the future the revenues are generated, the less they contribute because of the time value of money. Discounted payback analysis is still relatively easy to evaluate, and it is more suitable for comparing projects that have different durations.

Payback analysis, with and without consideration of the time value of money, is often criticized for being too short-term. These metrics determine only the time required to recover the initial investment. They do not consider any benefits that might occur following the break-even point, so a project that breaks even quickly and then generates no further benefits would rank higher than a project that takes longer to return the investment but represents a much longer, larger stream of subsequent revenues or benefits.

Net Present Value

Total net present value (NPV) is another method to measure project ROI. NPV follows the same process as the discounted payback analysis, but it does not stop at the break-even point. NPV includes all the costs and all the anticipated benefits throughout the expected life of the project deliverable. Once all the project costs and returns have been estimated and discounted to the present, the sum represents the total present value for the project. This total NPV can be used to compare possible projects, even projects with very different financial profiles and time scales, basing the analysis on all expected project benefits.

Total NPV effectively determines the overall expected return for a project, but it tends to favor large projects over smaller ones, without regard to other factors. A related idea for comparing projects normalizes their financial magnitudes by calculating a profitability index (PI). The PI is a ratio, the sum of all the discounted revenues divided by the sum of all the discounted costs. PI is always greater than one for projects that have a positive NPV, and the higher the PI is above one, the more profitable the project is expected to be.

Even though these metrics require additional data—estimates of the revenues or benefits throughout the useful life of the deliverable—they are still relatively easy to evaluate.

Internal Rate of Return

Another way to contrast projects of different sizes is to calculate an internal rate of return (IRR). IRR uses the same estimates for costs and returns required to calculate total net present value, but, instead of assuming an interest rate and calculating the present value for the project, IRR sets the present value equal to zero and then solves for the required interest rate. Mathematically, IRR is the most complex ROI metric, as it must be determined using iteration and "trial and error." For sufficiently complicated cash flows, there may even be several values possible for IRR (this occurs only if there are several reversals of sign in the cash flows, so it rarely happens in project analysis). These days, use of a computer (or even a financial calculator) makes determining IRR fairly straightforward, if good estimates for costs and revenues are available. For each project, the interest rate you calculate shows how effective the project is expected to be as an investment.

ROI Estimates

All of these ROI methods are attempts to determine the "goodness" of financial investments, in this case, projects. Theoretically, any of these methods is an effective way to select a few promising projects out of many possibilities or to compare projects with other investment opportunities.

Due to their differing assumptions, these methods may generate inconsistent ranking results for a list of potential projects, but this is rarely the biggest issue with ROI metrics. In most cases, the larger, more fundamental problem is with input data. Each of these methods generates a precise numeric result for a given project that is based on the data. For many projects, this information comes from two sources that are historically not very reliable: project planning data and sales forecasts. Project planning data can be made more accurate over time using metrics and adjustments for risk, at least in theory. Unfortunately, project ROI calculations are generally made before much planning is done, when the project cost data are still based on vague information, or the estimates come from top-down budget goals that are not correlated with planning at all.

Estimates of financial return are an even larger problem. These estimates are not only usually very uncertain (based on sales projections or other speculative forecasts) but also much larger numbers, so they are more significant in the calculations. For product development projects, in many cases revenue estimates are higher by an order of magnitude or more, so even small estimating errors can result in large ROI variances.

ROI metrics can be very accurate and useful when calculated retrospectively using historical data, long after projects have completed. The predictive value of ROI measures calculated in advance of projects can never be any more trustworthy than the input data, so a great deal of variation can occur.

Key Ideas for Project Risk Analysis

❏ Survey contributors and stakeholders for risk assessments.
❏ Use worst-case estimates, contingency plan data, or PERT analysis to determine project uncertainty.
❏ Estimate project scale in effort-months.

Panama Canal: Overall Risks (1907)

When John Stevens first arrived in Panama, he found a lack of progress and an even greater lack of enthusiasm. He commented, "There are three diseases in Panama. They are yellow fever, malaria, and cold feet; and the greatest of these is cold feet." For the first two, he set Dr. William Gorgas to work, and these risks were soon all but eliminated from the project.

For the "cold feet," Stevens himself provided the cure. His intense planning effort and thorough analysis converted the seemingly impossible into small, realistic steps that showed that the work was feasible; the ways and means for getting the work done were documented and credible. Even though there were still many specific problems and risks on the project, Stevens had demonstrated that the overall project was truly possible. This was quite a turnaround from John Wallace's belief that the canal venture was a huge mistake.

With Stevens's plan, nearly every part of the job relied on techniques that were in use elsewhere, and almost all the work required had been done somewhere before. Project funding was guaranteed by the U.S. government. There were thousands of people able, and very willing, to work on the project, so labor was never an issue. The rights and other legal needs were not a problem, especially after Theodore Roosevelt manipulated the politics in both the United States and in Panama to secure them. What continued to make the canal project exceptional was its enormous scale. As Stevens said, "There is no element of mystery involved; the problem is one of magnitude and not miracles."

Planning and a credible understanding of overall project risk are what convert the need for magic and miracles (which no one can confidently promise to deliver) into the merely difficult. Projects that are seen as difficult but *possible* are the ones that succeed; a belief that a project can be completed is an important factor in how hard and how well people work. When it looks as though miracles will be necessary, people tend to give up, and their skepticism may very well make the project impossible.

CHAPTER 10

MANAGING PROJECT RISK

"Let us never negotiate out of fear, but let us never fear to negotiate."

—JOHN F. KENNEDY

It is rare to encounter a project where everyone involved feels things are adequately under control. There never seems to be enough time, funding and staffing seem too low, and there are generally a few technical challenges yet to figure out. Managing project-level risk involves understanding all of this well enough early in your work to set realistic project expectations and, if necessary, to negotiate at least minor changes to the project. While it is never possible to deal *completely* with project risks and issues, shifting things to minimize the worst problems may be sufficient. Once a project is seen to be feasible, hard work, with a bit of inspiration, cleverness, and luck, is often enough to let you close the rest of the gap.

The main point of this chapter is to deliver on the title of the book—to provide techniques for failure-proofing your project. Managing project risk begins with the risk assessments and plans of the preceding chapters. This chapter builds on that foundation, discussing how to effectively use risk and project data to influence necessary changes, to clearly communicate project risks, and to adopt ongoing risk management practices that detect new risks promptly and minimize problems throughout the project.

Most of the content of this chapter falls into the "Risk Response Planning" portion of the Planning Processes in the *PMBOK®* Guide, but it goes beyond that material to include concepts from other Planning Processes. The principal ideas in this chapter include:

❏ Project documentation requirements
❏ Project start-up
❏ Selection and implementation of project metrics
❏ Management reserve
❏ Project baseline negotiation
❏ Project plan validation
❏ Specification change management

Project Documentation Requirements

One of the only things less interesting than assembling project documentation is reading a lengthy description of what it "must" include. Since technical projects come in all sizes, shapes, durations, and complexity, the requirements for project documentation—the written descriptions for project deliverables, plans, and other relevant information—vary a great deal. Whether the documentation is lengthy and elaborate or fairly informal, it serves as your basis for project execution and control. Project teams that fail to put adequate documentation in place know too little about their projects, and they carry more risk. In addition, when you lack data, you have a much lower chance of influencing necessary changes to your project, because your proposals and negotiations will not have enough facts supporting them. While it is certainly possible to overinvest in project documentation, it is far more common on technical projects to do too little. Prudent project risk management tends to err on the side of capturing more, rather than less, data.

Project documentation is most effective when it is available in "layers." At the most detailed level, there is the thorough, *Encyclopedia Britannica* version of the project plan needed by the project team. For others, such lengthy detail is neither necessary nor appropriate. You also need clear, summary-level documentation that can be used in discussions with sponsors, stakeholders, and others who are less involved with the project but who will take part in project discussions, negotiations, decisions, escalations, problem solving, and other project communication.

Thorough project documentation created during your planning and risk assessment gives you a foundation for validating your project plan. It also provides the leverage you need to negotiate project modifications when it is necessary to transform a project that would almost certainly fail into something more realistic. The ultimate goal of this process is to set your project plan of record consistent with both the project objective and a realistic plan. Ongoing project risk management also requires periodic plan reviews and an effective change management process, and these also rely on thorough documentation.

PROJECT DOCUMENTS

Project documents fall into three categories: definition documents, planning documents, and periodic project communications. Definition documents are generally assembled earliest. They include:

❐ A high-level project overview

❐ A scope statement and a summary of the project objective

❐ The project proposal (or "data sheet," project charter, or whatever the overall description of the project may be called)

❐ Project sponsorship

❐ Project staffing and organization information

❐ Significant assumptions and project constraints

❐ Methodologies or life cycles to be used

❐ Procedure for managing specification changes

Additional necessary documentation may include detailed specification documents, a high-level project financial analysis, the project budget, detailed release or acceptance specifications, any market research reports or user investigations, and any other specific project data required by your organization.

Planning documentation is also assembled in the earliest project stages, but it may be modified and augmented throughout the project as a result of approved changes or new information. Typical project planning documents are:

❐ The project work breakdown structure (WBS) and activity list

❐ The project schedule

❐ The project resource plan

❐ Functional plans (for quality, support, test, and other aspects)

❐ The risk register and management plan

❐ Planning assumptions and constraints

Periodic project communications accumulate throughout the project. They include:

❐ Status reports

❐ Meeting minutes

❐ Specification change notices

❐ Project review

❐ Phase transition or stage-gate reports

❐ Interim and final project retrospective reports, and "lessons learned"

Project documents are most useful when they have a consistent, easy-to-read format, so you should adopt an appropriate existing format (or define one) and stick with it. Especially for lengthy documents, use a format that begins with a high-level summary or abstract that is no longer than half a page of text. It is always risky to bury important information on page 43 of a project report. For each project document, identify an owner (often the project leader) who will be responsible for creation, maintenance, and distribution. Define how and when document changes can or should be made. When there are approved changes, you need to assign responsibility for providing up-to-date documents and for marking old versions obsolete.

Documents have value only if the people who need them have ready access to them. Storing documents on-line (with appropriate access security) is an effective way to ensure that all team members have access to and are working from the same information. Establish a centralized location for any paper documents (or several, for geographically separated teams) that is well known and easily accessed. Whether your project documents are in a notebook, in a file cabinet, or on a server or use some other medium, keep them available and current.

Project Start-Up

One of the most significant problems on technical projects is lack of team cohesion, particularly for projects that have geographically separated teams. Completing a difficult project requires teamwork, trust, and a willingness to look out for and help the others on the project. Under tension, chains tend to break at the weakest link; projects staffed by "virtual" teams have nothing but weak links.

One method for countering this problem and minimizing the risks that result when projects must be staffed by people who do not know each other is to hold a project start-up workshop. A start-up workshop (sometimes referred to as a project launch, a "kickoff" meeting, a planning workshop, or a project initiation meeting) is an event intended to initiate the project processes and to build teamwork. A well-run start-up achieves a common understanding of the project goals and priorities and avoids wasted time and redundant efforts. It also builds a more cohesive team that will get a fast, efficient start on the project.

Typically, you will want to hold these workshops very early in the planning process, at the start of project execution, and before each major new phase of the project. The precise objectives vary somewhat for workshops held at these different times, but all start-ups focus on team building and on common project understanding. Achieving these objectives substantially reduces many types of project risk.

J<small>USTIFY AND</small> P<small>REPARE FOR THE</small> W<small>ORKSHOP</small>

One reason given for not holding start-up workshops is cost. Particularly for global teams who must travel to take part in a face-to-face workshop, costs and travel time can be significant. But the cost of *not* doing a project start-up is also high; serious problems and loss of productivity can result whenever people are uncooperative or misunderstand information in complex projects. For technical projects, it is not a choice between the expense of a project start-up workshop and saving money; the choice is between investing a relatively small amount of time and money early or spending a lot more time and money later in the project. Establishing common objectives and language for the project and building relationships among the project team members minimizes risk and creates the environment needed for a successful project.

The most effective start-up meetings are held in person at the beginning of the project. On longer projects, the exercise is best repeated at least every six months. Face-to-face meetings are best for team building, and periodic renewal of acquaintances establishes the foundation that allows distance collaboration and other means of communication to work smoothly and well. When the timing or cost aspects of a project start-up genuinely make an in-person meeting impossible, at least plan and hold a meeting, or a series of meetings, using videoconferencing or other teleconferencing technology. Such a meeting is much less effective for team building and generating trust, but it still contributes to better common understanding, and it is much better than doing nothing.

As the plans for project start-up take shape, allow some time during the meeting for some nonwork activities to let people get to know one another better. If the workshop takes place over multiple days, consider using evenings for team dinners or other events. Even for "virtual" meetings, invest some time in activities that encourage people to connect, such as individual discussions of hobbies and interests or sharing other personal information. Having distant team members interview one another before the meeting and then asking each person to report some of the information gathered to start the meeting is very effective in building the personal relationships that difficult projects depend on. Exchanges of pictures, items of interest, or even food with distant team members involved in the meeting are also good ways to connect people.

Productive project start-up workshops are organized well in advance. Put sufficient effort into details such as the agenda, a facilitator, the information required, the place and time, and the people who should participate. Set an agenda that includes introductions, discussion of project objectives and deliverables, exploration of planning information, defining of team roles, and other project aspects that you need to cover. Specific project start-up workshop agenda items vary depending on the timing of the meeting, the size of the project, and the length of the workshop. Include sufficient time on the agenda for discussion of each topic, and clearly specify any outputs or decisions expected for each part of the workshop listed in the agenda. For small projects, a start-up meeting might only require half a day. For large programs, a series of workshops could run for a week, or even longer. When working with global teams, allocate additional time to accommodate factors such as language and culture. Prioritize the agenda to cover the most important items first, and review the agenda in advance with your project sponsor.

Some of the objectives and benefits of a start-up workshop are difficult to achieve when the project leader is also the facilitator. The facilitator's main job is to keep the team focused on the agenda. The project leader is better able to participate in the meeting and contribute to the results if he or she is not also facilitating. One alternative is to ask a leader from another project to facilitate and then to reciprocate later by offering to facilitate his or her meeting. This not only allows you to participate more fully in your start-up but also leads to broader awareness of other projects, lowering organization-level risks. Another option is to use a professional facilitator.

The meeting objectives also require up-to-date project information, in a form that is easily distributed and used for the workshop. Assemble project documents and distribute any necessary data in advance of the meeting. For specific outputs that are listed on the agenda, be sure to provide any examples, formats, and templates that are available.

Determine the people you need to participate in the workshop for it to be successful. Include all of the core project team, as well as others who will make significant contributions. Schedule the meeting to minimize timing conflicts for the attendees. Invite all the participants, and get their commitment to attend the full workshop. Select your meeting place to minimize distractions and interruptions. Meetings held off-site, away from the normal workplace, allow you to accomplish more in less time.

HOLD THE WORKSHOP

Begin the meeting with personal introductions, and work to ensure that the people attending start to get to know one another. Each person has a role in the project, and his or her introduction should include a summary of what that role will be, and why it is important to the project. Long meetings tend to meander, so set meeting ground rules and enforce them throughout to focus the meeting and keep it productive. Open the start-up workshop with a review of the meeting agenda, project objectives, and other necessary background information to set expectations and to gain common understanding of the project.

Throughout the workshop, have someone capture issues, questions, action items, and other data produced by the team. As the workshop progresses, work together with the attendees to review, develop, and improve the project definition and planning documents. During all the discussions and presentations, strive for common understanding of the project objective, project priorities, the major project deliverables, the roles and responsibilities of contributors, and at least a high-level version of your project plan. Depending on the timing of the workshop, the focus may be on development of these items or on review and understanding, but team buy-in for the project is always a primary objective.

Toward the end of the workshop, review the issues and assumptions captured, and assess them for project risks. Risk identification is a significant byproduct of start-up workshops, so explicitly add any newly uncovered risks and significant issues to your risk list for further analysis and follow-up. Wrap up the workshop by identifying all assignments, due dates, and owners for all action items and other required additional work. Close the meeting by thanking the participants for their contributions.

Follow Up After the Workshop

After the workshop, provide all the participants with a written summary of the meeting's outcomes and decisions. Integrate the work done during the workshop into project documents as appropriate, and put the updated documentation where it can be referenced and used. Follow up on all action items and other assignments made during the workshop, by either bringing them to closure or adding them to your project plan.

Selecting and Implementing Project Metrics

Project metrics are very important for project risk management. Some metrics relate to risk triggers, and others may provide trend data that foreshadows future project problems. The value of project metrics depends on what, and how much, is measured.

A project is a complex system, so one metric generally is not sufficient to adequately monitor the overall process. Using too few metrics may also lead to inappropriate conclusions, resulting in undesirable decisions or behaviors. Defining too many metrics also causes problems, starting with the excessive cost and effort required to collect them. When there are too many data, it is easy to overlook important information hidden in the jumble. Strive to define the minimum set of project metrics that you need to give a balanced view, consistent with the goals and values of your organization.

There are examples of many useful metrics in Chapter 9. Selecting a few appropriate measures and collecting data regularly provides useful information for both your current project and future projects.

Selecting Metrics

Useful metrics are objective; if they are evaluated by several people, each person will get the same result. Good metrics are also easy to understand and to collect. Clarify how and what you need to measure, and verify through discussion that everyone involved understands the process consistently. Define the units and precision to be used for the measurements, and use the same units for all collection, evaluation, and reporting. For example, you might decide that all measurements for duration estimates will be rounded to the nearest full workday. Also, determine how often to measure. You need to collect data frequently enough to support the results you desire, but not so often that the collection represents higher than necessary overhead. Capturing data too often also displays "noise," variations in the data that have little or no meaning.

Prioritize any metrics you are considering, using criteria such as criticality, contribution to potential process improvement, linkage to desired behaviors, or availability of data. Collect only metrics that make a meaningful difference; do not collect data just because you can. An effective set of metrics also provides tension—improvement of one measure may diminish another one. Opposing a metric measuring speed of execution with another measuring defects or quality results in more appropriate behavior than either measurement by itself. Work to minimize "gaming" of the metrics by eliminating factors that might improve the measurement without achieving any desired results. It is possible to subvert almost any metric, so define them in terms that minimize differing interpretations and loopholes.

For project metrics that measure factors that are under the control of the project team, use input and computational definitions that are unambiguous and not subject to change. Avoid metrics based on subjective interpretations.

Finally, work to ensure that any metrics collected are used primarily for process monitoring and improvement, not as a basis for punishment. Metrics are powerful tools for identifying opportunities for beneficial change and determining trends, but the quality of the data that people provide will be less useful if they know that they will also be used to evaluate their performance. Once metrics are identified with processes used to rank and cancel projects, the reliability of future data deteriorates substantially. Use metrics for process control and improvement, not to generate criticism of the project team. If any personal information is involved, ensure that the measurements are kept confidential.

IMPLEMENTING METRICS AND COLLECTING DATA

Before you start to use a metric, discuss it with everyone who will be affected by it. For project metrics, work to get consensus from all members of the project team on the definition, the planned collection and use of the data, and the meaning of the results. Get commitment from everyone who will collect or supply data in advance, and seek agreement not to "game" the metrics.

Once a set of metrics is defined, the next step is to define an acceptable or desirable normal range. For well-established metrics, baselines are probably already documented. For new measures, or for metrics used in a new application, you need to establish the initial data range. While you can begin with an educated guess as a provisional baseline for a new metric, you should use the first several cycles of data collected to confirm it. Use this initial data only to validate or to correct the baseline. Until you have established the baseline using measurements, resist the temptation to make decisions and process changes.

Document each metric and its parameters, and provide these data to everyone affected. Include information such as the name of the metric, the intended objective, data required, measurement units, measurement frequency, the method for data collection, any formulas used, the target acceptable range, and who is responsible for making the measurement.

After setting a measurement baseline, collect project data as planned, and use the information to guide your project decisions. Set baselines for diagnostic metrics early in projects, using current data or data from similar earlier projects. For retrospective metrics, set baselines using existing data from earlier projects, or wait until several completed projects have collected the data required. For predictive metrics, establish corresponding retrospective metrics (for example, validate financial ROI predictions against actual performance), and establish norms that plausibly connect to the desired results. With all metrics, you should remain skeptical; review the data, and confront any suspected "gaming" of the measurements. Periodically reevaluate all metrics, especially after significant organizational or process changes. Following changes, review the baseline and acceptable range for each metric. Validate any necessary adjustments with new baseline measurements before considering additional system changes.

Throughout the process, make the measurements visible. Report the status of measured factors as planned, to all project stakeholders who need the measurements or are affected by them. Be prompt in evaluating and reporting the data to ensure timely feedback and early detection of significant variances.

Management Reserve

Imagine a large target with a big, red, circular bull's eye in the center. If you stand two meters away from the target and aim a target rifle right at the center, you should have no difficulty hitting the middle of the bull's eye. If you were to repeat the shot, but this time from two *hundred* yards away, the situation would change. For the second shot, aiming at the bull's eye would no longer be effective, because you could no longer rely on the projectile to fly in a straight line. If you were to aim at the center of the target, you would hit below its center. The parabolic arc that controls the flight of the bullet was described with precision hundreds of years ago by Sir Isaac Newton, and the principle is so well understood that even the average middle manager would not be tempted to give the bullet a lecture on "flying smarter, not harder." Everyone knows that you need to aim higher than the point you wish to hit, to compensate for the effects of gravity.

Simple, short projects are analogous to the first shot. Setting a date and planning to hit it works more often than not, because the time window is brief, the work is fairly obvious, and the risks are small. For most technical projects, though, the analogy of the second shot is better. The longer duration, with substantial unknowns and risks, is a very different situation. As with gravity for the flying bullet, risk has an effect on the trajectory of a project. Project plans that set deadlines to line up *exactly* with the final planned activities, even if the plans are based on reasonable, realistic estimates, have little chance of completing on time. The "force" of risk makes this sort of schedule unreliable.

Management reserve is a general concept for managing project risk that reduces uncertainty. Reserve—in time, in budget, or in both—based on *expected* risk may be used to develop credible schedules. Establishing reserves is not about padding estimates or making scheduling choices to accommodate sloppiness or team sloth; it is about using risk assessment information to set appropriate buffers at the project level to allow the project to deliver on commitments. In effect, management reserve is about setting project objectives with ranges, with the size of the range, or reserve, defined by project-level risk assessment.

Management reserve is based on two factors: known risks, with contingency plans or worst-case scenarios (this includes any known risks you may have elected to passively accept—that you have decided *not* to manage), and unknown risk. The first factor, discussed in detail in earlier chapters, comes from planning data. Unknown risk, by definition, is risk you are unable to anticipate and describe. Explicit planning for unknown risks is not possible, but metrics from earlier projects can provide guidance on the magnitude of exposure. Using project risk assessment data and metrics, you can estimate appropriate schedule and budget reserves. In effect, management reserve is a generic contingency plan for your overall project. Reserve is *never* allocated to the activity level, and it is managed by the project leader, not by activity owners.

SCHEDULE RESERVE

Management reserve for schedules may be implemented in several ways. The simplest method is to estimate the amount of expected schedule exposure and then to develop a plan that supports completion of the project earlier than the required completion date by that amount. In dealing with problems, the project can slip by any amount less than the reserve and still meet the project commitment. The published project schedule could show only the more aggressive, target completion date, or it could show the target date as a milestone followed by a dummy activity and then the committed deadline. The dummy activity has a name such as "allowance for risk," and it has a duration estimate equal to the schedule reserve.

For known risks, the amount of reserve needed for a given project can be estimated using methods that have been described in earlier chapters of this book. From Chapter 4, the idea of worst-case estimates provides one source. Using the "most likely" duration estimates establishes one possible project end date. Schedule analysis based on the worst-case estimates calculates a second end date for the project further out. The difference between these two dates can be used to determine the required reserve. How you do this depends on your confidence in the data, but it is common to set up half of the difference as a reserve—managing the work using the "most likely" schedule, but setting the project deadline to be a date midway between that schedule and the worst-case end date.

A second method for determining schedule reserve relies on data from your contingency plans. This process uses the method discussed in Chapter 9 to aggregate activity risk data. In this case, you would track and manage your project using the project plan as a target, but your committed deadline would be later by a duration defined by the cumulative *expected* consequences of having to use your contingency plans.

A third way to assess schedule reserve using data from known risks, also discussed in Chapter 9, relies on PERT or PERT–type analysis. The histograms or expected distribution can also be used to estimate required reserve, by determining the duration between the "most likely" (30 to 50 percent likelihood) date and some higher probability point farther out that is consistent with your project's risk tolerance. Again, your plan supporting the "most likely" dates will be used to manage the work and define the early point of a range window of acceptable dates. The upper boundary of the window will be the project commitment.

Estimating schedule reserve using any of these ideas is still incomplete. These estimated allowances for reserve are based only on known risks, so, without some consideration of the magnitude of your unknown risk, the reserve allowance will be too small. If you have metrics that measure typical schedule impact from unknown risk, incorporate this into your estimate of required reserve.

One very common example of reserve for unknown risk is explicit in many kinds of project plans. At the end of many construction and relocation projects, there is an activity scheduled called a "punch list," or something similar. The purpose of this activity is to fix and close out all the defects, problems, omissions, or other issues that accumulate on a list during the project. At the start of the project, a duration estimate based only on the list would logically be zero—there is no work yet identified. Since a duration estimate cannot be based on explicit knowledge of the work, it is based on the history of dozens, or hundreds, of similar projects. Experience from earlier work tells you how much time and effort, on average, you can expect between completion of the final scheduled activity and customer sign-off. Metrics that measure unscheduled effort, the number of activities added during projects, underestimated activities, and other indicators of plan incompleteness are all useful for estimating typical "unknown" risk.

An alternative method for estimating the schedule consequences of unknown risk is the project appraisal idea discussed in Chapter 9. The comparison projects include the effects of unknown risk, whereas your planned current project does not. Part of any difference shown in an assessment is due to unknown risk.

The amount of required schedule reserve varies greatly depending on the type of project. A reserve of only a few days may be appropriate for short, routine projects. For complicated, aggressive projects, target dates may need to be established weeks, or even months, before the committed deadline to deal with the many possible problems and potential sources of slippage. Whether the reserve is short or long, remember that it, like schedule float, belongs to the project as a whole. It is available only for problem solving, not for personal convenience. Using reserve established to manage project risk for other purposes (especially for scope creep) *increases* project risk.

How schedule reserve is best handled varies. On some projects, reserve is openly discussed and managed by all. Schedules posted and distributed reflect its existence, and the status of remaining schedule reserve is discussed in status meetings with other topics. On other projects, the management of reserve is more covert. As far as the teams on these projects know, the deadline for the project is the date that follows the final activity in the plan. While this has the desired effect of focusing attention on getting the work done as promptly as possible, it is inconsistent with open and honest project communications. While managing the reserve openly is usually the better method, it is easily undermined unless you effectively guard against two potential issues: scope creep and Parkinson's Law.

Scope creep is always an issue on technical projects; the more time the team spends thinking about and doing the work, the more ways they come up with to make it "better." In projects that possess a time buffer for risk management, the temptation may become overwhelming to add and modify the project scope, since "we have the time available." On all projects, risk management depends on disciplined and thorough control of changes, and this is particularly true of projects that have visible schedule reserve. Schedule reserve should be used only to accommodate project changes that are a direct result of project problem solving and issue resolution. Schedule reserve is not a tool for project "improvement."

The second issue, Parkinson's Law—work expands to fill the time available—also presents a significant challenge. Misuse of schedule reserve, particularly unused reserve still available late in the project, is a constant temptation. One method for guarding against this is to establish the available window of time for project completion and to set up rewards for the team proportionate to any *unused* reserve at the end of the project. Incentives for avoiding misuse of the reserve can be very effective, but they need to be developed carefully so that they are effective in discouraging misuse and scope creep but not *so* desirable that the reserve is not applied when necessary to solve problems and deal with risks. In setting up incentives, you need to discover what kinds of rewards your team will value. The best leaders make recognition for good performance fun, and rewards meaningful. Use rewards that encourage teamwork. *Individual* rewards, particularly of money, can erode teamwork and cooperation.

The best methods for reserve management ensure that all decisions are ultimately in the hands of a project leader who will apply the available reserve only to deal with real-time problems, issues, and conflicts. This way, the established reserve operates to counteract the effect of risk and helps aggressively scheduled projects complete on or before their committed deadline.

Budget Reserve

Reserve for resources uses project resource analysis and risk data. Budget reserve at the project level can be used to expedite work, add additional resources, or take other necessary actions to stay on schedule.

The amount of reserve needed is estimated similarly to the schedule reserve discussed earlier, from analysis of known risk using worst cases, contingency plans, or PERT analysis. For unknown risk, estimate reserve using metrics derived from earlier projects. Base your determination of required budget reserve on the best data you have available.

Again, it can be a challenge to be aware of the budget reserve while resisting the temptation to use it for project modifications that have nothing to do with risk. It is usually somewhat easier on technical projects to manage budget reserve than schedule reserve, because decisions concerning money and resources are generally made by the project leader, and sometimes even higher in the organization.

USING MANAGEMENT RESERVE

While determining a prudent allowance for schedule and/or budget reserve is the first step, establishing these requires discussion, negotiation, and approval from project sponsors and stakeholders. You need all the planning and other data you used to calculate required reserves, but this is not sufficient. You also need to identify and factor in your project constraints. Requesting schedule reserve that is not consistent with a hard completion date for the project probably makes no sense, nor would a proposed budget reserve that exceeds the expected benefit for the project. Work to keep your analysis consistent with the goals and objectives for the project, and understand that when your estimate for reserve exceeds what is logical for the project, project risk is very high, and it may be an indication that your project is doomed. Abandoning such a project in favor of better alternatives could be the best decision.

Project Baseline Negotiation

Managing project risk nearly always involves some shift in the project objective. In the unlikely event that your bottom-up plans and risk assessment are wholly consistent with the project objective, no negotiation is necessary; validating the plan and documenting the baseline is all that you need to do. For most projects, however, there are issues to confront, often significant ones.

Project negotiation serves a number of purposes. The most obvious one is to shift an unlikely, perhaps impossible, objective enough to bring it in line with a realistic plan. Other reasons for negotiation include building awareness and support for the project from sponsors and stakeholders, setting limits on project scope, and managing expectations.

STRONG SPONSORSHIP

Risky projects need all the help they can muster, so work to get and retain high priority and visible support for your project. Projects that have substantial risk are generally undertaken because there are large potential benefits expected, and you should make sure that all discussions of the project emphasize the positive results that will come from the project, not just the risks, problems, and challenges. Build awareness of your project, early and often, so that your management will continue to support the project in their words and actions. Particularly on risky projects, you need commitment for quick resolution of escalated issues, protection of the project team from conflicts and nonproject commitments, and approval for any requested management reserve. You may also need sponsor approval for training to acquire new skills and to streamline or change processes. Projects are surrounded by organizational "white space," generally managed by the project sponsor. The sponsor can lower risk for the project by aggressively removing organizational barriers and administrative overhead and by dealing with organizational and business factors that may inhibit fast execution of the project. Conversely, management can exacerbate risk by contributing to these factors and initiating new work that requires people currently assigned to your project. Strong, continuing sponsorship is one of the key factors that separate risky projects that succeed from those that crash and burn.

SETTING LIMITS ON PROJECT SCOPE

Another goal of project negotiation is to set boundaries for the project. A great deal of risk for technical projects, as was discussed in Chapter 3, arises from the fact that there may be any number of different conceptions for what, exactly, your project is supposed to produce. Even though you and your project team probably have a fairly clear definition as the planning and risk analysis come to closure, there still may be residual "fuzziness" in other quarters. The project scope must be just as clear as the deadline to everyone involved.

The project documentation prepared for discussions with sponsors should be unambiguous about what the project will include and specific in outlining what it will *not* include. Setting limits on scope early, using "is/is not" scope definition descriptions that are understood by all, either validates the project team's conceptions or triggers discussions and necessary adjustments. Either way, doing this early in the project is the best course; it lowers risk and results in consistent expectations for all parties.

FACT-BASED NEGOTIATION

Project baseline negotiation requires your definition and planning documents. Initial discussions focus on summaries, so writing clear, informative summaries is essential. In preparing project information for discussion, include a high-level objective summary, a milestone project schedule, a high-level WBS, a project appraisal, and a summary of major assumptions and risks. If your planning shows a major mismatch between the current project plan and the requested project objective, you should also have several high-level proposals that describe project alternatives.

With these data in hand, your next step is to set up a meeting with the project sponsor to discuss the project, the results of your planning, and, if necessary, the alternatives. Begin the discussion with a presentation of your planning results. Whenever your project plan is inconsistent with the originally requested project objective, you need to negotiate changes. Changes to consider include requesting additional resources, extending the deadline, getting contributors with more experience or more training for the people you have, reducing project scope, or any number of other options.

Having data is critical for your success, because the balance of power in such negotiations is not in your favor. While it is relatively easy for sponsors and managers to brush aside concerns and opinions, it is much more difficult for them to dismiss hard facts. When there is a significant difference between project expectations for timing and resources as seen by the project team and their management, a half-page project appraisal (described in Chapter 9) can be a good starting place for the discussion, showing why the requested project is not likely to be done as quickly or inexpensively as desired. ("Remember this project? That's the one we had to do in two months, and it ended up taking six.") When the issue is a request to do a project much faster than is possible, your project Gantt chart, showing all the activities and durations, is an effective tool. When the deadline requested is far too short to accommodate the work, hold up the chart, and say that you can do it on schedule only if the sponsor selects which activities to delete. Most sponsors will back down and be willing to begin a productive discussion of alternatives, rather than randomly removing work they probably do not understand. Any project information backed up by historical, documented data can be a good starting point for a fact-based, not emotion-based, negotiation.

Reducing project risk through negotiation is best done with the ideas outlined by Roger Fisher, William Ury, and Bruce Patton of the Harvard Negotiation Project in their book *Getting to Yes*. Their process of principled negotiation is effective for "win-win" negotiations, where all parties get at least some of what they seek. In project negotiations where only the sponsor "wins," everyone has actually lost. It does no one any good to force a commitment to an infeasible project. The team and project leader lose because they are stuck on a doomed project. The sponsors, managers, and customers lose, too, because they do not get what they expect and need. Principled negotiation, done early, is essential for dealing with failure-prone projects.

Some useful ideas for project negotiations include separating the people from the issues and focusing on interests, not positions. By sticking to facts and mutually understood needs, you raise the discussion beyond "This project is *hard*" on the project side and "You are the best project leader we have" on the other. While both of the statements may be true, neither one actually addresses the real issue—that the project objective, as stated, is not possible. As you prepare for negotiation, develop project alternatives that provide for mutual gain, such as exploring opportunities that could extend beyond the original project request or segmenting the project into a sequence of smaller projects capable of delivering value earlier. In your negotiations, base decisions and analyses on objective criteria. Brainstorm, problem-solve, and get everyone involved in seeking better options. Ask lots of questions, and focus on resolving the issues, not just arguing about the project.

One of your best assets in all of this is your knowledge. As a result of your project planning, no one alive knows more about the project than you do. You also have a track record and credibility, built up over a body of prior work. The managers and project sponsors are aware of this; that is why they requested you to lead the project. Proceed with negotiations using your technical and planning expertise, and the experience of your project team.

Lay out the consequences of accepting a commitment to a project with excessive residual risk in clear, fact-based terms. By using conservative assumptions to support the analysis of the potential project problems, you will end up with one of three possible results. The most desirable outcome is shifting the project objective in line with, or at least closer to, your plan. For other projects, realistic analysis of the work and risks may lead to the conclusion that the project is not a good idea, and it is taken no further. Either of these outcomes avoids a project destined to fail.

The third possibility is that your data may not be sufficiently compelling or that your sponsors pay no attention to them. In this case, you may end up forced to commit to an infeasible project, with no realistic plan to support it. Should this happen, document the situation for future reference, to make it less likely to recur. Then you can either try your best and hope for miracles or consider finding a way out of the project.

Project Plan Validation

Following discussion and negotiation, validate that you have consensus on the project. Verify that you have a plan supporting the project objective that is acceptable to the project sponsor and other stakeholders, as well as to you and your project team.

Use the project documents from the planning processes, with any negotiated modifications, to establish the project baseline plan of record. Before finalizing the plan, review it to ensure that it includes periodic risk reassessment activities throughout (at least at major phase milestones). During these reviews, additional risks not apparent at project start will be identified, and your contingency plans can be updated.

Publish the final versions of the project documents and distribute them so that the project team can access and use them to manage progress throughout the project. Put your project documents on-line if possible so that everyone has access at any time to current versions. If a computer scheduling tool is to be used for project tracking, save the project schedule as a baseline and begin tracking activity status in the database.

When you set the project baseline, freeze all specifications. Set both the project scope definition and your baseline plan at the same time, and change neither one without using your established process for making changes. Freezing the schedule and resources on a project while allowing the scope to continue to meander is a massive source of project risk.

For risk visibility, create a "top-ten list" of the most significant known risks for the current phase of your project, and post it where the project team will be aware of it—in the team workplace, on the project Web site, or at another prominent location. Commit to periodically reviewing and updating the list throughout the project.

Specification Change Management

Once the project plan is accepted and you have frozen the specifications, carefully consider all changes before accepting them. After the project documents are signed off by all appropriate decision makers—the project sponsor, customers, stakeholders, and others—it becomes very risky to allow unexamined changes in the project. Although new information flows around technical projects continuously, maintaining specification stability is crucial for project success. Unmanaged change leads to slipped schedules, budget problems, and possibly even scope problems due to unintended consequences, as seen in the PERIL database.

Having a process for submission, analysis, and disposition for each proposed change lowers the risks, especially if "reject" is the default decision for submitted change requests. An effective change management process puts the burden of proof on each change request; all changes are considered *unnecessary* until proven otherwise.

Another requirement for effective change control is to ensure that people responsible for the change process have the authority to enforce their decisions. Change reviewers need to have sufficient involvement with the project to effectively understand the probable consequences of a change, both positive and negative. Change approvers also need to have knowledge of the project, and they need the power to say "no" (or at least "not yet") and make it stick. For reasons of efficiency, some change processes establish change screeners, who initially examine any proposed change and determine when (or even if) a change deserves further consideration.

CHANGE PROCESS

Change control processes need to be documented, in writing, especially on fee-for-solution projects. The formality of the actual process adopted varies a great deal with project type, but at a minimum, it should include:

- ❒ Logging and tracking of all change requests
- ❒ A defined process for analyzing all proposed changes
- ❒ Documented criteria for accepting, rejecting, or deferring changes
- ❒ Communication of decisions and status

Change Submission

Ideas for change generally begin in problem solving or from recognition of an opportunity. Submissions of proposed changes should be in writing and include information such as:

- ❐ Why the change is necessary
- ❐ An estimate of expected benefits from the change
- ❐ The estimated impact of the change on schedule, cost, and other factors
- ❐ Specific resources needed for the change

Less formal systems may require only brief summaries; more elaborate change management processes often require specifics in a defined format and may also require additional information and specific documentation.

All changes submitted, even in systems that are relatively informal, need to be logged. Maintain an up-to-date list of submitted change proposals throughout the project, with current status information available to the project team. Following submission, examine each submitted change request for form, completeness, and reasonableness. If the information is unclear or key data are missing, return the request to the person who submitted it for amendment. Provide the change request information to those responsible for evaluation, review, and approval.

Change Analysis

Analysis of changes should include at least two aspects, impact assessment and cost/benefit analysis. Impact assessment parallels the processes used for impact analysis of risks. It begins with high-level categorization of change impact:

- ❐ Small (minor effect on the deliverable or project plan)
- ❐ Medium (functional change to the deliverable but little project impact)
- ❐ Large (major change to project objective and the deliverable)

Specifics of impact are also important. It may be necessary to carry out a new, detailed planning analysis of the project for significant changes, examining costs for additional research and development, equipment modification, acquisition or retrofit costs, changes required in documentation, any required training, the cost of purchasing new parts, and scrapping of any old components not needed. Consider the impact of the change on any legal contracts for purchasing of materials or outsourced services. Changes may also have impact on commitments made to customers or users concerning availability or features.

Finally, analyze the schedule impact of the change. Assess the duration impact of any new activities on project completion and the effect of undoing any work that the change renders unnecessary.

Cost/Benefit Analysis

Each change presumably has credible benefits, or it would not be under consideration. The expected benefits need to be estimated so that they can be contrasted with the expected costs and other consequences.

Changes generally fall into one of several categories. Many proposed changes resolve problems encountered on the project or fix something that is not functioning as required. The benefits of these changes relate to the avoided expense or time slippage that will persist on the project until the problem is solved. Other changes arise from external factors such as new regulatory or safety requirements, the need to comply with evolving standards, or actions by competitors. These types of change, which are solving real problems, complying with company requirements, and reacting to adverse shifts in the environment, are often unavoidable. Your project deliverable will lose much, if not all, of its value unless the changes are made. The consequences of both making and not making the change are usually clear from your project planning data.

Project changes aimed at making the project "better" are on less solid ground—changes that add something to the deliverable, alter something about the deliverable to improve it, or introduce new processes or methods to be used for project work. The benefits of these changes are more speculative, and thus more difficult to analyze. Credible estimates for increased sales, revenue, or usefulness as a result of the change are difficult, and they tend to be very optimistic. While some opportunities for change may result in very significant benefits, many changes intended to improve technical projects generate unintended consequences and lead to benefits that are far smaller than expected. The impact to the project may also be very hard to estimate, particularly if the change involves adopting a new approach to the work. Effective change management systems are skeptical of these modifications and tend to reject them. When outright rejection is not possible, the system should at least be adept at saying "not yet," allowing the project to complete as planned and then embarking on a follow-on effort to pursue the new ideas.

In all cases, a rational consideration of the net benefit of the change—the reasonably expected benefits less the estimated costs and other consequences—is the central focus of the decision process. This analysis should apply to *all* submitted changes, regardless of their origin. If customers submit changes, the specific consequences in terms of timing and cost must be visible to them, and generally borne by them, as well. If a project contributor submits a change, he or she should provide ample documentation for it and expect to fight hard to get it approved. Politically, the most difficult situation on technical projects arises from the changes requested by sponsors and management. While it is never easy to say "no" to the people you work for, the existence of a documented process that has been approved to manage project change is a vital initial step, and clear, data-supported descriptions of the consequences of requested changes are also crucial. As with risk management generally, managing change risk effectively relies on thorough, credible project planning data.

Disposition

For each potential change, you have four options: approval, approval with modification, rejection, and deferral. The process for making a decision on each change request uses the results from the analysis and documented information on project objectives and priorities to make a business decision. The primary criterion for the decision is generally the assessment of benefits versus costs, weighing the relative advantages and disadvantages of each change. The process for this may be relatively informal, taken up during regular project meetings as a part of normal business (with all required analysis done in advance, *not* during the meeting), or part of formal meetings periodically convened specifically to consider changes. The level of formality scales with the project, but two aspects of the decision process are universal. The first requirement is to make decisions promptly. Change requests, particularly those that address problems, need quick attention. The value of a change can diminish significantly as it sits, so ensure that all changes are considered and closed without undue delay, generally within a week. The second need is for consistent adherence to agreed-upon requirements for decisions. Some change systems are based on approval by a majority of those involved; some require unanimity; and still others grant veto powers to some approvers who have greater authority. Effective change systems avoid having too many approvers, in order to minimize scheduling problems and shorten debate, and they provide for alternate approvers whenever a designated approver is not available.

You should always begin with the presumption that changes are unnecessary and reject all changes that lack a compelling, credible business basis. Even for changes that have some benefits, carefully examine them to determine whether some parts of the change are not needed or whether the change might be deferred to a later project. Seek substantial credible net benefits even for changes you decide to approve with modifications or to defer. Approval and acceptance of changes should be relatively rare and reserved for the most compelling requirements for problem solving or other significant business needs. The more a project is subject to change, the higher the risk. Whatever the decision, close out all requests quickly, within the documented time goals established for the process. Also, promptly escalate any issues or conflicts that cannot be resolved at the project level.

Communicate the Decision

As each decision is made, you need to document it in writing. Include the rationale for the decision and a brief description of any project impact. Prepare a summary of the pending, accepted, and rejected change proposals for the project archive, and distribute the summary to project stakeholders and to your project team members. Also, consider any people impacted by the change who are not in your normal distribution for project information, and communicate the change status to them.

Whenever a change is not approved, respond to the submitter with an explanation, including the rationale for the decision. If there is a specific process for appeal and reconsideration, provide this information to the submitter as well.

Update all relevant project documents—the WBS, estimates, schedules, specifications and other scope documents, the project plan, charts, or any other project documents that an approved change affects. Distribute new versions to holders of original documents, and mark all earlier versions as obsolete. If documents are centrally stored in electronic form, replace them, and move the older versions to the project archive or clearly identify them as noncurrent.

Even for rejected changes, retain the proposals in the project archives. The "good ideas" may be worthy of consideration in follow-on projects or in a parallel projects. When your project is over, you can use the change history to reduce risk on future projects by carefully reviewing the process and the decisions made.

Key Ideas for Managing Project Risk

❏ Hold a project start-up workshop.
❏ Select and use several project metrics.
❏ Determine required project reserve.
❏ Negotiate and validate possible project objectives.
❏ Freeze scope and manage specification changes.

Panama Canal: Adjusting the Objective (1907)

Setting a concrete objective for a project is not necessarily a quick, easy process. In the case of the Panama Canal, although Theodore Roosevelt made the decision to build the canal and the Senate approved the commitment early in 1904, the specifics of exactly what sort of canal would be built were still not settled nearly two years later. All the data accumulated by John Stevens led him to the same conclusion ultimately reached by the French engineers—building a sea-level canal at Panama would be very difficult, if not impossible. He estimated that a lock-and-dam canal could be completed in nine years, possibly eight. A sea-level canal would require a minimum of eighteen years. He convinced Theodore Roosevelt of this, and he thought the matter was settled.

This, however, was not the case. In spite of the French experience, the lock-and-dam versus sea-level debate was still going strong in the U.S. Senate in 1906. Showing much of the same diligence and intelligence one might expect today, the Senate, with responsibility to oversee the canal project, took a vote on how to build the canal. By one vote, they approved a sea-level canal. One unavoidable observation from study of past projects is that things really do not change very much over time, and politics is rarely driven by logic.

John Stevens had just returned to Panama from Washington in 1906, and, although he was quite busy with the project, he turned around and sailed back to the United States. He met extensively with members of both the U.S. House of Representatives and the Senate. He patiently explained the challenges of a sea-level canal in a rain forest with flooding rivers. He developed data, drew maps, and generally described to anyone who would listen all the reasons why the canal could not be built at sea level. As was true earlier for the French, the main obstacle was the flooding of the Chagres River, which flows north into the Gulf of Mexico parallel to the proposed canal for nearly half of its route.

Stevens spent a lot of time with one ally, Senator Philander Knox. Senator Knox was from Pennsylvania—specifically, he was from Pittsburgh, Pennsylvania. Stevens worked with Knox on a speech in which the senator described in detail why the canal had to be constructed with dams and locks. By all reports, it was an excellent speech, delivered with great eloquence and vigor. (It was probably not entirely a coincidence that a sea-level canal required none of the locks, steel doors, and other hardware that would come from Senator Knox's friends in the foremost steel-producing city in the Americas.)

Despite of all this, there were *still* thirty-one senators who voted for a sea-level canal. Fortunately for the project and for Stevens, there were thirty-seven senators who were paying attention, and the design Stevens recommended was approved.

It had taken him more than a year, but finally John Stevens had his plan completed and approved. Defending the feasible plan required all of his data, principled negotiation, and a great deal of perseverance, but he ultimately avoided the costly disaster of a second failed canal project at Panama.

CHAPTER 11

MONITORING AND CONTROLLING RISKY PROJECTS

"Adding manpower to a late software project makes it later." —FRED BROOKS, author of *The Mythical Man-Month*

Apart from phrasing (the very 1970s *manpower* would be replaced by the more politically correct *people* or *staff*), it's hard to quibble with Fred Brooks's statement. In fact, the effect described by Brooks applies to projects of almost any type, not just software projects. Adding contributors to a late project never seems to help very much, because the first thing that new people on a project need is information, so they ask blizzards of questions. These questions are directed, of course, to the overworked people already on the project, which slows them down further. There are other reasons adding staff late in a project can be counterproductive, such as the need to build trust and to move through the team-building stages of "forming, storming, and norming." It is not the additional staff that is the real problem, though. It is additional staff *too late*. Monitoring and control of the work is essential to detecting problems such as insufficient staffing early enough to avoid the need for chaotic, and seldom successful, heroic measures. Disciplined monitoring and control finds and fixes problems while they are still small, so the project avoids serious trouble in the first place.

Risk management cannot end with the initial planning. Your project starts with its plan, just as a lengthy automobile trip begins with an itinerary based on maps and other information. But what trip ever goes exactly as planned? As the driver continues on the trip, small adjustments based on events and conditions are necessary. More serious issues such as vehicle problems or automobile accidents may result in major modifications to the itinerary. Throughout the trip, the driver must remain alert and reasonably flexible. Managing risk in projects is about detecting things that are not proceeding as planned in your project. Like the driver who must remain alert and responsive to things that happen on the road, the project leader uses tracking, reviews, and reapplication of the planning concepts discussed in the preceding chapters to adjust to the prevailing project conditions, seeking to bring it to successful closure.

Effective management of project risk relies on frequent and disciplined reassessment of new information and status as the project proceeds. Particularly on longer projects, you cannot know everything about the work at the beginning, so periodic project reviews are necessary to keep the project moving and productive.

Most of the content of this chapter falls into the "Risk Management and Control" portion of the Controlling Processes in the *PMBOK® Guide,* but it also draws from "Performance Reporting," "Integrated Change Control," and from other Controlling and Planning Processes. The principal ideas in this chapter include:

❐ Application of the plan

❐ Project monitoring

❐ Status collection

❐ Trend analysis and metrics

❐ Issue resolution

❐ Communications

❐ Project archives

❐ Project reviews and risk reassessment

Applying the Plan

Once a project baseline is established, the project plan is no longer a work in progress. The plan becomes a road map for the work, and you can begin tracking status and updating your project database with actual results. This information is useful primarily in assessing progress, but it also allows you to improve your processes and efficiency through periodic project reviews, as well as through postproject retrospective analysis.

Risk management relies on systematic project tracking to

provide the information necessary for proactive detection of project problems while they are still small and easily solved. Project tracking helps you anticipate potential problems, allowing the project to avoid at least some of them. Disciplined tracking makes it difficult to ignore early warning signals and provides the data you need for effective response. Without accurate, timely information, project problems remain hidden, so they will occur without warning, inflicting serious damage to your plans.

Credible status data also can reduce the project worries and team stress that arises from a lack of good information. Even when the project status reveals bad news, the true situation viewed with credible information is nearly always less dire than the alternatives that people dream up when they lack data. In addition, detailed status often provides the information you need for recovery. Factual information also helps minimize both excessive optimism and pessimism, neither of which is helpful to a project.

Dogmatic collection of project status and routine comparison to the plan guards against a common project risk—"safe so far" project reporting. As long as the project deadline is still way out in the future, the project is not officially late. Even without any data, project reporting continues to say that the project is doing fine. Only at the deadline, or perhaps a little before it, does the project leader publicly admit that the project will not meet its schedule commitment. This is analogous to a man who falls off a ten-story building and reports, as he passes by each row of windows, "Safe so far!"

Projects become late *one day at a time*. Failure to detect this lag as soon as possible allows schedule and other risks to remain undetected, grow, and ultimately overwhelm the project.

In addition to frequent status collection, longer projects also need project reviews, performed every three to six months, to manage the work that extends beyond a reasonable planning horizon. A project review provides the opportunity to detect new risks, fine-tune the project plan, and make necessary corrections and shifts in the overall project.

Project Monitoring

Project monitoring can begin as soon as there is a clear, validated baseline plan that has been approved by the project sponsor and accepted by the project leader and team. Other prerequisites for effective project tracking are a functioning communications infrastructure, functioning tracking methods, and thorough project planning data available to all team members and stake-holders.

DECISIONS RELATED TO MONITORING

You need to make decisions about project status collection and storage as part of the initial project infrastructure for your project.

You need to commit to an appropriate frequency and method for status collection. Tracking on technical projects is usually done weekly, with status collected from all project contributors via electronic mail, but many other options are possible for this. For very short or very urgent projects, more frequent data collection may be warranted. For long projects, less frequent data collection may be appropriate, but a cycle longer than two weeks is inconsistent with good risk management. In addition to electronic mail, data collection methods include printed forms, discussion during project team meetings, reporting by telephone, and one-on-one meetings between the project leader and project team members. Some projects also do this informally, but any choice that does not generate a written record increases project risk arising from garbled or incomplete information.

On large, complex, multiteam programs, consistent data collection is essential, and the volume of status information can become quite a burden. One way to respond to this is to set up a project office that is responsible for assembling, summarizing, and analyzing the data consistently for all the project teams. This ensures that you will have current, consistent data and also permits use of more complex scheduling tools without the cost of so many copies and the considerable effort that would be required for all the project leaders to master the tool.

Project reports and meetings are generally synchronized with status collection, so reporting is generally done on a weekly basis and distributed via electronic mail. Project status meetings, also usually weekly, should be face-to-face when possible; for distributed project teams, use the best available telecommunications methods. The frequency and methods used vary from project to project, but risks rise steeply when reports, meetings, and other communication are more than two weeks apart.

Decisions on how and where to store the project status information are also important. Whether the data are hard copy or on-line, all project team members should have access to them. Determine the tools and systems to be used for collecting and storing the data and provide appropriate security so that team members who need to update project information, but not others, are able to modify the data.

The precise details for these decisions related to project monitoring will affect your ability to manage risk, so commit to methods and frequencies that will best serve your project.

PROJECT STATUS

Project status information is of two types: hard data (facts and figures) and soft data (anecdotal information, rumors, and less specific information). Both types of data are useful for risk management. Hard data include the project metrics discussed in Chapter 9, and most of them are diagnostic—telling you how the project is proceeding. Some of the hard data collected will relate to, or may even be, a risk event trigger, and other data may reveal dangerous trends. Soft data can tell you the causes for your project status; they may also provide early warnings of future problems and risk situations.

Hard Data

Hard schedule data include metrics that assess information on activities and milestones, including revised start and completion estimates for future work. Other hard data track resource information related to effort and expenses, results of scope testing and investigation, and other information on project deliverables. Hard data collection needs to be routine, easy, and not too time-consuming. On most technical projects, people are so busy that if collecting hard status information is not simple, it will not get done. At a minimum, collect:

❐ Schedule data, such as activities completed and activities scheduled but not completed, milestones completed or missed, actual activity start and finish dates, and duration remaining for incomplete activities

❐ Resource data, including actual effort consumed, cost data, remaining effort for incomplete work, and missing resources

❐ Data regarding issues, problems, and specification changes

Soft Data

Additional information of a less tangible nature also permeates your project. Information about the project contributors may alert you to potential threats to needed resources, individual productivity, and other potential sources of project risk. Changes in the work environment, a rumored reorganization, or personal problems among individual team members may also adversely affect upcoming project work. Soft project data issues include:

- ❏ Conflicts arising from expected new projects or other work
- ❏ Falling productivity of individual team members
- ❏ Suspected changes to the project environment
- ❏ Changes need by your project that seem threatened
- ❏ Potential problem situations with a common, persistent root cause
- ❏ Frequent situations requiring more authority than you have
- ❏ Long delays getting resolution of escalated issues and decisions

You should collect metrics for hard data systematically, on the frequency you set for your project, and make the results available to the project team. Use hard data to detect any issues or shifts in project assumptions. Collect soft data continuously, but share them only as appropriate. Do not spread or add to the project archive any unsubstantiated rumors or confidential information specific to individuals.

THE STATUS CYCLE

Project monitoring depends on a four-stage cycle that repeats periodically (generally weekly) throughout the project. The first stage is inbound communication, collecting of project status information. The second stage of the cycle compares the status to the plan, evaluates the metrics, and analyzes any variances. The third stage responds to any issues or problems detected. The fourth and final stage is outbound communication, keeping people aware of what has happened in the project.

The monitoring cycle provides for analysis and planning after collecting project status information but before project reporting. This lets you include your responses to any issues or problems in your project status report. Any bad news you report will be received better if it is accompanied by credible plans for recovery.

Collecting Project Status

Collecting project status is primarily your responsibility as the project leader. Confine status collection to the data that you need, keep the process simple, and make your use of the data visible. Basic status for the scheduled project activities is an effective minimum. One easy way to obtain it is to provide a list of current open activities to each activity owner via electronic mail with a request for two responses—an indicator and a date. Possible indicators are "Not started," "Continuing," and "Done." The date provided with the indicator is the expected start date for activities not yet begun and the finish date (expected or actual) for the other two. Additional data, such as effort or cost information, are also useful, but for routine periodic status collection, simplicity improves both the quality of the data and the willing cooperation of the team. A detailed, five-page form that collects every possible project metric is of no use if no one fills it out or everyone treats it as a joke. Risk management requires data, so do what you can to keep them flowing.

There are a number of factors that can impede status collection. One pitfall is to collect project status only "when there is time." As typical technical projects proceed, the work intensifies, and problems, distractions, and chaos build. It becomes tempting to skip a status collection cycle. Especially during times of high stress and significant problems, it is risky to lose information. You may even find it necessary to *intensify* data collection during problems or near project completion.

Another thing to guard against is collecting data and then not using the information. After you collect status, at least incorporate a summary of it into your overall project status report. When you fail to use what is available, or when it looks like you are not using it, your team members will either stop sending it or will put no effort into supplying meaningful data. At least once in a while, recognize the work required to submit status, and thank people for it.

Perhaps the most common problem in status collection is handling bad news. When someone reports that his or her work is not going well, your first temptation is to find a chair and break it over his or her head, or at least to yell a lot. One of the hardest things a project leader has to learn is not to shoot the messenger. You need to respond positively, even to bad news. Thanking people for bad news is never easy, but if you routinely punish team members for providing honest data, you will quickly stop hearing what you need to know, and project risks will escalate. It is much better to mentally count to ten and then offer a response such as, "Well, I wish you had better news, but I appreciate your raising this issue promptly. What will help get you back on schedule?" It is never too soon to begin thinking about how to respond to the problem or issue.

Particularly when the status is coming from distant team members, or from people you do not know very well, screen the information carefully to ensure that it is realistic and meaningful. It takes a lot more effort to get regular, high-quality information from remote contributors, so be persistent, make multiple requests when necessary, stay up late or get up early to speak with team members on a regular basis, and verify the status data submitted as thoroughly as you can. For work done at a distance, probe for evidence of progress that supports the reported status, such as the results of evaluations, interim tests, walkthroughs, and investigations or samples of prototypes, mock-ups, or partial systems.

Risk management requires current, factual project information, so be persistent and diligent in obtaining it.

Metrics and Trend Analysis

After collecting status, look for project problems by analyzing variances. Variance analysis involves comparing the status information you collected with the project baseline plan to identify any differences. Variances, both positive and negative, need to be analyzed for impact; positive variances may provide clues for improved execution that might be applied to future work, and negative variances need attention so that they do not send the project spiraling out of control. Trend analysis on the metrics can also identify aspects of the project that may cause future disruptions.

DIAGNOSTIC METRICS

After contrasting the status data with the plan, the first thing to do is to validate the differences, particularly large ones. Before spending time on impact analysis, check with the people who provided the data to make certain that the problems (or, for positive variances, the apparent benefits) are real. For each difference, determine the root cause of the variance, not just the symptoms. Work with both hard and soft project data to understand why each variance occurred. Metrics seldom slip out of expected ranges in isolation; the project schedule, resources, and scope are all interrelated, so problems with one of these parameters tend to affect the others. Variances may also display patterns and trends over time that can be used to anticipate future problems and emerging risks.

Once you have determined the underlying cause of each variance, you can decide how to respond. Dealing with the root cause of a problem also prepares you to deal better with future situations that may cause similar problems later in the project. In variance analysis, focus on understanding the data; never just look for someone to blame.

Schedule Metrics

Schedule variances are generally examined first, whether positive or negative. If there are positive variances—work completed early—there may be an opportunity to pull in the start date of other work. It is also worthwhile to discuss the early finish with the activity owner to see whether it is the result of an approach or method that could be applied to similar work scheduled later in the project or whether you could shorten any duration estimates.

The more common situation is an adverse variance, which for critical activities will impact the start of at least one scheduled project activity. Unless an activity that comes after the slip can be shortened, it will affect all of the activities and milestones later in the project, including the final deadline. Even for noncritical activities, adverse variances are worth investigating; the slip may exceed the flexibility in the schedule, causing the same impact as a critical path activity that slips. For any adverse variance that impacts a schedule dependency, promptly notify the affected team members (and, if necessary, other projects) that their work will be delayed.

Whether or not the slipped activity is critical to the schedule, seek the root cause of the slip. If the delay is due to faulty analysis or inappropriate assumptions, any duration estimates for similar work later in the project could also be too short. On technical projects, there may be many essentially repetitive activities, so if the estimate for one proves to be too short, there is a good chance that they all may be too optimistic. Another consideration is the possibility of a similar problem within any of your contingency plans; it is a good idea to repair any defects in your recovery plans whenever they become apparent.

Finally, schedule variances may be due to root causes that were not detected during risk analysis. If the root cause of a slip suggests new risks and project failure modes, note the risks and set a time for additional risk analysis and response planning.

Resource Metrics

Resource variances are also significant, but dealing with them may not be as urgent. Metrics related to the concept of earned value are particularly useful in examining resource use throughout the project. Earned value metrics, such as the cost performance index (CPI), measure the effort or money consumed by the project in relation to the plan. If the consumption is low (CPI greater than one) but the schedule progress is adequate, there may be a possibility of completing the project under budget. If it is too low and the schedule is also slipping, the root cause is likely to be inadequate staffing or too little of some other resource available. Whenever project progress is too slow because of insufficient resources, escalate the situation to higher management promptly, especially if your project is being denied access to committed resources.

Whenever resources are being used in excess of what is expected—that is, when the CPI metric is less than one—the variance is almost certainly a serious problem. The likelihood is strong that the project will ultimately require more resources to complete than the plan indicates, because it is very difficult to reverse resource overconsumption. Even as early as 20 percent through the project schedule, a project with a "burn rate" that is too high has essentially *no chance* of finishing within budget. Using more resources than planned may cause your project to hit a limit on staff, money, or some other hard constraint, and halt the project well before it is complete. Publicly admitting to this sort of problem is never easy, but if you delay in delivering the news, it will make the inevitable discussions even harder. The longer problems like this persist, the larger they tend to become. There are also fewer options later in the project for resolving the problem, and the project sponsors and other managers will have much less sympathy for you near the scheduled end of the project.

Some resource issues are acute, having impact on only a short portion of the project, while others are chronic and recur throughout the work. Chronic situations not only create project budget problems; they also may lead to frequent overtime and constant pressure on project staff. Risks associated with late project activities grow with lowered motivation and other staffing issues. Chronic resource problems may also have an impact on existing contingency plans, and their root causes may reveal the need for additional risk response planning.

Scope Metrics

While schedule and resource variances are the most common results of status collection, some of the status data collected relates to the project deliverables. The results of tests, integration attempts, feasibility studies, and other work will either support the expectations set out in the project requirements, or they will not. Significant variances related to scope may indicate a need to propose project changes. Major variances may well foreshadow project failure.

If a scope-related metric exceeds the result expected, you should explore whether the project might be able to deliver a superior result using the same time frame and budget. It may also be possible to deliver the stated result sooner or less expensively. While this situation is relatively rare, it does happen, and making the best choice may not be obvious. Discussion with the project sponsors, customers, and other stakeholders is prudent before adding something to the project scope "just because you can." Assess the value and utility of any additional product feature before incorporating it into the project.

When scope data indicate a problem that can be resolved with additional work, the impact may be to the project schedule, resources, or both. These possibilities, along with an analysis of what realistically could be delivered consistent with the project budget and deadline, all need consideration in light of the data, so the most palatable option (or options) can be proposed as a change request to modify the project objective.

If you cannot resolve a scope problem with extra work, your only options are to propose a change that would result in a different, but possible, deliverable or to abandon the project. As with recognition of a resource overconsumption problem, scope under-delivery issues are always difficult to deal with. Some projects choose to hide the problems, hoping that someone comes up with a brilliant idea to close the gap between what is desired and what can credibly be delivered. This is a very high-risk strategy and seldom works out. The best course is to surface the issues as soon as you have validated the data. If you do this early, project options are more numerous, the total investment in the project is still relatively small, and expectations are less "locked in." While still painful and unpleasant, this is a lot easier than dealing with it later. When a project proves to be demonstrably impossible, the optimal time to change (or kill) it is early, not late.

In addition to the impact on the current project, scope problems may also affect other projects. Project teams that depend on aspects of your deliverable that are unrealistic or who are working with similar flawed assumptions also need to be informed so that they can develop alternate strategies or work-arounds.

Once you have completed the variance analysis, document the impact. List the consequences of each variance in terms of:

- ❐ Predicted schedule slip
- ❐ Budget or other resource requirements
- ❐ The effect on the project deliverable
- ❐ Impact on other projects

Once you have determined the source and magnitude of the problem, you have a basis for response.

Trend Analysis

Trend analysis does not necessarily need to be part of each monitoring cycle, but periodically it is a good idea to examine the trends in the status data. When the resource consumption rates or cumulative slip for the project moves in a dangerous direction, the trend data will make it clear. The earlier you are able to detect and analyze an adverse trend, the easier it will be to deal with it. Trend data may reveal a need to adjust the project end date, raise the budget, negotiate for more resources, renegotiate contracts, or modify the project deliverables. If so, the earlier you start, the better your chances for success.

Trend analysis performed early in the project identifies the things that need to shift at a point where there is much more tolerance for change, even significant change; the concept of the project is still flexible in the minds of the project sponsors, stakeholders, and contributors. Ignoring or failing to detect adverse trends in the status data is very risky. If trend information indicates a problem and no action is taken, the trend is likely to continue and grow. Ultimately, something *will* have to be done. As it gets later in the project, the options diminish and the changes required to reverse the trend become more extreme and less likely to do much good. These actions may create additional problems and even lead to project failure.

Detecting and dealing with adverse project trends early enough avoids the late project changes and cancellations that are so demotivating for technical project teams. After having worked for months, or even years, on a project, the team may find even small changes to the deliverable devastating. Allowing everyone to identify with a very aggressive, high-tech, bleeding-edge objective for the bulk of the project and then having to chop the heart out of it at the last minute so that you can ship *something* on time is demoralizing and embarrassing. People identify with the work they do, so they take late project changes very personally. Team building and motivation on subsequent projects become very difficult. If this happens often, project staff members are trained not to care about the projects and not to trust the people who lead and sponsor them. Technical projects are successful not because they are easy; they succeed because people care about them. Anything that interferes with this raises project risk to insurmountable levels.

Detecting and responding to adverse trends so that you can

shift project expectations early into better alignment with reality is an important tactic for delivering on failure-prone projects.

Responding to Issues

At this point in the status cycle, any significant differences between the plan and actual project performance are visible. Treating plan variances as issues and resolving them soon after they occur, when they are still small, allows project recovery with minimum disruption. Responding to project issues resembles risk response planning, discussed in Chapter 8. In fact, for issues that you anticipated as risks, the response could be as simple as implementing a contingency plan. Other possible responses range from very minor staffing shifts or resequencing of project activities to major changes to the project objective, or even to project cancellation. The process for issue response closely resembles the "Plan-Do-Check-Act" cycle from quality management.

Base your response plan on the specifics of the problem. If the variance is small or there is a well-established contingency plan, it may be sufficient to delegate the response to the team members responsible for the work affected. If the situation is more complicated, many of the ideas from project planning and risk response come into play.

For significant problems, involve the right people. As with any project planning, everyone on the team brings his or her own expertise, ideas, and perspective. Larger project problems often require major project changes, so review, if necessary, the processes and requirements for change management.

PLAN FOR RESPONSE

Prepare to brainstorm ideas to respond to the issue by checking the contingency plans already available and reviewing any responses that were used to recover from similar situations on earlier projects. Clearly state the problem and its root cause or causes, and focus your planning on solving the real problem, not just dealing with the symptoms. Be creative and let ideas flow; even ideas that seem impractical may trigger someone to think of a workable response. Don't simply accept the first idea someone comes up with. Develop a number of ideas, especially for larger issues.

SELECT A PLAN

Once ideas for responding have been generated and captured, analyze and rank them. Consider the consequences of each potential response on project schedule, resources, and scope. Probe for possible unintended consequences, both in your project and for other related work. Even ideas that seem very good can sometimes lead to consequences that make things worse overall.

The best of the options developed may not present any obvious problems or require any significant project changes (sometimes the "brute force" option of just working some additional overtime is the path of least resistance). However, if the recovery plans that seem to make the most sense do require changes, the next step is to submit each option you are considering to the change management process for review.

For even more significant response plans, those that modify the basic project objectives, the analysis process could also involve fundamental replanning. If so, get buy-in from the project team and stakeholders for the revised plan, validate the new objective and baseline with the project sponsor, and update the affected documents.

IMPLEMENT AND MONITOR THE CHANGES

Once a response plan is accepted, implement it. Communicate the plan and the information on required project changes to the project team and any other people involved.

After taking the actions in the response plan, monitor to see whether you have solved the problem. If the actions are ineffective, plan for additional responses, looking for a better solution. The situation is similar to the way a fire department treats a fire. Initially a new fire is "one alarm," and one fire crew is sent out. When the fire is too large, or it spreads, the fire alarm escalates to two alarms, and then, if needed, to three or more. The escalation continues until the fire is brought under control. Ongoing project risk management requires the same diligence and persistence.

Significant project changes often lead to unintended consequences. During the status cycles that follow big changes, be particularly thorough in your data analysis and look for unexpected results.

Communication

The final step in the status cycle is to let people know how the project is doing. This includes the use of project status reports and status meetings, as well as less formal communication. Successful projects depend on a solid foundation of clear, frequent communication. Without effective communication, project risks may not be detected, let alone managed.

COMMUNICATION CHALLENGES

Communication on projects presents a number of growing challenges, many of which relate directly to observed risks on technical projects. These include distance, time differences, languages and culture, and the need to work cross-functionally with many diverse disciplines. Each of these makes effective communication, which is never easy anyway, more and more difficult.

Distance is a well-known barrier to communication. It restricts both the type and amount of communication possible and reduces informal interaction to almost none. On global or distributed projects teams with people who work at a distance, no one can just "stop by" to share information. Even with project teams that are local to each other, increasingly people are working from their homes or other locations apart from other team members.

As projects become increasingly global, time differences also interfere with communication. Even phoning people on global projects can be difficult; whenever you need to talk, it is the middle of the night for them, and they are probably asleep. Communication tends to be mostly written, with rare exceptions when one part of the project team can make itself available outside its normal work hours. Again, this challenge is not unique to global teams. "Flextime" and other policies that allow people to set their own work schedules erect a barrier even for teams that work in the same time zone.

Different languages and cultures are another growing communication challenge for technical projects. Global work involves people who speak different languages and who have different ways of working and communicating. Sharing complicated technical project information in this sort of environment is never easy, and omissions and misunderstandings may be frequent. In many locations, such as California, Singapore, India, and much of Europe, even projects with co-located teams face this challenge. Technical project teams are made up of individuals with different first languages and cultural backgrounds. Cultural and linguistic diversity in technical work is becoming the norm, not the exception, for many types of technical projects.

Finally, few technical projects are *only* technical. Communication between people from different disciplines can be even more difficult than communication between people with different native languages. Cross-functional project teams involve people from very different educational and work backgrounds. Development, manufacturing, sales, marketing, support, and other functions all need to cooperate on projects, and their vocabularies, jargon, and perspectives are radically different. In addition, technical projects increasingly depend on consultants, partners, and suppliers from other companies, and these contributors bring their own communication idiosyncrasies.

As the project leader, you are the person primarily responsible for project communication, and you must rise to these challenges to minimize project risks. In today's projects, this requires discipline and effort.

Project Status Reports

The most visible communication for most projects is the written status report. Ongoing risk management depends on clear, credible project information that is understood by everyone on the project. Status reporting that is too cursory increases risk because no one has enough information about the project to know what is happening, leading to chaos. This may occur because the project leader is busy or distracted and provides too little data. It also may be the result of "need to know" project reporting, where the project leader sends out very brief notes to each team member containing data only on the portion of the project that he or she is involved with. It can even happen because the project leader dislikes writing reports. Whatever the source, projects with too little information become very prone to risks, particularly risks related to dependencies and interfaces.

On the other hand, status reporting that rambles on and on is no better. No one has time to read it all, and, although the information everyone needs is probably there, somewhere, finding it becomes vanishingly unlikely. One common reason for long reports is a project leader who solicits individual reports from the whole team, concatenates them into a compendium running to dozens of pages, and ships it all out once a week. It can also happen with project leaders who like to write and are not good at summarizing. Time can be a factor in this; there is much truth in the old saying "I didn't have time to write a short report, so I wrote a long one." Whatever the reason for verbosity, the result is increased project risk, because no one has the patience or time to digest the entire report.

The best reports start with a short, clear summary and include only current, relevant data. Reporting formats may be standardized in your organization or created for the project specifically, but a consistent format for the weekly report makes it easier to write, easier to read, and more useful for postproject analysis. Select a format that works for your project, and stick with it.

In written reports, strive to be concise, honest, and clear. If you commit to reporting project status every Friday (or some other frequency), do it. Work to summarize, interpret, and clarify information. Avoid stringing together random bits of project data in a stream of consciousness. Include the information needed by your project team, your management, and other stakeholders such as the customer, other project leaders, or others to whom you will distribute the report. Periodically discuss the project reporting with stakeholders, and note their key interests so that you can provide the information that they require. Any important data that people notice are missing will probably result in unnecessary and time-consuming telephone calls or other interruptions. Missing information that goes unnoticed can lead to serious project risks and problems.

Regardless of the recipient, begin every status report with a brief (twenty lines or fewer) executive summary. Include the most important information in the summary, such as key accomplishments, current issues, and planned next steps. Be aware that sometimes the summary is all that will actually be read and that some of the people who receive your report will not need or want any more detail than this.

Follow the summary with any additional information organized by declining relative importance and increasing detail. If different people in your distribution list need varying levels of detail, the hierarchical structure allows you to create additional reports by truncation, rather than by rewriting. Always reread your report for errors, omissions (a missing "not" here and there can cause no end of trouble), and language that is clear and easily understood by all report recipients. Avoid technical jargon, acronyms, and idioms that may be confusing or misunderstood. Attaching graphs, figures, and charts can simplify complex project information and statistics (but be sure to use a format for this that all recipients will be able to read).

In addition to the executive summary, a typical project status report may include:

❐ A short description of each major accomplishment since the last report, including a discussion of milestones achieved and any project changes. This portion of the report is an excellent place to "name names" and to recognize individual and team accomplishments. Technical projects often miss opportunities to thank people and recognize their hard work; here is one of the best places to reverse this tendency.

❏ Activities planned during the next status period. These items are included as accomplishments (or issues) in the following status report.

❏ Significant issues and problems, with your planned responses.

❏ A schedule summary, with planned, actual, and expected future dates in tabular or graphic format.

❏ A resource summary, with planned, actual, and expected future resource requirements, in tabular or graphic format.

❏ A detailed project analysis, including an explanation of any variances, a discussion of issues encountered, and plans for resolution.

❏ Risk analysis, including the known risks in the near project future and the status of any ongoing risk recovery efforts.

❏ Additional detail, charts, and other information as needed.

In written reports, include only status information that is substantiated, and use soft status data sparingly, if at all.

OTHER REPORTING

In addition to the project status report, other reporting may be required. Some reports may be periodic, similar to the status report, while others may be issued only occasionally.

Periodic reports common on technical projects include change control summaries, quality reports, testing and defect reports (particularly late in the project), personnel reports, contract status reports, and budget reports. Some of these reports may be written for the project by others, and some are created by the project leader or team. Regardless of the source of the report, effective risk management requires that you, as the project leader, check the information for accuracy and consistency and diligently correct any inaccurate information.

Other, less frequent reporting and presentation of project data may be required for management reviews, phase transitions, or other reasons. These reports and presentations generally include much of the same sort of information found in your project status reports, but they take a longer view of the project, both backward and forward. Again, one of your chief responsibilities as the project leader is to ensure scrupulous consistency with other project information.

These higher-level reports and presentations are a good opportunity to reinforce your project goals and objectives, to be positive about what the team has done, and to share your plans for the future. Presentations are a particularly effective way to renew strong project sponsorship, motivate the team, and renew enthusiasm for the project. On longer projects, all of these factors are significant sources of risk.

PROJECT STATUS MEETINGS

Project status meetings for technical projects are viewed by many as a necessary evil, and by everyone else even less positively. Technical people, for the most part, hate meetings, especially long ones. Considering the increase in project risk that results from inadequate communication, this is unfortunate. The discussions and exchanges that occur during project status meetings are essential for avoiding risks, and many potential problems never occur because of things that are discussed during status meetings. Regular status meetings, even via teleconferencing, are a potent tool for keeping difficult projects on track and risks under control.

Brevity

One key to improving attendance and participation in status meetings is to keep them short. Meetings are more interesting and energized if they focus only on project status—what has been accomplished and what issues are pending. Status meetings for some projects are lengthy, rambling affairs that cover a lot more than project status. In addition to discussions of general issues and business information unrelated to the project, there are frequent side trips into issue resolution and problem solving. While all of this may be necessary, none of it needs to be part of a project status meeting. General "staff meeting" issues may be of no value or interest to some of the project team, such as external consultants, and consume both time and money unnecessarily. Problem solving and issue resolution are unquestionably important, but they rarely require the entire project staff to be involved. While a few people are fascinated and engaged in the discussions, the rest of the people in the meeting will be falling asleep. Take problem solving and extended discussions off-line with smaller groups in follow-up meetings.

Agenda

Effective meetings are well structured, and they work from an established meeting agenda that they stick to. Useful goals for status meetings include always starting on time, setting time limits for the agenda items and enforcing them, and ending the meeting early as often as possible. An effective method for keeping meetings short is to schedule them just before lunch or near the end of the workday. Hunger and the desire to go home are excellent ways to focus people on the important issues and manage meandering discussions.

A typical project status meeting agenda might include:

- Introductions of any new participants
- Review of the meeting's purpose and agenda
- Recognition of recent major accomplishments
- Status of the project schedule (actual results compared with the baseline)
- Status of project resource use (actual results compared with the baseline)
- Discussion of plan variances and the status of action(s) taken
- New issues

Method

Meeting methods vary a great deal, and almost any method for periodic project discussion that the project team cooperates with can be effective. Face-to-face communication is generally best. When people can be in the same place at the same time, it minimizes misunderstandings and reinforces teamwork. Meetings in person also provide the best direct and immediate feedback to what is said; when you are face-to-face, you can ask questions and get answers immediately. Even when people work in the same location but at different times, meeting once per week should not be too difficult to arrange.

When people work in different places, frequent face-to-face meetings are not possible. Technology provides several other methods, but, without adequate planning and preparation, you will not get the most out of them.

Teleconferencing, like any meeting, requires advance planning so that any materials to be discussed will be available to all. Prepare any support materials the meeting will require, and send them via computer networking, electronic mail, fax, expedited shipping, or other means to all locations involved with the meeting so that all the information is available in time. Also, distribute the agenda for the meeting to all attendees, and get a commitment to participate from each person who needs to take part. Since, even with videoconferencing, it may not always be obvious who is speaking, start the meeting with introductions of all involved whenever there are new participants, and remind everyone to state his or her name before speaking during the meeting. When teleconferencing with people who don't know one another, it can be helpful to exchange pictures so that you have some idea of who is speaking.

For "real-time" work that involves visual images or applications—presentation slides, graphics, reports, or demonstrations of software—use videoconferencing or Web-facilitated meeting capabilities, and allow sufficient time for transmissions, explanations, and an occasional operational problem. When dealing with significant time differences, schedule meetings at a time that is as mutually convenient as possible. If there is no convenient time, as when dealing with a half-day difference between India and the western United States, do not schedule every meeting for the same time. Schedule the meetings so that all participants will be able to meet during their daytime at least once in a while. Spread the pain around; don't make the same team members lose sleep for every meeting.

For technology-assisted meetings, here are key considerations:

❏ Select technology that all the participants have access to and can competently use.

❏ Obtain buy-in from the entire project team to use the technologies for meetings, including external consultants, partners, and outside service suppliers.

❏ Test, in advance, for compatibility of electronic mail systems and other software applications that you intend to use. Make sure that everyone involved can receive attachments to electronic mail messages and open them using compatible versions of software. Warn everyone in advance if new software releases are scheduled, and repeat the compatibility tests after any upgrades.

However the meeting is conducted, record what is discussed for any absent team members and for the project information archive. Capture new issues and action items, with assigned owners and expected due dates. Distribute meeting minutes promptly to all project contributors, and to others as appropriate.

INFORMAL PROJECT COMMUNICATIONS

Never limit project communications to scheduled meetings. Some of the most important communication on technical projects takes place at coffee machines, in hallways, and during casual conversations. Project risks may surface far earlier in these discussions than in formal analysis.

Some of this communication involves the project leader, and successful project leaders create opportunities for frequent, unstructured conversations. The idea of "management by wandering around," popularized by Dave Packard and Bill Hewlett, is a particularly effective way to reinforce trust and build relationships within a project team. Even when teams are distributed and you are unable to talk frequently with people in person, there will be opportunities to do it once in a while, and you can rely on the telephone for the periods in between. A great deal of "soft data" and valuable project information surfaces during casual exchanges. Informal communications are also an important benefit of project celebrations. When one project team in California discovered a mutual interest in local wines, the members assigned letters to all their milestones. They had a great time working their way through the alphabet, sharing a bottle of wine (after work) from a winery with a name that started with the same letter as the completed milestone. Particularly on longer projects, you can schedule periodic "extracurricular" activities chosen by the team and have some fun. Eating together works well, and, depending on the team, so might a sporting event, the new big-budget science fiction movie, or some other recreation. Effective project leaders work to encourage interactions among project team members. Team cohesion, which correlates strongly with the amount of informal communication, is one of your best defenses against project risk.

Project Archives

In addition to distributing project documents and reports to your stakeholders and contributors, you also need to retain copies as part of your project management information system (PMIS). This archive not only serves as an ongoing reference during the project but also is essential for capturing the lessons learned during postproject analysis; it contains data that can improve risk management on future projects. For most technical projects, the archive will probably be stored on-line, but it is also prudent to keep a hard copy of key data because a great deal of useful information may be lost whenever older software applications are replaced, making the original source files useless.

A typical project archive contains:

❏ The documents created during the project, including the original scope definition documents

❏ A complete project roster that includes all the comings and goings of the project staff

❏ The initial baseline planning documents

❏ Each project status report

❏ Other periodic project reports and communications

❏ A change control history

❏ Copies of all revised project documents following authorized changes

There may also be a great deal of additional archived information specific to the project. This archive tells the history of the project from beginning to end. When the project is over, the final addition will be the postproject retrospective analysis and lessons learned.

The archive serves many purposes, not the least of which is helping to mitigate a very significant project risk—the loss of the project leader. If for any reason the project needs to continue without the original project leader, the information in a well-maintained PMIS is invaluable. The new project leader who takes on a project where a thorough PMIS exists still faces a daunting task but is light-years ahead of where he or she would otherwise be.

Project Reviews and Risk Reassessment

When you operate a complex piece of machinery such as an automobile, you frequently need to add fuel, check the oil and the air pressure in the tires, and make other minor adjustments. This is sufficient in the short run, but if you never do anything more, the car will soon break down. Periodically, you also must perform scheduled maintenance to change the oil, replace worn-out or poorly functioning components, check the brakes and other systems, and generally bring the vehicle back into good operational condition.

A project is also a complex system. The activities in the status cycle are necessary, like adding fuel to a car, but, unless the project is very short, they are not sufficient. Most projects also require periodic maintenance, in the form of a project review. The planning horizon for some technical projects may be as short as two to three months, or it may stretch to most of a year, but no project can plan with adequate detail beyond its planning limit, whatever it may be. Project reviews allow you to take a longer view, beyond the next status cycle, in order to revalidate the project objectives, plans, and assumptions. Successful project and risk management require cycles of review and regular reassessment to keep the project on track.

Another reason for periodic review relates to the dynamics of a distributed team. If you begin a project with a face-to-face start-up workshop, technological methods and long-distance meetings are very effective for coordinating work on separated teams—up to a limit. After about six months, established trust and relationships begin to break down, resulting in conflicts, errors, and loss of productivity. Desired behavior, such as collaborative problem solving, deteriorates into unproductive finger pointing and arguing. Periodic project reviews, which at least some of the distributed team members attend in person, are an excellent way to reestablish project team cohesion.

Even for co-located teams, the project review is an opportunity to reinforce the value of the project, recognize and reward significant accomplishments, and motivate the project team. Loss of interest on very long projects is one of the reasons that these projects are higher-risk. Reminding the team why the project matters and formally saying "thank you" is an effective way to reduce this risk.

The limited planning horizon and technical complexity also contribute to the greater project risk of lengthy projects, and project reviews are an effective way to better manage these factors. During the review, as you reassess the project, one of three scenarios will arise. Some reviews find few issues, requiring minimal attention, and the project continues as planned. Other reviews reveal changes or additional planning that is necessary, and the project continues, but only after the changes are made. The third possible outcome of a project review is a recommendation to cancel future project work. While this is not pleasant, it is better ultimately for everyone than continuing with a project that would eventually fail after spending even more time and money.

SCHEDULE THE REVIEW

Project reviews are generally most productive when they are scheduled to coincide with major project milestones or events. Some examples include life-cycle phase checkpoints and stage-gate transitions that follow a major change in project direction or occur when key project contributors leave or join the project or after a major business reorganization or change in management. Even in the absence of one of these events, however, you should schedule a project review at least every six months; for particularly risky projects, quarterly (or even more frequent) reviews may be prudent.

Allow sufficient time for a project review. A thorough review usually requires about the same amount of time as the project start-up workshop did. At minimum the review will take half a day, but most technical projects need a day or more. The most effective way to review a project is to get away from the usual workplace and assemble all key project team members face-to-face. Choose a time for the review by checking the calendars of the people you need to participate, and get their commitment to attend. If there are more than about twelve essential people, consider breaking the review into several smaller meetings with fewer participants that will focus on specific aspects of the project. These partial project reviews can be either conducted in sequence or held simultaneously and then followed by a larger general session where you summarize results, integrate the findings, and bring the review to closure.

Preparing for a review relies on information in the project archive, but it also may require new information, necessitating revision or new versions of the data used for scope planning. The universe does not remain static month after month as your project work proceeds, so for long projects you should update your market research, customer needs data, and competitive analysis information. Basic project assumptions and business strategies may also shift during the project, requiring adjustments, and more work may be necessary to assess new or evolving technological alternatives currently available to the project. Before your review, determine the information you need, and assign an owner to prepare it. Thorough preparation for a project review may entail significant effort, so scheduling reviews too frequently can create a lot of project overhead.

OBJECTIVES FOR THE REVIEW

The overall objective of the review is "scheduled maintenance" for the project. During the review, the principal focus is the course of the project moving forward. Major objectives should include:

- ❏ Thorough review of project objectives and specifications.

- ❏ Recognition of significant project accomplishments.

- ❏ Revalidation of project assumptions. Check the information you have on user needs, technology, competitors, and other data.

- ❏ Review of planning information, including identification of additional required project activities, reassessment of project estimates for remaining work, analysis of dependencies and project interfaces, and a review of the resource plan.

- ❏ Risk reassessment, including identification, reprioritization, and response planning for new and existing known project risks.

- ❏ Review of the cumulative impact of project changes.

- ❏ Review of the processes you are using on the project. Identify things you have done well, and plan for wider use of good practices. Review problems, and investigate process improvements needed for avoiding them in the rest of the project. Seek faster or more efficient ways to accomplish remaining project work.

- ❏ Collection of specific input from any key staff members who are leaving the project.

- ❏ Assignment of owners and time frames to all action items, new activities, and recommendations made.

Develop an agenda for the review, and assign specific expected outcomes and time allotments for each item on the agenda.

Conduct the Review

Begin the project review by clarifying the roles of the participants and setting the agenda. During the review, assign participants responsibility for capturing decisions and action items in writing, and maintain a separate list of any project issues that require later attention but are beyond the scope of the review meeting.

Focus initially on positive aspects of the project. Review accomplishments and project work completed, recognizing the people who have made noteworthy contributions. Identify the things on the project that have gone well, and consider how you could expand the use of these processes as the project continues.

Then, focus on any needed project changes. Reconsider the scope definition assumptions, and, when necessary, develop recommendations for changes necessitated by newly available market research, competitive analysis, or user interview data. Review all unanticipated activities you have added to the project to date and all the activities that were underestimated or were planned based on faulty assumptions. Review the future project plans using these data, and identify any additional project activities or other plan defects that are now apparent. Test the assumptions, estimates, and other data for future scheduled work in light of what you now know. Make note of any changes that are proposed for later analysis. Reexamine project decisions that you have made, the project environment, and the processes that you are using. The risk survey in Chapter 9, edited down, is an effective way to determine aspects of your overall project that could use improvement.

Discuss the problems and risks you have encountered in the project so far, and brainstorm methods for avoiding similar trouble in the remainder of the project. Also, review your existing risk list, and identify additional scope, schedule, resource, or other risks that are now visible in the project. Add the new risks to the list, and assess all of them, rank-ordering the risks on the basis of current information. Develop appropriate risk responses for any significant risks that have none.

Capture all suggestions, recommendations, and decisions made during the review, and close the review by summarizing the results. Assign owners and due dates for all added project activities and action items. For any change recommendations that are beyond your authority, delegate responsibility for preparing a change proposal. For recommendations that would change any of the overall project objectives, assign yourself the task of updating any affected project documents, and prepare to revalidate the project with your sponsor.

FOLLOW UP AFTER THE REVIEW

After the review, document what you discussed and learned. Summarize the findings and distribute them appropriately, generally to the same people who receive your project status reports. Submit all recommendations requiring changes to your change control process, and support their analysis with your data. When changes are approved, implement them as soon as practical. If a change you recommended is rejected, meet with the project team to investigate other ways to deal with the situation that the proposed change would have corrected.

If changes to the project objective are necessary, discuss your recommendations with your project sponsor. Support your proposal with compelling data, and seek approval, revalidating the project plan. You will need to replace any project plans and documents to reflect all recommendations that were approved and provide updated project plans to the project team. Archive all older versions of the project documents, marking them as obsolete.

After the review, use what you learned to get some attention for your project. Prepare a presentation to summarize the project's progress to date and your plans going forward. Invite stakeholders and people from related projects to attend. Use the presentation to report significant accomplishments and to publicly recognize the contributions by specific people and teams. In presenting information about the remaining project work, accentuate the positive, emphasizing the value and importance of the project. Use the presentation to renew enthusiasm for the project and motivate the project team.

Finally, personally thank your team members for their contributions. If team members work for other managers, acknowledge the contributions to them, too. When appropriate, suitably reward contributors for their efforts. Do not wait until the end of a very long project to recommend contributors for available recognition programs. Project reviews are also a good time to celebrate your accomplishments. Long projects, especially, need more parties.

Key Ideas for Risk Monitoring and Control

❐ Collect status dogmatically.
❐ Monitor variances and trends frequently throughout your project.
❐ Respond to issues and problems promptly.
❐ Communicate clearly and often.

Panama Canal: Risk-Based Replanning (1908)

Project monitoring and prompt responses when necessary were among the main differences between the first effort to construct the Panama Canal and the second one. No project proceeds exactly as planned, and the U.S. canal project was no exception. It was ultimately successful because the managers and workers revised their plans to effectively deal with problems as they emerged.

As the work at Panama continued, for example, it seemed that the more they dug, the more there was to dig. Mud slides were frequent, and between 1906 and 1913 the total estimates for excavation more than doubled. The response to this problem was not terribly elegant, but it was effective. Following the report of a particularly enormous mud slide in the Culebra Cut, George Goethals remarked, "Hell, dig it out again." They had to, many times. Some risks are managed primarily through persistence and perseverance.

As time passed, a number of factors not known at the start of the project came into focus. By 1908, it became clear that new materials, including the steels to be used on the canal, were making possible the construction of much larger ships. Goethals made two significant design changes as a result of this. The first was to commit to a wider excavation of the Culebra Cut, increasing it to nearly one hundred meters (from 200 feet to 300 feet) to accommodate ships wider than thirty meters sailing in each direction. Although this represented much additional digging, it also made the tasks of ongoing maintenance and dredging a little easier.

The second change was to the size of the locks. Relying on Goethal's estimates of the size of future ocean-going ships, the locks were enlarged to be 110 feet wide and 1,000 feet long. Although conversion to metric units of these dimensions is trivial, few do it, as this somewhat arbitrary choice became the single most important factor in twentieth-century ship building. These dimensions are the exact size of the rectangular-hulled PANAMAX ships, the largest ships that can transit the canal. Apart from oil supertankers (which are generally designed for use on a single-ocean, point-to-point route), very few ships are built any bigger than a Panama Canal lock.

In addition to making the locks larger, Goethals made another change to them. All the water used to operate the canal flows by gravity. Locks are filled from the manmade lakes above them and then emptied into the ocean. During the rainy season, this works well. In the drier parts of the year, the depth of the lakes falls, and the water level in the cut that connects them could fall to too low a level to permit ocean-going ships to pass. To save water, Goethals redesigned each of the twelve locks with multiple sets of doors, enabling smaller ships to lock through using a much smaller volume of water.

One additional significant change was adopted midproject,

primarily for security reasons. At the start of the twentieth century, the global political situation, particularly in Europe, was increasingly unstable. The geography of Panama has a long, gradual slope from the central ridge north on the Atlantic side and a much shorter, steeper slope on the south, facing the Pacific. On the steeper Pacific slopes, the locks in the original plan were visible from the water, and Goethals, a military man, feared that the canal might be closed down by projectiles fired from an offshore warship. To avoid this, he moved the Pacific locks further inland. The change actually made the engineering somewhat easier, as the new plan took better advantage of the more level land farther up the slope.

George Goethals managed risk through scrupulous management of all changes, insisting throughout his tenure that "everything must be written down." Once the plan was set, the debating stopped, and all the effort went to execution.

CHAPTER 12

CLOSING PROJECTS

"History repeats itself. That's one of the things
wrong with history."
—CLARENCE DARROW

Reviewing the records of technical projects, it is striking
how many consecutive projects fall victim to the same problems.
Common issues such as inadequate staffing, top-down imposed
deadlines that have nothing to do with the work, fixed commitments made with little or no analysis, and many of the other issues
listed in the PERIL database, discussed in the first several chapters
of this book, plague project after project. One definition of insanity
is repeating the same actions over and over, hoping for a different
result. More than a little risk in most projects is a direct result of
using the same methods for projects that have caused problems in
the past.

Getting better results requires process improvement. Using
a continuous cycle of measurement, small modifications, new measurement, and comparative analysis, you can discover ways to improve any process. By treating each project as a separate
experiment, you can, as part of project closure, examine the results
you obtained from the project processes that were used. Achieving
consistently better results and minimizing risks down the line requires you to identify what worked well, ensuring that these processes are repeated on future projects, and it also requires you to
isolate the processes that did not work and investigate ways to
change them. Any process change you come up with is probably a
better bet than repeating something that does not work. After the
changes, if the performance of your next project is still not good
enough, you can always change it again. Postproject analysis is a
powerful and effective tool for longer-term project risk management improvement.

Most of the content of this chapter falls into the "Administrative Closure" portion of the Closing Processes in the *PMBOK®️ Guide,* as well as other Project Processes. The principal content of this chapter focuses on:

❑ Project closure

❑ Project retrospective analysis

Project Closure

There are a number of closure activities common to most technical projects, but the specifics vary a great deal with the type of project. Project close-out generally involves:

❑ Formal acceptance of the project deliverables (for successful projects)

❑ The final written report

❑ Close-out of all contracts, documents, and agreements for the project

❑ Acknowledgement of contributions

❑ A postproject retrospective analysis to capture the lessons learned

❑ A celebration or other event to commemorate the project

The most relevant of these to risk management is the retrospective analysis, which is covered in detail later in this chapter.

Formal Acceptance

One of the greatest potential risks any project leader faces is, after finishing the work, to be asked, on delivery, "What's this?" Scope risk management seeks to avoid this situation through validation of the initial specifications and scrupulous management of changes. Definition of all final acceptance testing, aligned with the initial specifications, should be one of the first activities undertaken in technical projects, as part of scope definition and planning. Testing and acceptance requirements must also be modified as needed throughout the project in response to authorized changes. If final tests and acceptance criteria are defined late in the project, it is only through happenstance that the project deliverables will meet the requirements.

Managing this risk involves thorough specification of the deliverable and frequent communication throughout the project with the people who will evaluate and accept it. You can also minimize the risk greatly by engaging them in discussions and evaluations of any prototypes, models, incremental results, or other interim project deliverables. Detailed, validated scope definition is the best way to minimize late project surprises.

When your project is successful, get formal acknowledgment of this from the project sponsor and, as appropriate, from the customer or other stakeholders. For technical projects undertaken on a fee-for-service basis, generate the final billing information and ensure that the customer is properly and promptly billed. Even for projects that end in cancellation or fail to deliver on all of their objectives, you should obtain written acknowledgement whenever possible of the partial results or other accomplishments that you did successfully complete.

FINAL PROJECT REPORT

The main purpose of a final report is to acknowledge what has been done and to communicate to everyone involved that the project is over. Some years ago, two contributors on a distributed team called their project leader to report their status, because they had not heard from him in about a month. The telephone conversation started awkwardly. Following a long, embarrassed pause, the project leader finally asked, "Didn't I call you last month to let you know the project had been canceled?" Every project needs a final project report summarizing results and thanking contributors, whatever its final disposition.

A final project report is usually very similar in format to a regular status report, but it puts more emphasis on the overall project and the accomplishments of the contributors. The report is an excellent place to document and formally recognize significant contributions made by individuals (and groups) on the project team. While the final project report may be longer than the periodic project status reports, it should also begin with a high-level summary, and it often includes much of the same content that you reported throughout the project.

CONTRACT AND DOCUMENT CLOSE-OUT

For all internal agreements and external contracts that are specific to your project, complete any final paperwork required. Following final payments of all invoices, summarize the financial information, and terminate the agreements. If there are issues or problems relating to any contracts, escalate and resolve them as soon as practical.

Add the final project report to the project information archive, along with any other project documents and reports that are updated or created as part of your project close-out.

ACKNOWLEDGING CONTRIBUTIONS

It is a small world. When you work with people once, the chances are fairly good that you will work with them again. Managing risk in a continuing stream of projects depends on developing and maintaining trust, relationships, and teamwork. Recognizing the accomplishments and contributions that people have made is fundamental to this.

On technical projects, expertise and hard work are frequently taken for granted. When technical people finish difficult activities, often the only feedback they get is an assignment to another, even more difficult activity. Especially at the end of a project, you need to *thank* people, both in person and in writing. For people who work for other managers, acknowledge their contributions to their management, also. Keep your remarks truthful, but focus on positive contributions. If it is culturally appropriate, praise people and teams publicly, as well. If there are programs in place for specific rewards, such as stock options or other tangible compensation for extra effort, submit recommendations for deserving project contributors to reward them for their work.

CELEBRATION

Whatever the atmosphere has been in the closing days of your project, bring the project to a positive conclusion. Celebrate the success of the project with some sort of event. Even if the project was not a success, it is good to get people together and acknowledge what was accomplished. Celebrations need not be lavish to be effective; even in businesses that may not currently be doing well financially, project teams can get together and share food and beverages that they provide for themselves. Moving on to the next project or another assignment is much easier when people have a chance to bring the past project to a good conclusion. If your project has a global or distributed team, arrange a similar event for each location at roughly the same time.

Project Retrospective Analysis

Managing project risk on an ongoing basis requires continuing process improvement. Whether you call this effort a retrospective meeting, lessons learned, a postmortem, a postproject analysis, or something else, the objective is always the same: improving future projects and minimizing their risks. If the people who led the projects before yours had done this more effectively, your project would have had fewer risks. Help the next project leader out—it could be you.

The overall process for a project retrospective analysis is similar to the project review process discussed in Chapter 11, but the focus is broader. Project reviews are concerned primarily with the remainder of the current project, using the experiences of the project so far to do "course corrections." A retrospective analysis is backward-looking and more comprehensive, mining the history of your whole project for ideas to keep and processes to change in projects generally.

Before you schedule and conduct a project retrospective, get organizational commitment to act on at least one of the resulting change recommendations. Performing postproject analyses time after time that always discover the same process defects is worse than useless. It wastes the time of the meeting participants and is demotivating. Decide how you will use the resulting information before you commit resources to the analysis.

PREPARE FOR AND SCHEDULE THE PROJECT RETROSPECTIVE

Thorough postproject analysis requires you to have accurate, completed project data. As the final project documents are added to the archive, determine what information is necessary, and ensure that it will be available for review during your project retrospective meeting. Some of the information you will need is the actual and planned schedule and resource data, the project change history, logs of issues and escalations, project metrics collected, and your status reports. If some team members left during the project and are no longer available, assemble any information that may have been archived when they left so that their perspectives on the project will also be considered.

Schedule the retrospective analysis soon after the project, but not immediately after it. If it is too soon, final documents will be incomplete, and events from the last, chaotic days of work will dominate the analysis. Don't wait more than about two to three weeks after the project, though, or important memories, particularly the less pleasant ones, will begin to fade, and key contributors may no longer be around. Schedule the meeting when the people who need to participate are available, and get their commitment to attend, face-to-face if possible. Strive to have all contributors participate; absent project team members often end up as scape-goats for more than their fair share of the project's difficulties.

You may benefit from having more than one retrospective meeting. If allowing managers or customers to attend will stifle discussion, consider having separate meetings—one for just the project team and another for everyone. Large programs may require retrospectives at several levels to collect appropriate information, generally beginning at the individual project level and then building on the findings and observations in additional meetings up through the program hierarchy.

Allocate sufficient time. Even shorter projects can generate enough data to justify a half-day retrospective. Longer projects require longer retrospectives. The process is most effective when all the project contributors, including the project leader, can focus on the project, so consider using a facilitator to run the meeting and have someone from outside the project take notes.

Set an agenda, and publish it in advance to gather comments for additional topics and requirements. At a minimum, include:

- ❐ A general statement by each project team member about the project
- ❐ Positive results: things that went well and practices to repeat
- ❐ Desirable changes: processes that caused problems that need improvement, new practices needed, and ideas for avoiding disappointments
- ❐ Prioritization of recommendations
- ❐ Final thoughts

Encourage participants to come prepared with specific examples of what went well and what changes they would recommend.

RETROSPECTIVE SURVEYS

If your business has a standard retrospective survey form, plan to use it. A retrospective survey typically includes questions about project definition, planning, defect and issue management, decision making, teamwork, leadership, process management, management of dependencies and deliverables, testing, logistics, and general recommendations. Standard formats usually have lists of statements to be rated on a scale from "strongly agree" on one extreme to "strongly disagree" on the other, and spaces for written comments.

If there is no survey form or the one you have does not include much in the way of risk information, consider using or adding the following:

Postproject Risk Survey

Please evaluate each of the following statements using the scale:
1—Strong disagree   2—Disagree   3—No opinion   4—Agree   5—Strongly agree

1   2   3   4   5   The project developed and used a risk plan.

1   2   3   4   5   Project problems were dealt with quickly and were escalated promptly when necessary.

1   2   3   4   5   Schedule problems were dealt with effectively.

1   2   3   4   5   Resource problems were dealt with effectively.

1   2   3   4   5   Project specifications were modified only through an effective change control process.

1   2   3   4   5   Detailed project reviews were done on an appropriate basis.

1   2   3   4   5   Project communication was frequent enough.

1   2   3   4   5   Project communication was thorough and complete.

1   2   3   4   5   Project documentation was self-consistent and available when needed.

1   2   3   4   5   Project status was reported honestly throughout the project.

1   2   3   4   5   Reporting of project difficulties resulted primarily in problem solving.

1   2   3   4   5   The project had adequate sponsorship and support throughout.

In addition to discussing processes during the meeting, it is also useful to have all project contributors list at least one practice that they recommend keeping and one practice that they recommend changing, with their suggestion on what to change.

Send the survey to team members, and ask each person to think about and return the survey with his or her thoughts before the project retrospective meeting. In some situations, it may be necessary to use a survey in place of a meeting, but, before deciding whether a survey will be sufficient, consider the loss of feedback involved.

Conduct the Meeting

Start a retrospective meeting with a statement of objectives, and review the meeting agenda. Invite each participant to make a general statement about the project, allowing people to say, briefly, what is on their minds.

Before getting into deeper detail, review the ground rules for the meeting. Rules might include a goal to hear from everyone, roughly equally. Do not allow just one person or a small group to dominate the discussion. Explain that the purpose of the meeting is to identify opportunities and issues, not to solve problems on the spot. The goal is recommendations, not solutions. As the retrospective continues, maintain a focus on the processes; avoid attacking individuals and "blamestorming." Resolve factual disputes using project documents.

To capture ideas generated in the meeting, have several flipcharts, or enter notes directly into a computer connected to a projector. (Computer entry saves time after the meeting, but posted large sheets of paper serve to keep the data visible where everyone can see them as the meeting progresses.) Maintain one list for "Positives" and another for "Needed changes" (*not* "Negatives"). Use additional lists for issues that need attention but are beyond the meeting scope, for action items, and for other data that may emerge. Designate a scribe to be responsible for creating the lists and documenting the meeting. If you cannot arrange for a scribe who was not involved in the project, rotate the responsibility for capturing data so that everyone can focus on the content of the meeting, at least most of the time.

Probe for positive aspects of the project first, using the data from the project retrospective surveys and other feedback or through general discussion. Collecting positives about the project first reminds people of all the aspects that went well. (If you allow people to begin by discussing problems and project aspects that went poorly, it starts the session on a depressing note, and the gloom can sometimes expand to take all the time you have.) You should probe for specific opinions on project aspects that led to success. Capture what went particularly well on your project; identify new practices that you should repeat or extensions to existing processes that were valuable.

When most of the positives have been cataloged, focus on desirable changes. Identify process areas that need improvement and practices that should be simplified or eliminated. Consider project issues and problems that you had to deal with, and develop process recommendations to avoid them on future projects. Seek the root causes of disappointments or failures on your project, and brainstorm possible ideas for mitigating them.

As your discussions progress, continue to collect positives that emerge, along with any important off-agenda information. Across the whole project team, perceptions may differ about what worked well and what did not. If there are differences, note them, and rely on project data wherever possible instead of opinions. Attack the issues, not the people; generating a list of people to blame things on will not improve future projects.

Throughout the meeting, specifically draw out people who are not saying very much, capturing their thoughts, and include observations provided in writing by former project team members and any others who are unable to participate.

As the allotted time winds down, summarize the recommendations. Ask each participant to nominate one recommendation that he or she believes would make the most significant difference on future projects. Work as a group to develop consensus, if possible, on the most important change, or at least generate support from the group for one or two that top the list. If further analysis will be necessary, capture the activities with owners and due dates.

Close the meeting with reflections on the process, and encourage people to share what they learned from the project personally and how they plan to work differently in the future.

DOCUMENT THE RESULTS AND TAKE ACTION

Document the meeting in a concise format, with the top recommendation (or recommendations) and key findings in a clear, short summary at the beginning. Include the lists of information developed in the meeting after the summary. Distribute the project retrospective report to the participants for review and comment. When this is completed, put a copy of the results in the project archive, and share the findings with others who could benefit from the information, such as the leaders of similar projects.

Take the principal recommendations to your management, and request support for making necessary changes. Small changes can be fairly trivial to implement, but more significant ones may trigger new projects and require significant data, planning, and resources to initiate. If your recommendation is denied, discuss alternatives with the project team, and investigate whether there might be other ways to mitigate the problem that, although less effective, would be under your control.

In any case, take at least one issue emerging from every project and resolve to do something different in the next project you undertake to address the problem. Effective risk management requires your firm commitment to continuous process improvement. Resolve to spread new practices found to be effective, and periodically review the standards and processes that are in place to detect the need for change and evolution. Monitor all changes you make to see whether they are effective. Whenever a change fails to achieve its desired result or causes serious unintended consequences, try something different.

Process improvement rests on the "Plan-Do-Check-Act" cycle and requires persistence. Managing project risk means reusing what has worked before on your projects and fixing or replacing what has failed. *Every* project offers beneficial lessons learned.

Key Ideas for Project Closure

❏ Thoroughly and accurately document the project results.
❏ Recognize accomplishments and thank contributors.
❏ Conduct a project retrospective and *use the recommendations.*

Panama Canal: Completion (1914)

On August 15, 1914, the first seagoing vessel crossed Panama, and the Panama Canal opened all the way through. This huge accomplishment was reported far and wide as the biggest news of the day. The attention lasted only a short time, though, as soon World War I broke out in Europe and quickly overshadowed the canal story.

In retrospect: The eighty-kilometer (fifty-mile) lock-and-dam canal was completed, slightly more than ten years after the congressional act that initiated the work. About 5,000 additional lives were lost finishing the U.S. project. Some died from disease, but most of the loss of life was from explosives (making the total death toll as high as 30,000, including those who died in the 1800s). The canal opened six months *ahead* of the schedule set earlier by John Stevens, despite all the difficulties and changes. Even more remarkable, it finished at a cost $23 million *less* than the budget ($352 million had been approved). The total cost for construction was more than $600 million, including the cost of the French project. If this is not the only U.S. government project ever to finish both early and under budget, it is certainly the largest one to do so.

Most of the credit goes to George Washington Goethals. Although he acknowledged his debt to John Stevens, nearly all the work was accomplished while Goethals was chief engineer. After the opening of the canal, Goethals remained in Panama as governor of the Canal Zone to oversee its early operation and to deal with any problems. His thoughts on completion of the work at Panama, delivered in March 1915, were:

We are gathered here tonight, not in the hope of something to be accomplished, but of actual accomplishment: the two oceans have been united. The [mud] slides hinder and prevent navigation for a few days, but in time they will be removed. The construction of the Canal means but little in comparison with its coming usefulness to the world and what it will bring about. Its completion is due to the brain and brawn of the men who are gathered here—men who have served loyally and well; and no commander in the world ever had a more faithful force than that which worked with me in building the Panama Canal.

If you were asked to name a famous engineer, Goethals would be an excellent choice. While there are other engineers who have become famous as astronauts, politicians, and multimillionaires, Goethals is famous for *engineering*. His accomplishments in addition to the canal are substantial, and he remains a significant influence in civil engineering to this day. The lessons learned from this project are thoroughly documented (as with all projects undertaken by the U.S. Army Corps of Engineers). They serve as the foundation not only for the subsequent civil engineering projects of the twentieth century but also for much of what is now recognized as modern project management.

CHAPTER 13

CONCLUSION

"Whether you think you can do a thing, or not, you are probably right."   —HENRY FORD

    Risk management processes provide a way to learn whether your project is feasible—whether you *should* think you can do it. A feeling of confidence, based on credible information, is a powerful determinant of success, and project risk information is a key source of the data that people need. When the verdict of the risk assessment is poor, it leads you to better alternatives.

    This book contains a wide range of ideas and techniques for project risk management. It is fair to ask whether all of these are always necessary, and the answer to that is simple: No. Each is essential to *some* projects at *some* times, but it is hard to imagine any project that would benefit sufficiently from everything discussed in this book to justify your doing all of it. Besides, some of the concepts covered represent alternative approaches to similar ends and would be redundant.

    So, how much *is* appropriate? The answer to this, like the answer to every other good question relating to project management, is also simple: It depends. Technical projects vary so widely that there can be no "one size fits all" answer. The trade-off between the value of risk information developed and the effort and cost associated with obtaining it always makes deciding how much project risk management to do a judgment call.

    That said, there is at least one useful guideline. Do enough planning and risk management to convince yourself that the project is, in fact, possible. The quotation from Henry Ford is applicable to projects of all kinds. People successfully deliver on ridiculously difficult objectives with amazing regularity when they *believe* that they can. When people are confident that they will be successful, they persist until they find a way to get things done. Conversely, even the most trivial projects fail when the staff working on them lacks confidence. The staff's belief in failure becomes self-fulfilling; no one puts in much effort—why bother?

Demonstrating to all concerned that your project is at least plausible defines the minimum investment in project planning and risk assessment that is prudent. If you can do this with informal discussions and capture the necessary information on index cards or yellow sticky notes, do it that way and get to work. If your project warrants more formality, and most technical projects probably do, determine what you need to do to provide confidence to the project team, and establish a baseline for status tracking and change management. But remain practical. Getting more involved than necessary in computer tools and complex assessment techniques is just as inappropriate to project and risk management as doing too little.

The most successful strategy for making permanent process improvements is to define your objective clearly, in measurable terms, and then to make small process additions and adjustments over time, assessing whether they are effective and helpful. Continuing this strategy over a sequence of projects will result in good control of risk at an acceptably modest cost in time and effort. Adding a lot of new overhead to a project environment all at once is not only expensive but also distracts at least the project leader from other project issues, often creating more problems than it solves.

Think about all the ideas and techniques in this book in the same way that a craftsman views his tools. In the tool set there are tools that are used every day, tools that are used only once in a while, and even a few tools that have never been used, at least so far. The entire set of tools is important because even the unused tools have applications, and the craftsman knows that when the need arises, the right tool will be available.

If you are currently doing very little to manage risk, consider the suggestions that follow. If the situation improves, this may be enough. If problems persist, add a few more ideas, and keep trying. While risk can never be eliminated from projects completely, it can always be reduced, often with relatively minor incremental effort.

Scope Risks. Minimize risk by thorough definition of project scope. Every aspect of the project deliverable that remains fuzzy, ill-defined, or "flexible" represents a very real failure mode. If you do not know enough to define everything, convert the project into a sequence of smaller efforts that you can define, one after the other, and perform reviews and testing as the interim subprojects complete. As you proceed, refine the scope definition and the next steps. If actually breaking the project into incremental pieces is not feasible, use a straw-man specification to document as much specific detail as you can, and invite criticism. Always validate the scope definition with project sponsors, customers, and key stakeholders, and set the expectation that every scope change will require significant justification.

Schedule Risks. Project planning is the foundation for managing schedule risk, and planning for the immediate short-term activities (at minimum) is never optional. Starting from the profile for the work, identify all the project activities that are similar to past work that has caused trouble. For every project estimate, set a range based on your confidence, or, better yet, probe for the worst cases and document their consequences. For projects that carry significant risk, negotiate some schedule reserve, but establish a credible plan that could complete at a date prior to the committed deadline.

Resource Risks. Most resource risks relate to bottlenecks and constraints. Past project resource problems are likely to recur unless you develop plans to avoid similar situations. Perform sufficient resource analysis to reconcile your requirements and skill needs with the project budget and available staff. For particularly risky projects, negotiate a budget reserve.

General Risks. Examine your plan, and brainstorm probable risks with the project team. List known risks, and determine probability and impact for each risk, using at least "high/moderate/low" assessments. Prioritize and distribute a list of significant risks, even if you use the list only to make the project exposures visible. Develop prevention or recovery strategies, as necessary, for substantial risks.

The remaining minimum requirements for risk management relate to tracking and change control. Dwight Eisenhower said, "In preparing for battle I have always found that plans are useless, but planning is indispensable." Eisenhower recognized the fact that few things ever go exactly as planned, which is especially true for projects. The exercise of planning never predicts the future precisely, but it does provide what you need to measure progress and quickly detect problems. For risk management, tracking progress at least once a week for all current project activities is prudent. Failure to do this periodic monitoring allows project slippage and other problems to quickly expand and cascade, and they can soon become insurmountable. Dogmatic, frequent tracking of project work is crucial to ongoing risk management. Through disciplined tracking, you can detect many risk situations while they are small. Small problems can be resolved quickly, preserving the project plans and objectives; large problems can easily take a project down.

Project control is also central to risk management. During a running project, there are many things going on that a project leader cannot control. Use the controls you *do* have to your best advantage. One of the most important controls the leader does have is the process for managing project changes. Projects with no ability to control specification changes are almost certainly doomed. Another thing leaders control is the flow of information. Use project reports, meetings, and discussions to communicate risks and to keep project issues and progress visible.

Long-term improvement of project risk management relies on postproject analysis. Through this, you can assess project results and make recommendations for more (or different) processes devoted to risk management and project planning, execution, and control.

Failure-proofing difficult projects requires three things. The first, thorough planning based on stable specifications, is the primary subject of this book. The second is diligent tracking and control of changes, the topics of Chapter 11. The third requirement, which is project-specific and beyond the scope of this (or any single) book, is technical expertise.

Risk management is much easier when you are lucky, and this third element of success represents the most obvious way to boost your luck. To the best of your ability, staff the project with a range of skills, including specialists in each field that the project is likely to need. Projects with experienced practitioners are much better equipped to deal with the twists and turns in a typical project trajectory. Recovery from risks is quick and effective when there are a few battle-scarred veterans who know what needs to be done and what has worked in the past. It also never hurts to recruit at least some people for the project who have reputations as generalists known for their problem-solving talents. Once your team is together, you can boost your luck further by rehearsing contingency plans for significant potential problems, so that if you need to use them, you will be competent and efficient.

Through all of this, never lose sight of the main objective: to manage your project to successful completion. The project management ideas presented here are components of the *means* to this end. Treat the ideas and concepts of this book as your risk management toolbox. When it makes sense, use the processes just as they are described. You may need to tailor other ideas to make them work in your environment. If a risk management idea promises you little current value, hold it in reserve. Above all, persevere. Inside every project that seems destined to fail lies a perfectly credible one, waiting for you to break it free. Also remember that a little risk is not a bad thing; to quote Ferengi Rule of Acquisition 62, "The riskier the road, the greater the profit."

Panama Canal: The Next Project

Projects have a beginning and an end, but they are generally part of a continuum of activities stretching back into the past and forward into the future. For the remainder of the twentieth century, the basic operation of the Panama Canal was largely unchanged, except for ongoing maintenance, widening of the cut, and a new dam built upstream in the 1930s to ensure continuous operation through the drier seasons. A plan in the 1950s to replace the canal with Ferdinand de Lesseps's imagined sea-level canal using thermonuclear bombs for the excavation was taken seriously for a time, but (fortunately) it was shelved.

As the twenty-first century begins, so does a new era for the canal. Following the 1999 turnover by the United States, the canal is now operated by Panama. It remains a vital link in world shipping, but, to ensure its viability in the future, the first major operational change in the nearly ninety-year life of the canal—the addition of a third transit through the isthmus—is now in the planning stages. A new set of locks, parallel to the existing locks on the Atlantic and the Pacific sides of the canal, are proposed that will be nearly twice as wide, 40 percent longer, and 25 percent deeper. This new route will permit transit of larger ships in addition to quicker transit for the PANAMAX freighters that currently use the canal. The new locks will hold nearly four times the volume of water required to operate the current locks, and their use will require massive dredging to allow the existing lakes to supply enough water. The magnitude of this overall effort is comparable to the original project, so it will be interesting to see which of the earlier projects the new endeavor will most resemble.

SELECTED DETAIL FROM THE PERIL DATABASE

The following information is excerpted from the Project Experience Risk Information Library (PERIL) database.

Schedule Risks

❐ Each stakeholder approved the project individually, but, at the meeting to grant final approval, disagreements surfaced that delayed the project.

❐ Sponsorship was not sustained, delaying decisions and limiting resources.

❐ Access to management was limited. Decisions and escalations were too slow.

❐ The system for approving requests failed; ordering parts was delayed.

❐ Document reviews slipped due to conflicts and low priority.

❐ Required end-of-phase review was delayed.

❐ Disaster recovery tests were delayed at project end because the hardware needed was tied up with an actual customer problem.

❐ Test systems were shared by several projects, causing queuing delays.

❐ Flooding in a data center caused delay for restoration and cleanup.

❐ Customer-supplied hardware failed and required replacement.

❑ Needed equipment was shipped from a pool of hardware in another country and was delayed by customs.

❑ New technology planned into the project was not available on time.

❑ Needed systems were down for scheduled maintenance not in the plan.

❑ New systems were delivered to the wrong building and were lost for weeks.

❑ Parts of the development team had a twelve-hour time difference. Bugs took two to three extra days to fix, on average.

❑ System components were all shipped separately, so installation was delayed until the last one arrived.

❑ Defective parts were received, and all had to be reordered.

❑ Paperwork and customs delayed delivery on international shipments.

❑ The process for developing integrated circuits failed, creating delays.

❑ In error, parts were shipped by sea, not by air, from Asia.

❑ Some activities were assigned only by function, not by name. No one was actually working on them.

❑ A dependency on another project was not discovered until project end.

❑ Clear responsibility for work to be done by the project team and by the customer was never delegated. Confusion led to delay.

❑ A deliverable from one project was "done," but the receiving project could not use it.

❑ Lack of coordination between projects caused delay.

❑ Interdependencies in complex programs were underestimated and detected late.

❑ A move from a former location was planned, but the new space was not ready on time. An interim move to temporary space required extra time and money.

❑ Support for the operating system used was inadequate for timely solution of conversion and delivery problems.

❏ Scheduling was based on a small pilot installation, but, when scaled up, systems lacked capacity, and the project was delayed.

❏ An old application had to be modified for the project, but no one left knew it well enough, and there was no documentation.

❏ An unrealistic project deadline was set; slips were unavoidable.

❏ Planning a project for new customer was based on similar work for an existing customer. Differences in relationships, infrastructure, jargon, and other factors required 50 percent more effort.

❏ Development scheduled in parallel led to frequent rework.

❏ Chronic optimism on completion dates for work led to missed deadlines.

❏ Neophyte project staff lacked technical expertise and required extra training time.

Resource Risks

❏ Project was delayed because of a major program budget cutback.

❏ Project expenses for supplies were limited (running the project at the scheduled rate necessitated 50 percent more money per month).

❏ A key supplier proved unreliable, delivering components late.

❏ Third-party deliverables were of poor quality and required major rework.

❏ A supplier agreed to needed changes but failed to deliver.

❏ A supplier contract included no penalties for missed deadlines, so its work was chronically late.

❏ A supplier was changed near the end of a project, causing delay and cost overrun.

❏ A subcontractor went out of business, causing a two-month delay for replacement.

❏ A key supplier was purchased and reorganized. Ultimately, the project had to find a new supplier.

- ❐ The project had a slow start due to difficulty in finding a qualified supplier.

- ❐ Pricing negotiation with a supplier stalled project work.

- ❐ Qualification and paperwork caused delays in beginning to work with a supplier in another country.

- ❐ High turnover at a supplier led to delays and crisis management.

- ❐ Two projects with similar objectives were taken on in different locations at the same time. The redundancy caused interference and arguing.

- ❐ Legacy systems were not retired as planned; the project team was tied up in unplanned support.

- ❐ Testing on a prior project was late, causing planning delays until staff was available.

- ❐ "Rolling Sledgehammer": The prior project tied up (and exhausted) staff, so the current project started late and slowly.

- ❐ The project had funding, but, due to head count limits, no staff was available.

- ❐ An expert (on supply chain) was difficult to find, causing delay.

- ❐ Needed people were still on a prior project.

- ❐ A key person was reassigned to other work in midproject.

- ❐ Staff turnover was very high, leading to delays and extra training.

- ❐ The project leader resigned and was not replaced promptly.

- ❐ Project priority was very low, leading to high turnover.

- ❐ Committed resources were reassigned to other projects and not replaced.

- ❐ Loss of staff led to tripling of activity durations on the project.

- ❐ The project was desired by management but not by the project team. Even with heavy monitoring, project work was slow.

- ❐ Enthusiasm and motivation fell because of the length of the project, so activities took longer than estimated.

- ❐ A third-party expert required for work was not available when needed.
- ❐ Key people were shared by several projects; lots of queuing.
- ❐ Training at project end took double the time, as people who required training missed the classes they were assigned to. Additional training was required.
- ❐ Key decisions were stalled when system architect was not available.
- ❐ Illness during key project work hit most of the project staff.
- ❐ An unexpected shutdown was scheduled at year-end. Work was delayed, and rescheduling it was difficult.
- ❐ A key team member was grounded in the Middle East during a war.
- ❐ Key staff was lost to a customer "hot site."
- ❐ Organizational reorganization created chaos and ownership problems.
- ❐ Manufacturing problems diverted project contributors.
- ❐ An unannounced audit in midproject caused delay due to required preparation.
- ❐ An earthquake made part of the project team unavailable for work.

Scope Risks

- ❐ The customer reorganized, and new staffing led to changed requirements.
- ❐ Project priorities were unclear, and secondary, less important work was done instead of required activities.
- ❐ Information from many sites was required, but, even after it was collected, additional time and work were necessary to make it consistent.
- ❐ A "small" client-requested change was accepted, which led to unintended consequences and major delay for the project.
- ❐ System redesign was added late in a maintenance project, creating major delay.

❐ Poorly managed change made the project very late.

❐ A "priced to win" project was badly understaffed, and the deadline was much too short.

❐ Scope definition changed late in the project.

❐ An unanticipated software upgrade was required, causing planning and training delays.

❐ New software installed by IT did not work, and fixing it caused delay.

❐ An operating system release was canceled; the project had to use a prior version.

❐ The project was based on standards that were still in draft form. Several options were possible for the final standards, but project was staffed to pursue only one.

❐ Organizational policy changes made late in a project required unplanned work.

❐ Project documents and expectations were not aligned. Adjustments required much additional work.

❐ Work was done by contractors who had too little project information; components supplied required extensive rework.

❐ The system was only partly specified until near the end of the project.

❐ Documentation was not translated into all needed languages; project was delayed.

❐ The product was developed for multiple platforms but worked on only two initially. Some problems were eventually fixed, but several platforms had to be dropped.

❐ Some project work was assigned to multiple owners. Each assumed the others were doing the work, when no one was doing it.

❐ Proprietary data were necessary for the project, but the owners of the data were reluctant to provide them. After delay, some partial information was shared.

❐ New technology promised faster results, but it failed and led to redesign and rework.

❐ A custom system for a customer was designed to use an Intel-based PC. A model based on a new CPU chip was shipped, but it failed to work as the older model did. The system was finally installed using a salvaged older PC.

❏   PC board failure required redesign and refabrication.

❏   Components did not work as documented. Replacements and software workarounds were required.

❏   Tests were not scheduled for historically reliable parts, but they were mandatory for the project and had to be added, late.

❏   The deliverable failed the final test, requiring rework to fix it and an additional test cycle.

❏   Final tests were interrupted by faulty test equipment. Repair of the equipment took time, and all the tests had to be restarted.

❏   Test hardware did not work properly, and performing all tests manually required extra time and effort.

❏   Redesign was required late in the project to meet quality goals, causing a major slip.

❏   A complex system was designed in pieces, and integration failed. Redesign and rework caused delay.

❏   A process developed worked in prototype but did not scale to production, requiring time-consuming changes.

❏   Problems were detected late in the project, and a solution was developed on the basis of the presumed root cause. The actual cause was something else, causing a slip.

❏   A purchased component was never delivered ("vapor-ware"). A brute-force workaround was developed but took time and was difficult to support.

❏   A key application failed during a system upgrade project, requiring unplanned effort to fix it.

❏   International shipment of media containing needed software was on time, but the media were unreadable and had to be replaced.

❏   Purchased software was limited and inflexible. The project had to develop workarounds and additional software.

❏   Late in the project, a software virus destroyed several crucial (and not backed-up) files, requiring rework to rebuild them.

SELECTED BIBLIOGRAPHY

Abdel-Hamid, Tarek, and Stuart E. Madnick. *Software Project Dynamics*. Prentice-Hall, Inc., 1991. Includes useful information on task estimation, especially in a software environment.

Brassard, Michael. *Memory Jogger Plus +*. GOAL/QPC, 1989. Covers process summaries for structured brainstorming and other techniques useful for planning and analysis.

Brooks, Frederick P. *The Mythical Man-Month: Essays on Software Engineering*. Anniversary edition. Addison-Wesley Publishing Co., 1995. A classic in the field, reissued 20 years after its original publication. The first half of the book holds up very well, especially for estimation, resource planning, and planning overall. Not just for software projects.

Chapman, C. B., and Stephen Ward. *Project Risk Management*. John Wiley & Sons, 1997. This is a thorough and very process-oriented treatment of project risk.

DeMarco, Tom. *Controlling Software Projects*. Yourdon Press, 1982. Useful information on planning, especially on estimation for software projects.

Demarco, Tom. *Slack*. Broadway Books, 2001. The final section (of four) addresses project risk.

DeMarco, Tom, and Timothy Lister. *Peopleware: Productive Projects and Teams*. 2d ed. Dorset House, 1999. Contains a wealth of information for resource management, applicable to all kinds of projects requiring teamwork.

Fisher, Roger, William Ury, and Bruce Patton. *Getting to Yes*. Penguin Books, 1991. This book is an excellent description of how to conduct data-driven discussions and principled negotiations. Additional related material is in Ury's *Getting Past No*.

Glass, Robert L. *Computing Calamities*. Prentice Hall PTR, 1999.

Glass, Robert L. *Software Runaways*. Prentice Hall PTR, 1998. These books offer examples of failed projects, through republished accounts (by the original authors) that mainly come from the trade press in the 1980s and 1990s.

Hall, Elaine. *Managing Risk: Methods for Software Systems Development (SEI Series in Software Engineering)*. Addison-Wesley Publishing Co., 1998. Offers a good deal of helpful advice, especially concerning the psychology of projects.

Hiam, Alexander. *The Vest-Pocket CEO*. Prentice-Hall, Inc., 1990. Good process summaries, including Nominal Group Technique for brainstorming and Delphi estimation process.

Jones, Capers. *Assessment and Control of Software Risks*. Yourdon Press, 1994. Includes useful information on uncovering and dealing with specific types of project risk. Applies as well to nonsoftware projects.

Kerzner, Harold. *Project Management: A Systems Approach to Planning, Scheduling, and Controlling*. 7th ed. John Wiley & Sons, 2000. The standard reference on project management. All topics relating to planning are covered, at least in passing, in this large work. Very strong on planning, but the risk material included is fairly cursory.

McCullough, David. *The Path Between the Seas: The Creation of the Panama Canal, 1870-1914*. Touchstone Book, 1977. A fascinating story of two projects: one that failed spectacularly, and one that paved the way for modern project management.

Patterson, Marvin. *Accelerating Innovation: Improving the Process of Product Development*. Van Nostrand Reinhold, 1992. Good material on project risk and project portfolios.

Project Management Institute. *A Guide to the Project Management Body of Knowledge*. 2000 ed. Project Management Institute, 2000. A good, high-level reference for project information. One of its knowledge areas is risk management.

Project Management Institute. *PMI®* Practice Standard for Work Breakdown Structures. Project Management Institute, 2001. A collection of practices and examples for developing a project WBS.

Russo, J. Edward, and Paul J. H. Schoemaker. *Decision Traps: The Ten Barriers to Brilliant Decision-Making and How to Overcome Them*. Fireside, 1989. Good material on decision making and confidence. Relates to planning overall and especially to estimation.

Scholtes, Peter R. *The Team Handbook*. 2nd ed. Oriel Inc., 1996. Material on brainstorming and other techniques for building effective teams.

Schuyler, John R. *Risk and Decision Analysis in Projects*. Project Management Institute Publications, 2001. A thorough over-

By Car

* Left out of U.O.G. onto Llantwit Road

* 1st Left at Roundabout into The Broadway

* Straight on through traffic lights , alongside high wall on left and in front of Pontypridd station

* At huge roundabout take last exit signposted TOWN CENTRE, then follow the signs for YNYSYBWL

* Ashgrove Surgery on left , just after the Muni and before Bus station

To Park

* Turn left in front of bus station. Pass around back of bus station and enter Pay & Display car park on Right

By Bus

* Out of gate by Forest Hall to corner of Brook Street (no 15)

* Bus goes 20 past & 10 to the hour. Will take you direct to bus station next to Ashgrove

ASHGROVE SURGERY
MORGAN STREET
Pontypridd
01443 404444

WALKING & by TRAIN (ONE STOP to Pontypridd)

- Left out of UOG onto Llantwit Road

- 1st left onto The Broadway at roundabout

- Straight on at the traffic lights, alongside the high wall on the left

- **Opposite Pontypridd station** turn right into **Taff** street opposite

- Walk to the end of Taff street

- Police station is straight ahead

- Next to Police station up the hill on the left is the Main bus station

- Ashgrove surgery is right next door to the Bus station (Vantage Chemist attached)

view of techniques and tools for decision analysis, with some coverage of project risk analysis.

Smith, Preston G., and Guy M. Merritt. *Proactive Risk Management: Controlling Uncertainty in Product Development.* Productivity Press, 2002. Contains a good summary of the application of risk techniques to product development projects.

Ury, William. *Getting Past No.* Bantam, 1993. This book is a companion to *Getting to Yes* by Fisher and Ury. It focuses on data-driven discussions and principled negotiations when the other party has more authority and power.

Wheelwright, Steven C., and Kim B. Clark. *Revolutionizing Product Development: Quantum Leaps in Speed, Efficiency, and Quality.* Free Press, 1992. Includes material on multiproject resource planning and project portfolios.

Wideman, R. Max, ed. *Project and Program Risk Management: A Guide to Managing Project Risks and Opportunities.* Project Management Institute Publications, 1992. Provides a thorough review of the PMI PMBOK material on project risk, but not updated for the 2000 revision.

Yourdon, Edward. *Death March.* Prentice Hall PTR, 1997. Ed Yourdon is a noted expert in the field of software projects, and this useful book is filled with information on how and why projects get into trouble.

INDEX